1992

UNDERSTANDING
TEACHER DEVELOPMENT

edited by

Andy Hargreaves and Michael G. Fullan

CASSELL

TEACHERS COLLEGE PRESS

Teachers College,
Columbia University
New York

First published 1992 by Cassell
Villiers House
41/47 Strand
London WC2N 5JE
England

Published in the United States of America by
Teachers College Press
Columbia University
New York, NY 10027
USA

British Library Cataloguing-in-Publication Data

Understanding teacher development. — (Teacher development)
1. Teachers. Professional education
I. Hargreaves, Andy   II. Fullan, Michael G.
371.146

ISBN 0–304–32259–8
        0–304–32277–6 pbk

Library of Congress Cataloging-in-Publication Data

Understanding teacher development / edited by Andy Hargreaves and
Michael G. Fullan.
          p.   cm.
    Includes index.
    ISBN 0–8077–3189–7. — ISBN 0–8077–3188–9 (pbk.)
    1. Teachers—In-service training.   I. Fullan, Michael.
LB1731.U43   1992
371.1′46—dc20   91–43958
                                                                                              CIP

Typeset by Colset Private Limited, Singapore
Printed and bound in Great Britain by
Dotesios Ltd, Trowbridge, Wiltshire

Contents

Notes on Contributors

Michael W. Apple is Professor of Curriculum and Instruction and Educational Policy Studies at the University of Wisconsin, Madison. A former elementary and secondary school teacher and past president of a teachers' union, he has worked with governments, unions and dissident groups in a number of countries to democratize education. Among his books (all published by Routledge) are *Ideology and Curriculum* (1979, second edition 1990), *Education and Power* (1985), *Teachers and Texts* (1988), and *The Politics of the Textbook* (1991).

Richard Butt's interests include curriculum praxis, professional development, classroom change, science education and multiculturalism. Within these different areas he exercises a commitment to emancipatory forms of education and research. He currently uses autobiographical enquiry in understanding the sources, evolution, and nature of teachers' knowledge and teacher development. He is also developing classroom materials to help reduce racism and prejudice. He is a professor of education at the University of Lethbridge, Alberta.

Christopher M. Clark is Professor of Education in the Department of Counseling, Educational Psychology and Special Education at Michigan State University. His research interests include teacher thinking, planning and decision-making and the connections between educational research and the practice of teaching. He also serves as Professor in Residence at Whitehills Elementary School in East Lansing, Michigan, assisting with teacher professional development and exploring the uses and limits of technology in support of elementary education.

Michael G. Fullan is the Dean of the Faculty of Education, University of Toronto and former Assistant Director (Academic) of the Ontario Institute for Studies in Education. He has participated as a researcher, consultant and policy adviser on a wide range of educational change projects, and has recently been awarded the first Award of Excellence by the Canadian Association of Teacher Educators for outstanding contribution to his profession and to teacher education. His most recent book is *The New Meaning of Educational Change* (Teachers College Press, 1991).

Ivor F. Goodson is Professor of Education at the University of Western Ontario, where he runs the Research Unit on Classroom Learning and Computer Use in Schools (RUCCUS). He also acts as Distinguished Visiting Scholar at the University of Rochester. His most recent books are (with Rob Walker) *Biography, Identity and Schooling* (Falmer, 1990) and *Studying Teachers' Lives* (Routledge, 1991).

Andy Hargreaves is Professor of Educational Administration at the Ontario Institute for Studies in Education, Toronto. He is the author of many books on education including *Changing Teachers* (Cassell/Teachers College Press, forthcoming), *Curriculum and Assessment Reform* (Open University Press/OISE Press, 1989) and *Two Cultures of Schooling* (Falmer Press, 1986). He has researched extensively on teaching and school culture and is currently directing two projects on the relationship between school culture and restructuring in secondary schools.

Michael Huberman is Professor of Education at the Faculty of Psychology and Education at the University of Geneva, Switzerland, and has been Visiting Professor at several European, American and Canadian universities. He has also designed several professional development facilities. His present research interests lie in the areas of life-cycle research, qualitative methodologies and knowledge dissemination. His most recent books are *La vie des enseignants* (Delachaux et Niestlé, 1989; English edition in preparation), *Innovation Up Close* (Plenum, 1984) and *Qualitative Data Analysis* (Sage, 1984; French edition in preparation), the last two co-authored with Matthew Miles.

Philip W. Jackson is the David Lee Shillinglaw Distinguished Service Professor in the Departments of Education and Psychology, the Committee on Ideas and Methods, and the College at the University of Chicago, where he is also the Director of the Benton Center for Curriculum and Instruction. He has recently completed a study of the moral life of schools. He is editor of the forthcoming *Handbook of Research on Curriculum* (to be published by Macmillan, New York).

Susan Jungck is Assistant Professor of Education at National-Louis University in Evanston, Illinois. She has been involved in schooling at a variety of levels and has taught ethnographic research methods at universities in both Asia and Europe. She has conducted extensive research on the policy and practice surrounding the use of computers in education.

William Louden is Director of the Schools Professional Development Consortium, comprising educational employers, unions and universities in Perth, Western Australia. Formerly a high school English department head, he also worked as a Ministry of Education curriculum consultant. His research interests include teachers' knowledge and culture, collegiality, and constructivist approaches to the teaching of science and mathematics. He is the author of *Understanding Teaching: Continuity and Change in Teachers' Knowledge* (Cassell, 1991).

Antoinette Oberg co-ordinates and teaches in the Curriculum Studies graduate programme at the University of Victoria, British Columbia. Her research centres on questions about reflection and teaching for reflection.

Danielle Raymond is at the Faculté d'éducation, Université de Sherbrooke, Quebec. Her interest in the study of teachers' life histories stems from earlier work on the limited impact of pre-service training on experiential knowledge of teaching and learning. Her current research uses biographical approaches to study student teachers' knowledge of adolescents and classroom processes in high-school settings.

Heather-jane Robertson is Director of Professional Development Services for the Canadian Teachers' Federation. Her work involves policy analysis and project development on a wide range of public policy and educational issues affecting teachers and students. Her recent work includes participatory research and analysis of the unmet needs of female adolescents in schools, a study of gender and literacy, and the design of inservice education models for schools and organizations on developing cultures for change. She holds a M.Sc. Ed. (Future Studies) Degree from the University of Houston, where her research was primarily on school-based strategic planning. She is currently developing an extensive training package for teachers on the needs of immigrant and refugee students.

Dennis Thiessen is Associate Dean of the Faculty of Education, University of Toronto. His research focuses on teacher and student beliefs, professional socialization and educational change. He has written articles on curriculum change orientations, perspectives in teacher development, dilemmas of principals in school-based development, and the place of Canadian teachers in educational reform.

David Townsend is Associate Professor of Education at the University of Lethbridge. His interests include analysis of teaching, supervision, staff development and social studies education. At present, he is most actively involved in research and development projects that emphasize collaboration between school districts and the University.

Susan Underwood is a teacher on Salt Spring Island, British Columbia. Her graduate work focuses on questions concerning identity, difference and pedagogy.

Foreword

In Britain and Australia, they call it teaching. In the United States and Canada, they call it instruction. Whatever terms we use, we have come to realize in recent years that the teacher is the ultimate key to educational change and school improvement. The restructuring of schools, the composition of national and provincial curricula, the development of bench-mark assessments — all these things are of little value if they do not take the teacher into account. Teachers don't merely deliver the curriculum. They develop, define it and reinterpret it too. It is what teachers think, what teachers believe and what teachers do at the level of the classroom that ultimately shapes the kind of learning that young people get. Growing appreciation of this fact is placing working with teachers and understanding teaching at the top of our research and improvement agendas.

For some reformers, improving teaching is mainly a matter of developing better teaching methods, of improving instruction. Training teachers in new classroom management skills, in active learning, co-operative learning, one-to-one counselling and the like is the main priority. These things are important, but we are also increasingly coming to understand that developing teachers and improving their teaching involves more than giving them new tricks. We are beginning to recognize that, for teachers, what goes on inside the classroom is closely related to what goes on outside it. The quality, range and flexibility of teachers' classroom work are closely tied up with their professional growth — with the way that they develop as people and as professionals.

Teachers teach in the way they do not just because of the skills they have or have not learned. The ways they teach are also grounded in their backgrounds, their biographies, in the kinds of teachers they have become. Their careers — their hopes and dreams, their opportunities and aspirations, or the frustration of these things — are also important for teachers' commitment, enthusiasm and morale. So too are relationships with their colleagues — either as supportive communities who work together in pursuit of common goals and continuous improvement, or as individuals working in isolation, with the insecurities that sometimes brings.

As we are coming to understand these wider aspects of teaching and teacher development, we are also beginning to recognize that much more than pedagogy, instruction or teaching method is at stake. Teacher development, teachers' careers, teachers' relations with their colleagues, the conditions of status, reward and leadership under which they work — all these affect the quality of what they do in the classroom.

This international series, Teacher Development, brings together some of the very best current research and writing on these aspects of teachers' lives and work. The books in the series seek to understand the wider dimensions of teachers' work, the depth of teachers' knowledge and the resources of biography and experience on which it draws, the ways that teachers' work roles and responsibilities are changing as we restructure our schools, and so forth. In this sense, the books in the series are written for those who are involved in research on teaching, those who work in initial and in-service teacher education, those who lead and administer teachers, those who work with teachers and, not least, teachers themselves.

Understanding Teacher Development is a collection of research studies and broader discussions of teacher development from leading international scholars in the field. Some of the central principles of teacher development are identified and discussed by them. Teacher development is discussed in relation to self-development, teacher reflection, teacher biographies, cultures of teaching, teacher careers, teachers' work, gender identity and classroom practice.

The understandings of teacher development outlined here are both humanistic and critical. They link professional development to the teacher's self, the teacher's life, the teacher's career and the surrounding culture of teaching in which teachers work. They also ask critical questions about many of the things that pass for teacher development: whether they are sexist and patronizing, whether they are a masquerade for processes designed to extract extra effort from teachers for no further reward, whether they offer cooptation rather than collaboration, and so on.

The international experts in this volume celebrate many of the principles of teacher development but are also sharply critical of much of the practice. In that sense, they offer guidelines for optimists but also warnings for zealots. In its combination of optimism and realism, this book offers much to all those who are involved in the education and development of teachers — especially teachers themselves.

Versions of most papers collected here were first presented at an International Conference on Teacher Development at the Ontario Institute for Studies in Education (OISE) in February 1989. We would like to thank the Department of Educational Administration at OISE, the Faculty of Education of the University of Toronto, and the Social Science and Humanities Research Council of Canada for co-sponsoring the conference. Leo Santos and Lina Chilelli provided invaluable assistance in typing and preparing the manuscripts for publication.

Andy Hargreaves, Professor
OISE
June 1991

Chapter 1

Introduction

Andy Hargreaves and Michael G. Fullan

Much of the debate about school improvement and the raising of educational standards revolves around the issue of providing equal and sufficient 'opportunities to learn' for all children in our schools.[1] It has been found that streaming or tracking does not provide equal opportunities to learn for children in lower streams, since such children receive fewer resources, are allocated less well-qualified teachers, and spend less time being involved with instruction (as opposed to discipline or management) than their higher-stream counterparts.[2] Similarly, children with differing abilities and needs within the same class may not receive equal opportunities to learn if the style of teaching is inflexible or if it does not allow tasks to be differentiated and adjusted within the class, so they are appropriately matched to the varying needs of *all* pupils.[3] Clearly, providing equal and improved 'opportunities to learn' is at the heart of our efforts to improve both quality and equality in education. However, as Woods notes, 'opportunities to learn' also require 'opportunities to teach'.[4]

The importance of providing teachers with sufficient 'opportunities to teach' seems persuasive enough. What exactly might be meant by this is, however, open to a number of different interpretations.

- Having sufficient opportunities to teach may entail finding opportunities to learn and acquire the knowledge and skills of effective teaching (especially for mixed ability settings).

- It may entail having opportunities to develop the personal qualities, commitment and self-understanding essential to becoming a sensitive and flexible teacher.

- It may entail creating a work environment which is supportive and not restrictive of professional learning, continuous improvement, and (where such things as class sizes and resources are concerned) the opportunity to teach, and teach well, rather than merely survive.

These three views of what is involved in providing 'opportunities to teach' embody different approaches to training or improving the teaching force — to teacher development, that is. These may be called:

- teacher development as knowledge and skill development,
- teacher development as self-understanding, and
- teacher development as ecological change.

In order to highlight and justify the focus and emphasis of this book, this introduction describes these three approaches to teacher development, and where we and our contributors stand in relation to them.

TEACHER DEVELOPMENT AS KNOWLEDGE AND SKILL DEVELOPMENT

One way of providing teachers with 'opportunities to teach' is to equip them with the knowledge and skills that will increase their ability to provide improved opportunities to learn for all their pupils. Deeper knowledge of and greater confidence in teaching their subject(s); developing better expertise in classroom management so that more time can be devoted to instruction; knowing how to teach mixed-ability classes; being aware of and becoming proficient in new teaching strategies like co-operative learning or 'whole language' approaches to learning; and becoming knowledgeable about and able to respond to the different learning styles of their pupils — attention to all these things can certainly help teachers increase their pupils' opportunities to learn. A teaching force that is more skilled and flexible in its teaching strategies and more knowledgeable about its subject matter is a teaching force more able to improve the achievements of its pupils.

If we have always known this apparent truism that good skilled teaching produces better learning, we have not always been confident in or agreed upon what this 'good teaching' is, especially where classes of widely varying abilities and needs are concerned. Over the years, debates have raged with passionate inconclusiveness about the relative merits of progressive versus traditional methods, of active learning versus direct instruction and so on.[5] In recent times, however, a number of educational researchers and administrators have reached the view that we *do* now possess a well-founded knowledge base of what constitutes 'good teaching', and of what works and what doesn't in most mixed-ability classrooms. Confidence in or certainty about the validity of this knowledge base has in many cases become so strong that these researchers and administrators have felt able to advocate and sometimes promulgate widespread inservice training of teachers in these newly discovered skills and strategies.[6] As a result, skills training in the development of teachers has become big business. It is the prime focus of staff development efforts and the major consumer of staff development budgets. When we evaluate skills-based approaches to teacher development, we are not therefore evaluating just one of many equally available and widespread approaches. We are evaluating the overwhelmingly dominant approach to planned teacher development activity in modern school systems.

The advantages of skills- and knowledge-based forms of teacher development are well known. They are practical in that they focus on methods that are understandable to and usable by teachers in their own classrooms.[7] Where they are presented not just as one-shot workshops but with support and follow-up for teachers in their own classrooms, evaluations indicate positive support among involved teachers along with improved levels of use in the newly acquired skills.[8] Knowledge and skills-based approaches to teacher development are also favoured by administrators since they are clearly focused, easily organized and packaged, and relatively self-contained (thus they do not impact intrusively on other people's territories — like those of curriculum and programming in the school board, or those of overall administration and leadership within the school itself).[9]

Despite their administrative popularity and widespread use, however, knowledge- and skills-based forms of teacher development have also been strongly criticized. In some people's eyes they are not part of the solution to improving our schools, they are part of the problem. What are these criticisms?

First, knowledge- and skills-based approaches are usually imposed on teachers on a top-down basis by 'experts' from outside their own schools. In Hunt's words, they are 'outside-in' rather than 'inside-out' forms of teacher development.[10] Such methods often fail to involve the teacher, and therefore run the risk of not securing their commitment and generating teacher resistance. Moreover, when the inculcation of new skills is undertaken inflexibly and teachers are given little discretion over the degree or pace of adoption of those skills, this betrays a disrespect for teachers' professionalism and the quality of their classroom judgements.[11] Training teachers to train other teachers, or asking teachers to support or coach their colleagues in the implementation of new skills, can mitigate or even override many of these effects of top-down, 'outside-in' reform, but even here, the origin of the reforms is still ultimately extraneous. Little value is placed on teachers' own practical knowledge in the development of classroom skills.[12] As Clark points out in Chapter 5, teachers, in this approach, are people to be trained and developed. They are not viewed as people who can and should develop themselves.

Despite the dangers of teacher resistance, if there were indeed a confident and secure knowledge base of effective teaching there would still be a case for training new teachers in methods whose validity was well grounded in educational research. The only outstanding issue would then be that of managing the process of implementation with appropriate sensitivity, so that the teachers concerned would be listened to and the necessary adjustments made to the implementation process as a result.

The problem of research-based, top-down reform is more than a problem of human relations, however. It is also a problem of undue confidence and certainty that is often invested in the findings of educational research. This problem of over-confidence is the target of a second criticism of skills-based teacher development. Following positivistic principles of scientific endeavour, many advocates of skills-based programmes of teacher development place excessive reliance on the supposedly incontrovertible findings of educational research in order to justify the teaching methods they promote. In Chapter 3, Robertson sees in these appeals to the findings of 'hard research' a characteristically masculine discourse of certainty and over-confidence, which betrays incipient sexism in much skills-based staff development work.[13]

In a rapidly changing postmodern world characterized by indeterminacy and unpredictability, this faith in the certainty of educational research findings is both exaggerated and misplaced.[14] Environmental destruction has challenged our beliefs in science and technology as ways of accurately and reliably predicting and controlling our world in the rational pursuit of progress. The dismantling of the Berlin Wall has questioned much Marxist faith in the scientifically predicted inevitability of socialist transformation. Even in physical science, scientists are now increasingly discovering chaos where once they found only order.[15] In social science, the unpredictabilities are greater still because the bundles of matter we study here have their own subjective thoughts and preferences about how they should behave; because their behaviour varies substantially from place to place, and over time; and because, as Giddens points out, these behaviours are a product of and a response to our social research knowledge (with regard to school improvement, say) as well as an occasion for it.[16] Teachers and their classrooms are variable and changing things — even more so when others intervene in their work. This unavoidable indeterminacy in social research does not mean that we know or can know nothing. But it does mean that what we know about the virtues of co-operative learning, for instance, is tentative and provisional; that it is likely to change over time as our understanding and modification of co-operative learning itself changes; and that it will vary from one context to another (between experimental and 'natural' teaching situations; between specially sponsored innovations and ordinary classrooms; between enthusiastic teachers and less supportive ones; or between one subject and another).[17]

Indeterminacy in educational research is unavoidable. Because of this, the purpose of such research should be to generate critical conversations with the wisdom and expertise of current practice, rather than to authorize the imposition and implementation of new practices from elsewhere.

This use of positivistic research models (usually ones which draw on a psychological or managerial heritage) to legitimize bureaucratic interventions in education is characteristic of North American approaches to change and the appeals to scientific and technical rationality on which they often rest.[18] In other settings, such as Great Britain, no such rationales are deemed necessary. The assertion of political preference and bureaucratic mandates through such measures as the imposition of the National Curriculum, with all its implications for teaching methodology, are felt to be enough. Unpalatable as this politically generated imposition of skills-based training has been for many teachers, there is at least a transparent honesty in it. In view of all this, we believe there is a need to return to practices of educational research and enquiry whose primary purpose is neither to support nor disguise political and bureaucratic control, but to engage in critical dialogue with the existing and collective wisdom of practice.

Following closely from this criticism of over-confidence in the research base of skills-based training is a third, related concern that this approach to teacher development forecloses teachers' disagreement with the methods to which they are being exposed. The 'hard' research knowledge of experts is deemed superior to the 'soft' practical wisdom of teachers. Disagreement is discouraged, and where it does occur it is discounted or interpreted as 'irrational' resistance. In particular, disagreement is treated as a problem, not an opportunity; something to be managed rather than something to be encouraged in order to stimulate critical reflection about and collective change in practice.[19]

Elsewhere, one of us has pointed out the frequency with which people confuse issues surrounding the educational change that they are introducing with issues surrounding the process of change in general.[20] Such people confuse the process of change with the change as such. One commonly observed implication of this is that what looks like opposition to a particular change may be due more to anxieties about the process of change in general. But an equally important and less commonly voiced implication is that what might seem like teacher resistance to the change process in general, may sometimes be a perfectly rational disagreement with the particular change in question.

What we are articulating here is an important tension in the change and improvement process between *vision* and *voice*. The development of a common vision, commitment to shared goals, or developing clarity in and understanding of the goals being implemented by others, are commonly advocated components of the change and improvement process. These are seen as essential to developing confidence and consistency among a community of teachers. Other writers, such as Goodson in Chapter 7, point less to the development of vision than to the articulation of voice as a priority of professional growth.[21] For them, the teacher's voice is something that articulates his or her purposes or concerns; that connects the teacher's teaching to the person the teacher is, to the teacher's life. A prime purpose of professional development, it is argued, should therefore be to help teachers articulate their voice as a way of constructing and reconstructing the purposes and priorities in their work, both individually and collectively. Unfortunately, it is noted, owing to the bureaucratic pressures to implement particular changes, those teachers who may voice doubt about the change or who disagree with it may go unheard, or be silenced, or be dismissed as mere resistance.[22]

An exclusive emphasis on vision or voice alone is not helpful for constructive professional development. A world of voice without vision is a world reduced to chaotic babble, where all voices are valid and where there are no means to arbitrate between them, reconcile them or draw them together. This is the dark side of the postmodern world: a world from which community and authority have disappeared. It is a world where the authority of voice has supplanted the voice of authority to an excessive degree.[23]

A world of vision without voice is equally problematic, however. In this world where purposes are imposed and consensus is contrived, there is no place for the practical judgement and wisdom of teachers and other street-level bureaucrats; no place for their views to get a hearing. A major challenge for professional development and educational change is to work through and reconcile this tension between vision and voice. By privileging vision — especially imposed vision — over voice, much skills-based teacher development fails to address this fundamental challenge.

A fourth criticism of knowledge and skills-based approaches is that they overemphasize particular aspects of teacher development. There are three components to this overemphasis. First, as we have already indicated, resources are invested more in skill development than in personal growth or in creating a culture in the teaching community that supports professional growth and improvement.[24] As a result, the chosen skills are often experimented with in conditions of poor leadership, teacher isolation or excessive work pressures that cannot support their proper development or continuing use.

Second, staff development resources are disproportionately allocated to developers and trainers rather than to the recipients of training (in the form of release time, and so on). The concentration of resources on skill developers and trainers leaves fewer resources to help ordinary teachers to learn from each other, or to improve the environment for their professional learning.[25]

Third, knowledge and skills-based training tends to concentrate staff development efforts on school subjects and curriculum areas in the more conventional high-status academic domain — in mathematics, language arts (or English in the UK), science and so on. For example, most of the research on teachers' pedagogical content knowledge — the knowledge teachers have of how to teach their subject — has been conducted within mainstream subjects like English and social studies.[26] This focus on particular subjects unintentionally communicates a view that 'real teaching' or generic teaching skills are the skills to be found in those subjects. At the same time, skills that may be appropriate for other subjects like drama and art, and that may sometimes be usefully incorporated into 'mainstream' teaching, frequently get overlooked.

To sum up, skills-based staff development is an important component of the teacher development process. At present, however, it almost certainly consumes too much time, energy and resources within teacher development as a whole. Within this overall emphasis, skills-based teacher development is too often imposed on teachers rather than developed with them. It is too often based on excessive confidence in the supposedly proven wisdom of experts and research. It is too frequently treated as a matter of non-negotiable technical *skill*, rather than as an issue of professional *will* or of something whose worth should be discussed or debated.[27] And the skills in which teachers are trained are all too often implemented out of context — their appropriateness for the teacher as a person, for the teacher's purpose, or for the particular classroom setting in which the teacher works, being overlooked.

Our concern with knowledge and skills-based teacher development is not only that undue emphasis is often given to it. Nor is it simply a case of assessing the strengths and weaknesses of skills-based teacher development in the abstract. Skills-based teacher development does not take place in a vacuum. It is widely used in a particular context: one of technocratic and bureaucratic control, in which the rhetoric suggests bottom-up development, but the reality reveals top-down implementation. While skills-based teacher development has an important role to play in other contexts, its pervasive presence in a bureaucratic apparatus of implementation and control creates more problems than possibilities.

This book therefore focuses on forms of teacher development and understandings of teacher development that are more humanistic and critical in nature: forms that take account of the person in teacher development as well as the person's behaviour, and which address the characteristics of the system as well as the skills of the individual. We shall see, however, that while these alternative approaches to teacher development have their virtues, they are also not without their problems.

TEACHER DEVELOPMENT AS SELF-UNDERSTANDING

Teacher development, we have argued, involves more than changing teachers' behaviour. It also involves changing the person the teacher is.[28] Some argue that self-understanding in the form of reflection on one's personal and practical knowledge of teaching comes before meaningful and substantial changes in teaching behaviour.[29] Others argue that changes in behaviour usually precede changes in beliefs.[30] Whichever is the case, behaviours and beliefs are closely bound together. To focus on behavioural skills alone without reference to their grounding in or impact on attitudes and beliefs is misguided and liable to prove ineffective. Acknowledging that teacher development is also a process of personal development marks an important step forward in our improvement efforts.

For writers like Nias and Leithwood, the process of personal development that underpins teacher development has three important dimensions.[31] First, one's development as a person progresses through different stages. It may be that the highest levels of development here are not normally achieved until several years after most people enter teaching. One implication of this is that sometimes factors to do with *personal* development may inhibit the achievement of goals concerned with *professional* development. For example, many younger teachers may not have reached a level of personal maturity which combines a strong and integrated sense of self with an ability to relate to and work with others. This in turn may inhibit the development of collegiality, as certain teachers either resist being 'swamped' by their professional contemporaries or become overly dependent on them.

Second, the human life cycle also comprises characteristic phases of development that embody typical concerns.[32] Younger teachers, like younger adults generally, characteristically have a great deal of physical energy, few domestic commitments, a somewhat untempered idealism and a willingness, therefore, to invest strongly in work and innovation. Teachers in the mid-life span have much life experience behind them, are more aware of their mortality, may be facing declining physical powers, are often more intent on establishing a balance between their work and the rest of their lives and are thus more cautious about change. Men usually discover these necessities rather later than women. Teachers at different points in the life cycle have characteristically different orientations to change and improvement as well as different needs in terms of professional development.

Third, there are personal development issues specific to the teaching career itself. Promotion brings its rewards and incentives. Equally the denial of promotion can create careers that become 'spoilt', leading their bearers to become disenchanted, even cynical, as they no longer feel valued by their organizations.[33] This in turn may impact on classroom performance, as commitment and enthusiasm are withdrawn.

All these aspects of personal and professional development express the importance of personal factors in teaching, whether it be for the teacher's relations with colleagues, the teacher's orientation to change or the quality of the teacher's classroom instruction. The importance of the teacher as a person is receiving growing acceptance in the teacher development literature and among educational administrators. Leithwood, for instance, points to the importance of treating the teacher as a person in his discussion of the principal's role in teacher development.[34] And many other writers point to the importance of self-knowledge and self-understanding as a key to professional growth in the teaching force.[35] Many of the chapters in this volume express this humanistic emphasis on the teacher as a person, as a way for others to understand and work with teachers more effectively, and as a way for teachers to develop themselves.

In Chapter 4, Philip Jackson explains various ways of approaching teacher development. One is the way that know-how or technique may be passed from researchers to teachers or from teachers to each other. Another is the way of independence which, through shared decision-making and the like, frees teachers to be relatively autonomous professionals. A third way is that of role accommodation which supports teachers and gives them encouragement, sympathy, respect, even therapy, in the furtherance of their work. Arguing that all three ways have their place, Jackson proposes a fourth, less trodden path — one he describes as something akin to the way of wonder, or art, or altered sensibility. This fourth way, says Jackson, is a way of coming to view teaching, even one's own teaching, differently, and seeing in it deeper significances and possibilities than a usual passing glance might permit. Grasping the complexities and emotional depths in teaching is illustrated through Jackson's analysis of a teacher's last day of teaching. Perhaps not at all an exceptional teacher, certainly not an innovative one, Mr Kitteridge, the subject of Jackson's analysis, is portrayed as a teacher of considerably greater depth and complexity than superficial appearance suggests. Jackson shows us that through this sort of analysis or 'enriched understanding', through embarking upon his way of wonder, seemingly ordinary teachers like Kitteridge become quite extraordinary; and the apparent simplicities of technique can be stripped away to reveal remarkable complexities of judgement and mood. The seeming simplicity and ordinariness of much teaching is actually a complex and substantial achievement. Jackson's chapter illustrates this very well and shows us how we too can come to understand it better.

Christopher Clark reaffirms Jackson's position on the complexities of teaching in Chapter 5. There is much more to teaching than meets the eye, he tells us: a point that is validated by many things, including the accumulating body of research on teacher thinking. This research, says Clark, shows teachers in the main to be active, knowledgeable and ready to learn, rather than passive, deficient and resistant. On the basis of this research and insight, Clark makes a case for teachers taking charge of their own professional development as communities of thoughtful, reflective practitioners. In his support, Clark argues that adult development is more likely to be successful when it is voluntary rather than coercive; that standardized development programmes do not meet the needs and desires of many different teachers in many different settings; and that many of our best teachers already design their own professional development. Clark then outlines seven principles for self-designed professional development: documenting our beliefs so that we are better able to develop them; building on strengths rather than patching up weaknesses; outlining a broad five-year plan to establish some priorities; learning more consciously in small ways from each other (by exchanging classes, visiting a colleague's class, etc.) rather than from dramatic initiatives introduced from the outside; asking for help and support; doing things in style where possible rather than second class and on the cheap; and celebrating our successes. These, argues Clark, are some of the key principles for designing our own professional development.

Dennis Thiessen takes up one particular aspect of this self-development process in Chapter 6. He presents a case for more teacher development being classroom-based rather than being located in university seminar rooms, training workshops or staffroom discussions. Thiessen reviews many arguments in support of what he calls classroom-based teacher development. Classroom-based teacher development (CBTD), he argues, focuses on the classroom, on the teachers and students who should participate in and are the ultimate beneficiaries of any development process. They are the ones who have the power to make things happen where it matters most — in the classroom. Focusing and developing change here also avoids the problem of having to implement changes introduced from elsewhere. And CBTD provides a way of continually reflecting in and on practice. Thiessen's most striking argument here, though, is that CBTD not only enables teachers to learn from their own or their colleagues' practice. It also enables them to learn from their students by involving these students in the development and change process. In Thiessen's view, the humanistic approach to teacher development therefore involves not just the individual teacher, nor even groups of teachers, but the student too — the person for whom all this development, change and improvement activity is ultimately intended.

While Thiessen urges us to place our teacher development efforts squarely within the domain of classroom practice, Ivor Goodson, in Chapter 7, argues for another starting point. Particularly where teachers and researchers are to collaborate together, he says, classroom practice may be a particularly unpromising point of entry, focusing as it does on the area of maximum vulnerability for the teacher. Goodson instead suggests we begin by examining the teacher's work in the context of the teacher's life, a particularly rich source of dialogue and data. If we begin with the life, we find there the teacher not simply as a practitioner but as a striving, purposeful person as well. Issues of class, gender, lifestyle and life cycle — all these are formative influences upon the teacher and his or her teaching, claims Goodson. They are influences that should be acknowledged, influences that deserve a hearing. Indeed, says Goodson, the teacher's voice that articulates the life and its purposes should not merely be acknowledged. It should be actively sponsored as a priority within our teacher development work.

Drawing on his research study of 160 secondary teachers in Geneva, Switzerland, Michael Huberman, in Chapter 8, examines the effect of the teacher life cycle on teachers' approaches to instruction. Where Thiessen and Goodson separated the practice and the life from each other and made difficult choices between them, Huberman artfully brings them back together. Life cycle concerns, he shows, are deeply implicated in teachers' approaches to instruction. This is graphically illustrated with respect to a group of mid-career teachers whom Huberman terms *positive focusers*. These are teachers who focused their interests and commitments on particular parts of their work (a subject, or a grade level, perhaps), built up their outside interests and steered clear of school-wide innovation. Yet having found and defined their areas of interest and preference, the positive focusers were still open to and interested in 'tinkering around' with their practice, in making small changes and improvements in their own domain. They were proud of their classroom mastery and always sought to improve it further — but in their own way and in their own time. There are important lessons to be learned from this group for teacher development as a whole, argues Huberman. First, he advocates a *craft model* as the most appropriate model for career development — one which encourages and supports teachers in their craft-like tinkering-around in their own classrooms, as a way of expanding and improving their repertoires of instruction. Second, Huberman argues that inservice training will need to be designed to support these needs of craft-like tinkering. He suggests that workshops, peer coaching and so on are likely to prove too codified and scripted for most individualistic craftworkers. More productive moves might be made in extending teachers' networks so that they can learn from each other's skills, he says.

Danielle Raymond, Richard Butt and David Townsend take up Goodson's and Huberman's emphases on the importance of teachers' lives and teacher biographies and spell out their practical implications for understanding what underpins a teacher's practice, and for the processes of development that may be necessary to bring about changes in such practice. Through three richly described teacher case studies, Raymond and her colleagues illustrate how approaches to teaching are profoundly influenced by such things as ethnic background, social class origins, experience of working in other cultures, gender influences and range and type of previous teaching experiences. Early personal experiences are particularly formative, the authors find. Later professional ones can endorse or modify them in important ways. They suggest that one of the key contexts here is a collegial one which allows and encourages teachers to learn from each other, from people they value — but it is a context sadly lacking in many teachers' professional lives. Raymond and her colleagues explore some of the conditions for collegiality to develop and suggest *collaborative autobiography* as one way of realizing them. They go on to describe the principles and some practical examples of collaborative autobiography drawn from programmes which they have designed and in which they have participated. This process, they say, gives teachers a deeper understanding of their own and their colleagues' teaching and how it came to be that way. It also applies a point of leverage for change and professional development in the future.

In Chapter 10, Antoinette Oberg and Susan Underwood, professor and student respectively on the same postgraduate course, describe their reflections on their experience of the programme in which they both participated. The programme is an unusual one, based on the writing, exploration and rewriting of personal journals about one's teaching and oneself as a way of trying to discover the *grounds*, as the authors term it, of one's practice. The authors speak in turn, comparing their reflections on the experiences they underwent and constructed together. The process they describe is a process of self-development and also of collaborative understanding — an intense yet supportive relationship that pushes the self to levels of understanding it might never develop on its own. Oberg and Underwood give a new meaning to postgraduate study or university courses as things otherwise often considered academic, irrelevant and detached from reality. As Thiessen restores importance to the classroom as a place for teacher as well as student learning, Oberg and Underwood restore meaning and relevance to the graduate programme as a place of productive professional development. Each has its place — the classroom as the busy hub of practice, and the seminar room as a safe refuge for reflection on it.

Chapters 9 and 10 explore some of the ways in which collaborative work can assist reflection on practice, and the purposes or grounds that underpin such practice. In a chapter drawn from his intensive collaborative study with one teacher and her practice, Bill Louden takes our understandings of reflection and collaboration considerably further. Through argument and illustration, he shows that the notion of teacher reflection is much more complex than is often assumed. Reflection, Louden argues, may serve different interests — ranging from ones of a technical 'what works' nature, to interests of personal self-understanding, to interests in solving a particular problem, right through to interests of a critical nature that question the very context and purpose of one's work. Reflection, suggests Louden, may also take different forms — some rather introspective, others more spontaneous and still others consisting of more systematic kinds of enquiry. Louden's analytically sophisticated and empirically well-grounded chapter teaches us not to speak so glibly about the value of teacher development for teacher reflection when reflection can have so many (sometimes contradictory) meanings and purposes. More than this, Louden's chapter and the book from which it is drawn also teach us to be less glib when we talk about the benefits of collaborative research with teachers. The depth and intensity of his relationship with the teacher he studied reveal the extraordinary degree of collaboration that is required to understand a teacher's practice and its grounding in his or her life.

Taken together, these chapters reveal many of the benefits of teacher development when it is seen and presented as a process of self-understanding grounded in the teacher's life and work. This broad approach to teacher development has some important limitations as well, however, and has sometimes been subject to stringent criticism.

For one thing, humanistic approaches to teacher development can become self-indulgent, involving teachers, developers and researchers in relationships that are intensive and ultimately rewarding yet not easily replicated across other teacher groups. At the extreme, an intensive full-time collaborative relationship of the kind described by Louden is not at all applicable to other work settings. What Louden's case provides, therefore, is more a beacon for our intellectual understanding than a model for our professional development practice.

Humanistic approaches to teacher development can also be slow, time-consuming and costly,[36] and their outcomes can be unpredictable. This is not an argument against their use, but a caution against our having excessively high expectations of their benefits on a system-wide basis.

A more trenchant criticism of humanistic approaches to teacher development is that they do not replace bureaucratic procedures of technical control in the teacher development process, but disguise them as therapy. Holmes has put this argument most forcefully:

> The term *teacher development* is Orwellian. No one could be
> against teachers developing. But there is a critical difference
> between developing and being developed.[37]

'Helping teachers develop' (the title of Jackson's chapter) might presumably be seen by Holmes as a ripe target for such accusations of patronizing, therapeutic control. As candidates for 'development', teachers here might be regarded as belonging to the same category as children and Third World nations: people who need help and who are dependent on our superior insight and expertise. This danger of control masquerading as care is an ever-present one that requires continued vigilance on all our parts. The implementation-driven examples that Holmes cites are, however, more characteristic of technical–rational forms of teacher development than of their humanistic counterparts.

An equally trenchant criticism of humanistic approaches to teacher development is that by focusing on the person and not the context in which the person works, they overemphasize personal responsibility for change and draw attention away from controversial questions about the *context* in which teachers work, and the ways in which it enhances or inhibits personal or professional development. In this sense, it is argued, humanistic approaches to teacher development can be implicitly conservative. Thiessen, Goodson, Louden, and Raymond and her colleagues are keen to avoid that charge and explicitly discuss critical and contextual issues as a proper subject for teacher reflection. But across the field as a whole, the charge is not without foundation and does point to the need within teacher development for a complementary focus on the work context of teaching as both a condition of and target for development work.

TEACHER DEVELOPMENT AS ECOLOGICAL CHANGE

> Living in an enforced present tense is too much like being made
> to breast the rapids of a river. The attention has to engage with
> the raging white foam rather than the depths.
> Dennis Potter: *Ticket to Ride*. London: Faber & Faber, 1986,
> p. 38.

The seeds of development will not grow if they are cast on stony ground. Critical reflection will not take place if there is neither time nor encouragement for it. Teachers will learn little from each other if they work in persistent isolation. Creative experimentation with instruction and improvement will be unlikely if changes are implemented from the outside by a heavy-handed administration.

The process and success of teacher development depends very much on the context in which it takes place. The nature of this context can make or break teacher development efforts. Understanding and attending to the *ecology* of teacher development should therefore be an important priority for teachers, administrators and researchers alike.

There are two broad ways in which this ecological perspective is important for teacher development. First, the context of teachers' working environment provides conditions in which teacher development initiatives succeed or fail. Second, the context of teaching can itself be a focus for teacher development.

In the first case, many factors may help or impede teacher development initiatives. Shortage of planning time or time away from class may make it difficult for teachers to plan together or to act as peer coaches for each other, or to serve effectively as mentors for their junior colleagues, for instance.[38] Meagre resources can restrict access to supply cover and therefore opportunities for release time to work together, to attend workshops or to see other teachers teach. More generally, they can create a dispiriting environment of large class sizes and poor-quality texts and instructional materials, in which survival comes to take precedence over improvement.[39] Misallocation of resources can be equally problematic. We have already noted a persistent and regrettable tendency in staff development funding to invest the bulk of expenditure in 'expert' trainers rather than in those being trained.

Leadership is another particularly important contextual factor which affects the success of teacher development efforts. Directly, strategies of principals and headteachers that have been shown to support and promote teacher development initiatives include freeing up and hustling for time and resources to facilitate the initiative; leaders showing that they are themselves committed to the initiative and symbolizing this by being present at staff training sessions and other activities; avoiding attachment to quick training 'fixes' and instead committing themselves and their staffs to minimum three-year programmes of improvement to get them beyond the uncertainties and disappointments of early implementation difficulties, and so on.[40] More indirectly, effective leadership can help provide a supportive context for teacher development efforts in general, not just for specific initiatives. Relevant strategies here include involving staff in decision-making processes, valuing staff contributions and initiatives, and developing school cultures in which teachers work closely together and support each other in the improvement and change process.[41]

These are not the only contextual factors that improve the possibilities for success in teacher development initiatives. But they are among the most important. The absence of a supportive work context, of appropriate resourcing and positive leadership, can create serious and perhaps insurmountable difficulties for specific teacher development and educational change initiatives. The first two chapters of this book illustrate these kinds of difficulties very clearly. Both Michael Apple and Susan Jungck in Chapter 2 and Heather-jane Robertson in Chapter 3 document extensively how much of the present context of teachers' work is highly unconducive to teacher development or to educational improvement more generally.

Apple and Jungck argue that away from the spotlight of innovative projects among ordinary teachers in countless ordinary schools, the daily reality of teachers' work is far removed from the rhetorics of professionalism and empowerment that are often used to describe it. For most teachers, they argue, the context of teaching and teacher development is not one of co-operation and collegiality but of centralization, standardization and rationalization. Teachers here are not so much the empowered vanguard of change and improvement as the embattled victims of bureaucratic and technocratic control. Teaching, Apple and Jungck contend, is becoming de-skilled. Curriculum content and goals are being increasingly mandated and more precisely defined. Tests and accountability systems are proliferating and being imposed. Methods, texts and tests, they argue, are being taken out of the hands of the people who must put them into practice. These measures, they continue, are creating not empowered professionals but 'alienated executors' of others' plans. The de-skilling of teachers' work in an 'intensified' context of increased pressures and reduced support is illustrated through an ethnographic study of how teachers deal with a newly mandated programme in computer literacy. As one teacher concludes when reflecting on her response to the pre-packaged, pre-specified nature of the change she is required to implement: 'You don't have to be a teacher to teach the Unit'.

Apple and Jungck argue that the de-skilling of teachers' work at the elementary level is also primarily the de-skilling of women's work: women who often face considerable pressures and demands in their domestic lives as well as intensification in their professional ones. Gender issues in this sense form an important and inescapable part of the context of teaching. Heather-jane Robertson takes this point further in her chapter on *Teacher Development and Gender Equity*. The context of teaching and teacher development, she argues, is not a gender-neutral context. It is androcentric. It values what is associated with being male, with men's work, men's experience and stereotypically male characteristics and values, more than what is associated with being female and with women's work and experience. Moreover, she argues, androcentrism disguises male experience as universal experience, making gender bias in the very ways we operate both powerful and invisible. Androcentrism, she continues, is deeply implicated in much of the context of schooling, teachers' work and teacher development.

Robertson cites Joyce and Showers's work on staff development as an example of the ways that androcentrism is embodied in dominant approaches to teacher development; approaches of a more skills-based nature.[42] She illustrates how sexism is profoundly present in many aspects of Joyce and Showers's influential work. It is present in the stereotypically masculine over-confidence and spurious certainty that Joyce and Showers display in their reliance on the 'hard' findings of educational research, and on the 'external' knowledge base of experts against the internal 'knowing' of teachers. Sexism is also present, Robertson argues, in Joyce and Showers's view of 'developed' teachers as professionally voracious 'omnivores': a view which, she says, values male-like exploitation of the environment in an all-consuming professional life against more characteristically feminine responses of caution and caring where the professional and personal life are held in a more healthy balance. Finally, Robertson argues, the teaching strategies advocated by Joyce and Showers as a focus for staff development are treated by them as if they are gender neutral; as if their appropriateness for boys and girls respectively does not differ. They do not attend to male/female differences in learning styles, to gender bias in curriculum materials, in questioning strategies and in many other areas of instruction. By ignoring these differences, it is proposed, Joyce and Showers may unwittingly be promoting the achievement opportunities of boys against those of girls, and also signalling that gender issues are an inappropriate or relatively minor concern for staff development. For Robertson and for Apple and Jungck alike, andro-centric and bureaucratic approaches to administration and teacher development in general make empowerment and professionalism hollow symbols for all but a few teachers and their schools.

As we argued earlier, the context of teaching can be a focus as well as a con-dition for teacher development efforts. One of the most important focal points for creating a context that supports continuing professional development is the culture of teaching, which Andy Hargreaves discusses in the closing chapter.

Hargreaves argues that the culture of teaching is a key focal point for improvement and change. There is growing evidence that the development of collaborative school cultures, where teachers routinely support, learn from and work with each other, is related to successful implementation of educational change, a strong record in school-fostered improvement, good practices in pro-fessional development, and positive outcomes in pupil achievement.[43] Drawing on his own research and other work in the field, Hargreaves describes the charac-teristic of these collaborative work cultures, which are still a relative rarity in our schools but which may be beacons for others to follow.

While urging the development of collaborative cultures, Hargreaves also cautions against 'managing' the creation of such cultures in top-down, bureau-cratic, technically controlled and characteristically masculine ways. Although *collaborative cultures* may be part of the solution to teacher development, he says, their bureaucratic equivalent in the form of *contrived collegiality* may be part of the problem. Contrived collegiality, he argues, makes collaboration com-pulsory rather than voluntary, forced rather than facilitated, formal and sched-uled rather than informal and evolutionary, directed towards administrative priorities more than teacher concerns, predictable rather than unpredictable in its outcomes, and — because of all these things — predominantly masculine rather than feminine in its administrative orientation and style.

The conclusion of this last chapter in seeking to develop a context for teacher development serves as a conclusion for the book as a whole. The chapter ends in the form of a challenge to those seeking to develop collaborative cultures in their schools and school systems. It is a challenge to shift the balance of responsibility for teacher development and curriculum development from the centre to the periphery, from administrators to teachers, and from men to women.

CONCLUSION

In this first chapter, we have tried to show that understanding teacher develop-ment involves understanding not only the knowledge and skills that teachers should acquire but also understanding what sort of person the teacher is and the context in which most teachers work. Without an understanding of the person, and without the most profound alterations in the bureaucratic, androcentric, control-centred ways in which our schools and school systems are run, specific staff development efforts are likely to prove temporary and localized in their impact, and unsuccessful in their overall effects. Understanding teacher development is a necessary beginning. Reconstructing it is an equally indispensable next step. We hope this book helps promote this understanding and reconstruction and, in doing so, helps contribute to the future development of teacher development itself.

NOTES AND REFERENCES

1. On 'opportunities to learn', particularly within streamed settings, see Oakes, J., *Keeping Track: How Schools Structure Inequality*. New Haven, CT: Yale University Press, 1985.

2. See Oakes, op. cit., note 1, and Hargreaves, A. and Earl, L., *Rights of Passage*. Toronto: Queen's Printer, 1990.

3. Bennett, N., Desforges, C., Cockburn, A. and Wilkinson, B., *The Quality of Pupil Learning Experiences*, Hillsdale, NJ: Lawrence Erlbaum & Associates, 1984.

4. Woods, P., *Teacher Skills and Strategies*. Philadelphia: Falmer Press, 1990.

5. These debates also apply in many other instructional fields, such as co-operative learning and whole-language teaching.

6. As, for example, in Joyce, B. and Showers, B., *Student Achievement through Staff Development*, New York: Longman, 1988.

7. Fullan, M., 'Implementing the Implementation Plan,' in Wideen, M. and Andrews, S., *Staff Development for School Improvement*. Philadelphia: Falmer Press, 1987.

8. See Joyce and Showers, op. cit., note 6 on peer coaching. Also Seller, W., 'The in-school resource coaching model: a professional development strategy for planned change'. *Journal of Educational Administration and Foundations*, December 1977, pp. 30–42.

9. Little, J. W., 'District policy choices and teachers' professional development opportunities'. *Educational Evaluation and Policy Analysis*, 11 (2), pp. 165–80, Summer 1989.

10. Hunt, D., *Beginning with Ourselves*. Toronto: OISE Press, 1987.

11. Hargreaves, A. 'Individualism and individuality: reinterpreting the culture of teaching'. *International Journal of Educational Research*, forthcoming.

12. On the importance of personal and practical teacher knowledge, see Connelly, F. M. and Clandinin, D. J., *Teachers as Curriculum Planners: Narratives of Experience*. New York: Teachers College Press, 1988.

13. See Robertson, Chapter 3.

14. Harvey, D., *The Condition of Postmodernity*, Oxford: Basil Blackwell, 1989.

15. Gleick, J., *Chaos*. New York: Penguin Books, 1987.

16. Giddens, A., *The Consequences of Modernity*. Oxford: Polity Press, 1990.

17. See Slavin, R., 'The PET and the pendulum: faddism in education and how to stop it'. *Phi Delta Kappan*, 70 (10), pp. 752-8.

18. McNeil, L., *Contradictions of Control*. London: Routledge, 1986.

19. See Hargreaves, op. cit., note 11, and Hargreaves, A. and Dawe, R., 'Paths of professional development'. *Teaching and Teacher Education*, 4 (3), 1990.

20. Fullan, M. *The New Meaning of Educational Change*. New York: Teachers College Press, 1991.

21. See Goodson, Chapter 7.

22. For example, see Joyce, B., Murphy, C., Showers, B. and Murphy, J. 'School renewal as cultural change'. *Educational Leadership*, 47 (3), pp. 70-8, 1989.

23. See Harvey, op. cit., note 14.

24. See Little, op. cit., note 9.

25. Ibid.

26. As an example, see Berliner, D., 'Ways of thinking about students and classrooms by more and less experienced teachers'. In Calderhead, J., *Exploring Teacher Thinking*. Eastbourne: Holt-Saunders, 1987.

27. The distinction between skill and will is drawn by Hargreaves and Dawe, op. cit., note 19.

28. See Fullan, M. and Hargreaves, A., *What's Worth Fighting for in Your School*. Toronto: Ontario Public School Teachers' Federation, 1991.

29. See Clandinin and Connelly, op. cit., note 12.

30. See, for instance, Fullan, M., *The Meaning of Educational Change*. Toronto: OISE Press, 1982, and Miles, M. B. and Huberman, A. M., *Innovation Up Close: How School Improvement Works*. New York: Plenum Press, 1984.

31. Nias, J., *Primary Teachers Talking*. London: Routledge, 1989, and Leithwood, K., 'The principal's role in teacher development'. In Fullan, M. and Hargreaves, A., *Teacher Development and Educational Change*. Philadelphia: Falmer Press, 1991.

32. Sikes, P., Measor, L. and Woods, P., *Teacher Careers: Crises and Continuities*. Philadelphia: Falmer Press, 1985.

33. Riseborough, G. 'Teacher careers and comprehensive schooling'. *Sociology*, 15 (3), pp. 355–81, 1981.

34. See Leithwood, op. cit., note 31.

35. For instance, see Clandinin and Connelly, op. cit., note 12.

36. See Fullan, op. cit., note 7.

37. Holmes, M., 'Bringing about change in teachers: rationistic technology and therapeutic human relations in the subversion of education'. Paper presented to the International Conference on Teacher Development, Toronto, Ontario Institute for Studies in Education, February 1989.

38. For a discussion of the time implications of teacher development, see Hargreaves, A., 'Teachers' work and the politics of time and space'. *Qualitative Studies in Education*, forthcoming.

39. On teaching for survival, see Woods, op. cit., note 4.

40. Little, J. W., 'Seductive images and organizational realities in professional development'. *Teachers College Record*, 86 (1), pp. 84–102, 1984.

41. See Leithwood, K. and Jantzi, D., 'Transformational leadership'. Unpublished paper, Toronto: OISE, 1990, and Hargreaves in this volume.

42. See Joyce and Showers, op. cit., note 6.

43. The benefits of collaboration are outlined in Rosenholtz, S., *Teachers' Workplace*. New York: Longman, 1989.

Chapter 2

You Don't Have to Be a Teacher to Teach This Unit: Teaching, Technology and Control in the Classroom

Michael W. Apple and Susan Jungck

TEACHING IN CRISIS

With all of the rhetoric about teaching and professionalism, about enhancing teachers' powers and about raising pay and respect, the reality of many teachers' lives bears little resemblance to this rhetoric. Rather than moving in the direction of increased autonomy, in all too many instances the daily lives of teachers in classrooms of many nations are becoming ever more controlled and ever more subject to administrative logics that seek to tighten the reins on the processes of teaching and curriculum. Teacher development, co-operation and 'empowerment' may be the talk, but centralization, standardization and rationalization may be the strongest tendencies. In Great Britain and the United States of America — to take but two examples — reductive accountability and teacher evaluation schemes and increasing centralization have become so commonplace that in a few more years we may have lost from our collective memory the very possibility of difference. Indeed, there are areas in the USA where it has been mandated that teachers must teach *only* that material which is in the approved textbook. Going beyond the 'approved' material risks administrative sanctions.

An odd combination of forces has led to this situation. Economic modernizers, educational efficiency experts, neo-conservatives, segments of the new right, many working and lower middle-class parents who believe that their children's futures are threatened by a school system that does not guarantee jobs, and members of parts of the new middle class whose own mobility is dependent on technical and administratively oriented knowledge have formed a tense and contradictory alliance to return us to 'the basics', to 'appropriate' values and dispositions, to 'efficiency and accountability', and to a close connection between schools and an economy in crisis.[1]

While we need to be cautious of being overly economistic (and indeed we have argued at great length against such tendencies in other places[2]), it is still the case that educators have witnessed a massive attempt — one that has been more than a little successful — at exporting the crisis in the economy and in authority relations *from* the practices and policies of dominant groups *on to* the schools. If schools and their teachers and curricula were more tightly controlled, more closely linked to the needs of business and industry, and more technically orientated, with more stress on traditional values and work-place norms and dispositions, then the problems of achievement, of unemployment, of international economic competitiveness, of the disintegration of the inner city and so on, would largely disappear.

In the USA, a multitude of reports told us that because of the inefficiency of our educational system and the poor quality of our teachers and curricula, our nation was at risk. In Great Britain a similar argument was heard. Teachers were seen to be holding on to a curriculum that was 'ill-suited to modern technological and industrial needs and as generally fostering an anti-industrial ethos among their students. In all respects, schools and teachers were portrayed as failing the nation'. Industry was turned into a 'dirty word', a fact that supposedly contributed greatly to the nation's industrial decline.[3]

As one of us has argued at greater length elsewhere,[4] there is immense pressure currently not only to redefine the manner in which education is carried out, but also what education is actually *for*. This has not remained outside the classroom but is now proceeding rather rapidly to enter into classroom life and alter our definitions of what counts as good teaching. As we shall see in the second, more empirical part of this chapter in our analysis of what happens in computer literacy classes — one of the newly formed high-status areas of curriculum and teaching during the 'educational crisis' — this can have a serious impact on the reality of teaching.

Among the major effects of these pressures is what is happening to teaching as an occupation and as a set of skilled and self-reflective actions. Important transformations are occurring that will have significant impacts on how we do our jobs and on who will decide whether we are successfully carrying them out. Seeing what is happening will require that we recapitulate a set of arguments about the relationship, in teaching, between the complicated processes involved in how one's work is controlled (what has been called 'proletarianization') and the struggles over what counts as, and who has, skills.[5]

TEACHING AS A LABOUR PROCESS

In order to understand this argument we need to think about teaching in a particular way, to think of it as what might be called a complicated *labour process*. It is a labour process which is significantly different from that of working on an assembly line, in the home, or in an office. But, even given these differences, the same pressures that are currently affecting jobs in general are now being increasingly felt in teaching. In the general sociological literature, the label affixed to what is happening is the 'degradation of labour'.[6] This degradation is a 'gift' from our dominant economic and ideological arrangements.

In society as a whole there has been an exceptionally long history of rationalizing and standardizing people's jobs. In industry, a familiar example of this was management's use of Taylorism and time-and-motion studies in their continual search for higher profits and greater control over their employees. Here, complicated jobs were rigorously examined by management experts. Each element that went into doing the job was broken down into its simplest activities. All planning was to be done by management, not workers. The consequences of this have been profound, but two of them are especially important for our discussion.[7]

The first is what we shall call the *separation of conception from execution*. When complicated jobs are broken down into atomistic elements, the person doing the job loses sight of the whole process and loses control over her or his own labour, since someone outside the immediate situation now has greater control over both the planning and what is actually happening. The second consequence is related, but adds a further debilitating characteristic. This is known as *de-skilling*. As employees lose control over their own labour, the skills that they have developed over the years atrophy. They are slowly lost, thereby making it even easier for management to increase control of one's job because the skills of planning and controlling it oneself are no longer available.[8] A general principle emerges here: in one's labour, lack of use leads to loss. This has been particularly the case for women's labour. Women's work has been particularly subject to the de-skilling and de-powering tendencies of management.[9] These tendencies are quite visible in a multitude of work places throughout the USA, from factories and clerical and other office work to stores, restaurants and government jobs, and now even teaching. More and more of these seem to be subject to such 'degradation'.

How is this process now working through the job of teaching? At the outset, it is important to realize that it has taken teachers decades to gain the skills and power they now have. Even though in many school systems teachers in reality have only a limited right actually to choose the texts and other curricular materials they use, these conditions are still a good deal better than in earlier periods of our educational history, when text and curricular selection was an administrative responsibility. The gains that teachers have made did not come easily. It took thousands of teachers in hundreds of districts throughout the USA, constantly reaffirming their right to determine what would happen in their classrooms, to take each small step away from total administrative control of the curriculum. This was even more the case at the elementary school level, where the overwhelming majority of teachers have historically been women. Women teachers have had to struggle even harder to gain recognition of their skills and worth.[10]

Yet while curriculum planning and determination are now more *formally* democratic in most areas of the curriculum, there are forces now acting on the schools that may make such choices nearly meaningless. At the local, state and national levels, movements for strict accountability systems, competency-based education and testing, systems management, a truncated vision of the 'basics', mandated curricular content and goals and so on, are clear and growing.

Increasingly, teaching methods, texts, tests and outcomes are being taken out of the hands of the people who must put them into practice. Instead, they are being legislated by national or state departments of education or in state legislatures, and are being either supported or stimulated by many of the national reports, such as *A Nation at Risk*, which are often simplistic assessments of, and responses to, problems in education, and ones which demonstrate the increasing power of conservative ideologies in our public discourse.[11]

For example, at the time of writing, in the USA nearly forty of the fifty states have established some form of state-wide competency testing. Many of these systems are quite reductive and more than a little unreflective. While this is meant ostensibly to guarantee some form of 'quality control', one of the major effects of such state intervention has been considerable pressure on teachers to teach simply for the tests.[12] It is part of a growing process of state intervention into teaching and the curriculum, and signifies another instance in the long history of state intervention into the work of a largely female labour force.[13]

As has been demonstrated at considerable length in *Teachers and Texts*, much of the attempt by state legislatures, departments of education and 'educational managers' to rationalize and standardize the process and products of teaching as a collection of measurable 'competencies' and so on is related to a longer history of attempts to control the labour of occupations that have historically been seen as women's paid work. That is, we do not think it is possible to understand why teachers are subject to greater control and to greater governmental intervention, *and what the effects of such mandates are*, unless we step back and ask a particular kind of question. By and large, *who* is doing the teaching?

Historically, teaching has been constructed as women's paid work. In most Western industrialized nations approximately two-thirds of the teaching force are women, a figure that is much higher the lower one goes in the educational system. Administrators are overwhelmingly male, a figure that increases significantly the higher one goes in the educational system. Thus, both statistically and in terms of its effects, it would be a mistake of considerable proportions to ignore the gendered composition of teaching when we discuss the rationalizing ethos increasingly surrounding it.[14]

These rationalizing forces are quite consequential and need to be analysed structurally to see the lasting impact they may be having on teaching. In much the same way as in other jobs, we are seeing the de-skilling of our teachers.[15] As noted above, when individuals cease to plan and control a large portion of their own work, the skills essential to doing these tasks self-reflectively and well atrophy and are forgotten. The skills that teachers have built up over decades of hard work — setting relevant curricular goals, establishing content, designing lessons and instructional strategies, 'community building' in the classroom, individualizing instruction based on an intimate knowledge of students' desires and needs and so on — are lost. In many ways, given the centralization of authority and control, they are simply no longer needed. In the process, however, the very things that make teaching a professional activity — the control of one's expertise and time — are also dissipated. There is no better formula for aliena-tion and burn-out than loss of control of one's labour (though it is unfortunate that terms such as 'burn-out' have such currency, since they make the problem into a psychological one rather than a truly structural one concerning the control of teachers' labour).

Hence the tendency for the curriculum to become increasingly planned, systematized, and standardized at a central level, totally focused on competen-cies measured by standardized tests (and largely dependent on predesigned commerical materials and texts written specifically for those states that have the tightest centralized control, and thus the largest guaranteed markets)[16] may have consequences that are the exact opposite of what many authorities intend. Instead of professional teachers who care greatly about what they do and why they do it, we may have alienated executors of someone else's plans. In fact, the literature on the labour process in general, as well as that specifically related to women's paid work, is replete with instances documenting the negative effects of tight systems of management and control and the accompanying loss of skill, autonomy, craft and pride that results.[17] As is too often the case, educational bureaucrats borrow the ideology and techniques of industrial management without recognizing what can and has happened to the majority of employees in industry itself.[18]

These kinds of interventionist movements will not only have consequences for teachers' ability to control their own work. It is also becoming very clear that they are having some very problematic results in terms of the kind of content that is being stressed in the curriculum.

A simple way of thinking about this is to divide the kinds of knowledge that we want students to learn into three types: knowledge 'that', 'how', and 'to'. Knowledge 'that' is factual information, such as knowing that Madison is the capital of Wisconsin or Baton Rouge is the capital of Louisiana. Knowledge 'how' is skills, such as knowing how to use the library or how to enquire into the history of, say, women or unions in the USA. Knowledge 'to' is dispositional knowledge. That is, it includes those norms, values and propensities that guide our future conduct. Examples include knowing to be honest, to have pride in one's racial heritage, to want to learn more after one's formal schooling is over, to be intel-lectually open-minded, or to see oneself as part of a democratic community and to act co-operatively. Each of these is important; but if we were to place them in some sort of hierarchy, most of us would agree that knowing an assortment of facts is probably less important than higher-order skills of enquiry. And these in turn are made less significant than they should be if the person is not disposed to use them in educationally and socially important ways.

With control over content, teaching, and evaluation shifting outside the classroom, the focus is more and more only on those elements of social studies, reading, science, and so forth that can be easily measured on standardized tests. Knowledge 'that' and occasionally low-level knowledge 'how' are the primary foci. Anything else is increasingly considered to be inconsequential. This is bad enough, of course, but in the process even the knowledge 'that' that is taught is made 'safer', less controversial, less critical. Not only is it a formula for de-skilling, it is also a contraction of the universe of possible social knowledge into largely that which continues the disenfranchisement of the knowledge of women, and of people of colour and labour, knowledge that is increasingly important given the levels of exploitation and domination that exist not only within our nations but between them as well.[19]

So far we have discussed at a very general level certain of the social dynamics that threaten to transform curricula and teaching. This discussion cannot be complete unless we add one other significant concept, the idea of *intensification*.[20]

Intensification is one of the most tangible ways in which the working conditions of teachers have eroded. It has many symptoms, from the trivial to the more complex — ranging from having no time at all even to go to the bathroom, have a cup of coffee or relax, to having a total absence of time to keep up with one's field. We can see it most visibly in the chronic sense of work overload that has escalated over time. More and more has to be done; less and less time is available to do it. This has led to a multitude of results.

Intensification leads people to 'cut corners', so that only what is 'essential' to the task *immediately* at hand is accomplished. It forces people increasingly to rely on 'experts' to tell them what to do and to begin to mistrust the expertise they may have developed over the years. In the process, quality is sacrificed for quantity. Getting done is substituted for work well done. And, as time itself becomes a scarce 'commodity', the risk of isolation grows, thereby both reducing the chances that interaction among participants will enable critiques and limiting the possibility that rethinking and peer teaching will naturally evolve. Collective skills are lost as 'management skills' are gained. Often the primary task is, to quote one teacher, to 'find a way to get through the day'. And, finally, pride itself is jeopardized as the work becomes dominated by someone else's conception of what should be done.

As already noted, with the growth of interventionist styles of management and a focus on reductive accountability schemes in many nations, more and more curricula and the act of teaching itself are dominated by prespecified sequential lists of behaviourally defined competencies and objectives, pre-tests and post-tests to measure 'readiness' and skill levels, and a dominance of pre-packaged textual and often worksheet material. The amount of paperwork necessary for evaluation and record-keeping is often phenomenal under these conditions. As has been documented elsewhere, increasingly common situations such as these often require teachers to be busy with these tasks before and after school and during their lunch hour. Teachers come in very early and leave very late, often still to be faced with two hours' more work at home every night.[21]

This is exacerbated by the fact that, given the pressures now being placed on schools, what has actually happened is that not only are curricula and teaching more tightly controlled but more, not less, has to be accomplished. Nothing has been removed from the curriculum. Instead, elements have been added on. One of the best examples has been the addition of 'computer literacy' programmes in many school systems. In most districts, nothing has been dropped from the already immensely crowded curriculum, and teachers are faced with the predicament of finding the time and physical and emotional resources to integrate such programmes into the school day. This may have even greater implications for female teachers, as we shall point out in the following section.

It is important to say here, however, that — as with other labour processes — one of the effects of these processes of de-skilling and intensification is the threat they pose to the conception of teaching as an 'integrated whole activity'. Concerns of care, connectedness, nurturing, and fostering 'growth' — concerns that have historically been linked to skills and dispositions surrounding the paid and unpaid labour of women — are devalued. In essence, they are no longer given credit for being skilled at all, as the very definition of what counts as a skill is further altered to include only that which is technical and based on a process 'which places emphasis on performance, monitoring and subject-centered instruction'.[22] As we shall see, such transformations can occur all too easily.

Concepts such as de-skilling, the separation of conception from execution, and intensification can remain abstractions unless we can see how they represent processes that have a real and material existence in day-to-day school life. Many teachers are experiencing these dynamics as very real alterations in their lives inside and outside the classroom. In the next section of this chapter, we shall situate these processes within the activities of a group of teachers in one particular school that was subject to a long-term and comprehensive ethnographic study by one of us of the growth and effects of a mandate to make all students 'computer literate'. The introduction of such a new curriculum emphasis was officially to help students and teachers become more technically literate. Yet it had a number of unforeseen effects that often led to the opposite. The new curriculum mandate to develop computer literacy was a response by this particular school system to the calls from a variety of groups for a more technically orientated curriculum that would teach the skills needed for access and mobility later on. It occurred in an educational, economic and political context in which the state department of education, business and industry and many middle-class parents were placing considerable pressure on schools to develop immediately programmes that guaranteed not only a computer literate school population, but to make such 'literacy' a requirement for graduation from secondary school and to establish closer links between educational and economic goals.[23]

As we shall see later in this chapter, gender relations, the changing labour conditions of teachers, and the organizational and material realities brought about by the fiscal crisis of the state have directly impinged on the construction of classroom life. In this site, the intensification of the teachers' workload, the lack of availability of sufficient resources, the organizational structure of the school as it had evolved over time, and the complicated reality of gendered labour all combined to create a situation in which few teachers were fully satisfied with the outcomes.

INSIDE THE CLASSROOM

Lakeside–Maple Glen School District has decided, in the face of national trends and considerable pressure, to make its curricula more responsive to recent and rapid social and technological change.[24] It wants to ensure that its curricula are more responsive to the 'needs of the economy' and the perceived future labour market. Computers are one of the keys in the school district's strategies for accomplishing this. Yet this district has also taken the stance that such curriculum programmes should not be imposed from above, even given the considerable pressure being placed on it. Rather, teachers themselves must be deeply involved in the curriculum development process.

This latter point about giving more responsibility to teachers is important. All too often, the critical literature has assumed that pressures toward de-skilling, the separation of conception from execution, and intensification must be imposed continually from the outside through administrative mandates, centralized curriculum determination, or externally produced and controlled evaluation plans. This is not always the case, and in fact it may ignore the complexity of decision-making on the ground, so to speak. Because teachers have always sought ways to retain their day-to-day control over classroom reality, and are not passive receivers of top-down strategies, complexity must be recognized.[25] In fact, as we shall document in this section, these external conditions do not totally determine the reality of curriculum and teaching. Teachers may indeed still have space for manoeuvring. However, these pressures may actually also create a context that makes it seem unrealistic and not in their *immediate* interests for many teachers to do other than participate in recreating conditions that foster continued difficulties in their own labour. To a large extent, this is exactly what happened here.

One of the first curriculum programmes to be developed and implemented under the District's new Computer Literacy Project was the ten-day Computer Literacy Unit (CLU). It was to be added on in every middle school seventh-grade maths class.

Mr Nelson, a middle school maths teacher and the district computer 'expert', and Mr Miller, another middle school maths teacher, were given summer curriculum compensation to develop the seventh-grade unit, which they and three other seventh-grade maths teachers were expected to implement in the autumn. Although Mr Nelson and Mr Miller had conceptualized the unit before the autumn, they had not specifically planned each daily lesson or assembled the necessary materials to be used. They began in the autumn with most of what became their unit outline completed:

Day 1 – History of and parts of a computer

Day 2 – Operation of a computer and computer vocabulary

Day 3 – Interaction with a computer (lab)

Day 4 – Input to a computer

Day 5 – Output from a computer

Day 6 – Flow charting

Day 7 – Introduction to programming in BASIC

Day 8 – Writing a program in BASIC (lab)

Day 9 – Group activity — a computer simulation (lab)

Day 10 – Test and effects of computers upon society

Mr Nelson and Mr Miller met frequently during the first six weeks of school to work on the unit, a comprehensive task which consisted of preparing daily lesson plans, procuring worksheets, filmstrips, tape recordings, audio-visual equipment and rescheduling the computer laboratory. The unit was developed with a number of 'givens' in mind, givens that bear on our earlier arguments.

One 'given' that Mr Nelson and Mr Miller considered was that the school's seven computers were being used in the computer laboratory for the eighth-grade computer elective courses, and were not available when several of the seventh-grade maths classes met. They recognized therefore that most of the unit would have to be taught without the use of computers — a major obstacle, because they believed that 'hands on' computer experiences were very important. Through elaborate planning, the teachers were able to schedule three of the ten days in the computer laboratory, not very much considering that there would be about 25 students sharing seven computers on those Laboratory days.

Minimal computer access, a problem of considerable moment in many budget-conscious school systems, affected the curriculum and the teaching because skills and concepts most effectively developed through using a computer had to be taught in more vicarious ways, such as observations and lectures, or eliminated altogether. For example, too few computers and too little time in the computer laboratory meant that most students were never able to write a program in BASIC, even though it was a specific objective and represented the general active hands-on experiences that were consistent with the district goals.

A second 'given' which influenced how the unit was developed was stated by Mr Miller: 'You have to remember that we have faculty in this department who don't know much about computers. We needed a program that everyone could teach.' Mr Nelson explained that a crucial factor in developing the unit was that teachers who know nothing about computers would be able to 'teach it'. He said, 'You see, we really needed to develop a canned unit.' The three other maths teachers, all women, were not involved in developing the unit and only found out about it in the autumn. One woman, Ms Wilson, a recent graduate who was newly hired on a part-time basis, had no computer experience and was quite apprehensive about having to teach a computer literacy unit. Another woman, Ms Linder, had some computer experience but had been away on a year's leave of absence and had only just learned of the required unit. The third woman, Ms Kane, was experienced in the department but had no experience with computers. Thus the unit was 'canned', so that these or any future teachers would be able to 'teach' it.

A third 'given' resulted from the organization of the maths department. It was a regular practice in the Department to test all seventh graders after the first ten weeks of school and transfer those with 'superior ability' to an eighth-grade maths class. Selection by 'talent', with all its stratifying implications, was not an invisible process at work here. This schedule therefore determined that the unit would have to be completed in all seventh-grade maths classes by the tenth week of school. In order to be able to share the computers and other equipment, and schedule the computer laboratory, half of the maths classes had to implement the unit during weeks seven and eight and the other half had the unit during the ninth and tenth weeks of school. This schedule placed tremendous time pressures on Mr Nelson and Mr Miller to complete the unit quickly.

Given these time pressures and the intensification of their own work, Mr Nelson and Mr Miller had to assemble the materials rapidly, and communications with the other maths teachers about the unit were minimal. What they did was to examine some commercially prepared computer literacy curriculum materials that were available.

The foundation of the unit that they planned consisted of two filmstrips and a prepackaged commercial curriculum consisting of tape-recorded lessons and co-ordinated worksheets. The topical outline that had been partially completed was finalized on the basis of some of these tape recorded lessons and worksheets. The unit became very structured, detailing the objectives, the equipment needed and the lesson plan for each day. The plan specified that six days were to be spent in the classroom, mostly listening to the commercial tape recordings and completing the worksheets. Three days were to be spent in the computer laboratory — two for interacting with instructional software and one for writing a computer program. A unit test was planned for the last day, and after the test a film about the social implications of computers would complete the unit. Because of the bulk of all the worksheets and equipment, the curriculum was usually rolled around from room to room on a 'cart' or trolley.

In many ways, the 'curriculum on a cart' may be viewed as an efficient, practical and sensible solution to the several 'givens' within the school. What occurred inside the classrooms, however, documents how the realities of teachers' lives inside and outside the school and what is happening to the job of teaching carries with it contradictions that are very serious.

A Curriculum on a Cart

Students and teachers expressed enthusiasm about the two-week computer unit because it represented something new and popular. There were five teachers teaching a total of 11 heterogeneously grouped seventh-grade maths classes and, as we noted above, owing to the time pressures, the unit was not prepared and ready to go until it was time to begin teaching the unit. The female teachers had little or no time to preview the unit. In essence, they experienced it as they taught it.

In all classes the unit began with some enthusiasm and two film strips and two worksheets. Students were shown a film strip which focused on the history and development of computers and were given a timeline of events for note-taking. The content emphasized dates of events, such as the invention of the transistor and computer terminology. There was little class discussion because the film strips took up the whole period. Homework consisted of a WordSearch worksheet with hidden names of computer parts.

To give a sense of daily activity, let us focus on Day 5. The daily routine that occurred on Day 5 was representative of all days in which worksheets and tape recordings were predominant. Day 5 is distinct, however, in that it represents a middle point in the unit and events on this day illustrate how the routine use of tape recordings and worksheets was beginning to have an impact on the teachers' and students' initial enthusiasm for the unit, on the teachers' sense of skill, and on the intensification of their work.

Day 5   As the students come into class today, one boy shouts out, 'Are we going to the lab today?' The teacher answers, 'We've got those sheets again and the tapes . . .'. Invariably, when hearing that it was a worksheet day, students would start to grumble, one rather loudly, 'That man's dejected', 'I hate this, this is boring', 'Do we have to do this all the time?', 'I cannot stand this class', 'This isn't computer class, this is worksheets . . . what do we learn, nothing . . . how to push a button' (referring to the tape recorder). One student turned to one of us and, referring to the worksheets, complained, 'We know this stuff already, maybe not these fancy words . . . but we know this stuff.' Although the students complained about the tapes and the worksheets, they did not disrupt the class routine. They came into class, made a number of enquiries and remarks, took their seats and co-operated with the teachers. Their attitudes were for the most part ignored or made light of by the teachers, who appeared to regard a certain amount of negativism and complaining as typical adolescent behaviour in school.

The first daily procedure in every class was the distribution of worksheets, which took about ten minutes because there were so many of them. Teachers usually passed around a stapler and this became the occasion for individual entertainment as students dawdled with it, withheld it from the next student, slid it on the floor and generally used it to attract attention and delay beginning the worksheets.

The teachers began the lesson by turning on the first tape-recorded lesson for the students. A man's voice read the captioned information on the worksheets and students were instructed to follow. He then explained how to complete the worksheet and said 'now turn off the tape and complete the worksheet'. Teachers who, given the immense workload of paperwork, used this time to do independent work at their desks, frequently missed this directive and the students would shout, 'Turn off the tape.' After a few minutes the teacher would turn the tape recorder back on and the narrator would read the answers while students were supposed to correct their worksheets. As the unit progressed many students would just wait for the answers to be read and would fill in their papers at that time. After a worksheet was completed the narrator would then say, 'If you want to continue . . .' which was an invitation to go on to the next worksheet. This invitation invariably met with responses such as 'but we don't!'. One teacher said in a singsong voice, 'Oh we do, we do'. After one of the first classes, this teacher said, 'I don't think this was a good day, the kids didn't really get much out of this . . .'. This was a surprising remark at first sight because the students had been very attentive, completed the worksheets and the day had progressed according to the lesson plan. It expressed, however, the teacher's intuitive sense that this material, as conveyed through the tapes, was not very effective.

As the tape recorder droned on, students found many quiet and unobtrusive diversions. Students would comb their hair, clean dirt from their sneakers, day-dream, doodle and sharpen pencils. One girl worked all period getting a sweet wrapped in crinkly paper out of her pocket, unwrapped and into her mouth, all unnoticed. These activities were generally quiet and private, and students in all classes during this unit were outwardly very orderly. These diversions were rarely disruptive. Most of the students, however, were very quiet and completed their worksheets.

Mr Miller said that the Maths Department had the reputation for being quite strict and seventh graders, still new to the school, might be a little intimidated by it. The students were also repeatedly told that (a) after this unit the teachers were going to determine which students would be transferred to an eighth-grade maths class, and (b) they should complete and keep their worksheets because they would be able to use them during the unit test. For many, the possibility of being advanced to the eighth-grade maths class — determined by their behaviour, their accumulated grades including their test score on this unit, and a maths achievement test — contributed to their 'good' behaviour during this unit.

Teachers also passed the time during the tape-recorded lessons in various ways. Some would correct papers from other classes and catch up on the seemingly endless backlog of routine paperwork. At first, these taped lessons seemed to be tolerated, probably because they gave teachers some extra preparation time, which in this school was limited to only 45 minutes a day. But by Day 5, it appeared that even the opportunity to catch up on other work was not totally absorbing. One teacher paced around the room, stared at a poster for five minutes, stared out of the window and finally stopped near one of us and said, 'I'm sick of these tapes!' One teacher dozed off during a tape. On Day 5, as on most days, the teacher's main role was to distribute the worksheets and manage the tape recorder. If all the daily tapes and worksheets were used and completed as specified on the lesson plan, then there was little or no time for questions or discussions. In all classes, other than supervising the use and distribution of the instructional materials, the teachers had little to do, as the tapes and worksheets established the content and form of the lesson.

However, teachers did not always sit passively by and watch; they intervened in the planned lessons. Mr Miller turned off the tape one day to explain a concept. He later told one of us, 'We have to discuss and clarify some, smooth the rough edges of these worksheets.' However, because of this interruption, he never did get back on schedule and complete the taped lesson. Ms Wilson lost a day owing to a school assembly and tried to consolidate two days by 'talking through' some of the lessons herself. 'We have to catch up today, so we can go to the lab tomorrow.' They couldn't catch up, however, and ended up skipping some tapes. Ms Linder stopped a lesson to clarify a mathematical formula, the inclusion of which irritated her because, as she later said, 'If I had seen the lesson first ... I would have taken that out, seventh graders don't know that, it shouldn't be in there.' On Day Six she modified the flow chart assignment by asking her students to write a flow chart on the topic of 'their choice' which she later explained to one of us would be 'more interesting for the students'.

Mr Nelson explained that computers are 'dumb' because they perform on the basis of how they are programmed and cannot reason or use common sense. He gave several examples of the kind of errors that have been made by computers, such as astronomical billing errors that most humans would immediately recognize as erroneous but which of course a computer could not. Nelson frequently supplemented the lessons in order to increase student interest and understanding. While he too strove to maintain the schedule, he was sufficiently knowledgeable to supplement and enrich the daily lessons.

Mr Miller took time one day to illustrate the difference between 13- and 16-sector disks. The computer program selected for use in the Lab was on a 13-sector disk. The students would therefore have to go through some extra procedures in the laboratory the following day and he wanted them to understand why. The point was not that this explanation about sectors was important, but that Mr Miller's explanation represented an attempt to demystify the computer, to help the students understand why the computer responded the way it did. In fact it was the 'mystical' aura of the computer that the general goals of the CLU were attempting to avoid. Naturally, teachers unfamiliar with computers could not explain these kinds of things, and the male teachers did more of this than did the women teachers. In the other classes, the sector incompatibility was not explained and the students were just told to 'first use this disk, then use the program disk'.

The male teachers did more explaining in class than did the female teachers, primarily because they were more knowledgeable about computers and familiar with the unit. However, they too were committed to following the lesson plans, and their diversions to 'smooth out the rough edges' invariably lost them time. Completing daily lesson plans was important to all the teachers because (a) the daily lessons were too long to make up the next day, (b) the schedule for the computer laboratory and the completion of the unit were fixed, (c) some lessons were sequential in nature, and (d) the final unit test was correlated to the information on the tapes and film strips. Therefore, the time that it would take teachers to explain the 'whys' of computers was inevitably brief or not taken at all. To take the time would jeopardize the completion of the two-week unit.

Two points are important here. One is that while the teachers did, to varying degrees, stop the tapes and clarify, explain or enrich the lessons, none attempted to (a) eliminate a lesson, (b) change the nature of the lessons, or (c) change the unit. The second point is that, in the context of a pressured and crowded curriculum and an intensified labour process, when teachers did interject discussions they invariably fell behind schedule. This made the pace of the unit even faster as they later tried to catch up. Thus teachers felt that they had to maintain the schedule because the unit was a requirement for which they and the students were responsible. Therefore the completion of the CLU became highly dependent on following the unit plans, and this instrumental goal usually took precedence over teacher- or student-originated activities, even when teachers became more than a little uncomfortable. Knowledge that, and low-level knowledge how, dominated almost 'naturally' in this situation.

Computer Laboratory Days: Hands On?   The three days in which the students met in the computer laboratory were quite a contrast to the classroom days, because the students were using the computers. On Day 3 the students were to select and use programs from a specially prepared demonstration disk. The general enthusiasm was dampened only by the fact that the students had to work in groups of three or four to a computer, and in the 45-minute class period each individual did not get very much 'hands-on' computer time.

On Days 3 and 9 the plan was that half of the class should work with the teacher at one computer using a simulation program, while the rest of the class shared the six remaining computers and were to complete a Laboratory worksheet and write their own programs, mainly because, given their workload, the teachers did not have time to offer them individual help. Ms Linder recognized this and later said that she did not like this lesson plan because, by working with the large group on the simulation game, she was not able to circulate and help those students who were trying to write programs.

The computer laboratory days were by far the most favoured by students and were planned to provide 'hands-on' experiences. Yet, since there were only seven computers to be shared, students had to work in groups of two, or on Day 3 in groups of three and four. Because periods were 45 minutes long, most students spent more time observing computer use than actually using a computer. Many educators claim that it is preferable to have students work in pairs rather than individually at a computer, because it promotes peer interaction and learning. We do not wish to reject that claim. However, in this study when groups became larger than two they usually became dysfunctional because individual interest waned as students were unable to sit and observe comfortably around the small computers. Invariably, some students would sit and engage in unrelated conversations while waiting for 'their turn', which some never got. Therefore, actual hands-on computer time was very limited.

Even with this disadvantage, however, students were in the laboratory and were generally enthusiastic about being there. If their computer use was more vicarious than actual, they were at least observing computers. The computer laboratory days were active and exploratory in nature and this provided a major contrast to the classroom days.

The Final Unit Test   The CLU final test on Day 10 was a short answer summary of the worksheets, tapes and film strips. The students could use their notes and worksheets to complete the test which was composed of matching, listing and fill-in-the-blank short answer items such as the following:

> Name three ways of putting information on printouts _____
> The first computer was built in Philadelphia and was named ____
> Put the outcome of each program on the output line.

Reflecting on the relatively reductive nature of the test, Mr Nelson said that he questioned whether the test really measured what was most important. Ms Linder did not really like the test:

> 'I felt that the final test could be better, some of the items were
> ambiguous and all the vocabulary stressed at the beginning was
> too technical.'

Ms Kane felt that there should have been a review sheet of the 'really important things' rather than having the students study and use all their notes during the test. Ms Wilson said that the students 'did well' on the test and the other teachers referred to the test scores as acceptable. In general, the teachers did not seem to place much emphasis on the test or its results, although the students, who had been repeatedly warned that 'this unit will be tested and your score will count in your quarter grade', did seem to take it seriously and worked carefully on the test.

Teachers' Reconstructions   In later interviews and a departmental meeting, teachers talked about how they felt about the unit. Mr Nelson, one of the developers, said 'I felt hamstrung, I would probably do things differently, but I felt that I had to pilot it.' Since Mr Nelson had computer expertise, he was not as dependent on the unit, and he, more than most, expanded the daily lesson plans.

Interestingly, use of the prepared CLU was not felt by all the teachers to be a required or even likely practice in the next years. Mr Nelson did not feel further pressure to use the unit in the future and he explained that it now exists as a 'resource for those who want it' and that as long as the objectives are 'covered' it didn't have to be done the same in every class. This is consistent with everday practice in the Maths Department, where all the teachers use the same standard textbook and cover the same objectives, so, as Mr Miller said, 'you know that each student has been exposed to the same things'.

However, it is important to state that many of the teachers may indeed still choose to *continue* to use the 'curriculum on a cart' in its current form, even though they recognize that it is minimizing their ability to affect the curriculum and that they are relatively 'hamstrung'. As noted earlier, the unit provided some extra time that teachers could and did use to catch up on routine paper-work and planning. For instance, when Ms Kane was asked how she felt about the use of the tapes she said:

> 'Well, it was good . . . I mean naturally it got boring and
> monotonous, but I would just tune out during those times. I used
> that time to work on a new unit, or on some school committee
> work, and I'd do other things during those tapes. I'd try not to
> show boredom to the kids, but I really didn't mind it, after all it
> was only for two weeks . . . If I'd change things next year, I'd
> lecture more but I'd still use a lot of those tapes, maybe not all,
> but a lot of them.'

We cannot understand this response unless we situate it into the reality of teachers' workloads. Ms Kane taught five seventh-grade maths classes in a row and, while she acknowledged that these tapes were boring for her, she essentially took advantage of these two weeks to gain time and relieve the pressures of keep-ing up with the planning and grading for five maths classes. She was aware of the fact that the unit marginalized her own curriculum autonomy, but she did not overtly resist her designated role in it. Instead, she interpreted and used the unit to compensate for her otherwise intense routine. She recognized the unit for what it was; she used the extra time that it gave her and she was not negative in assessing her role in the unit.

Her colleague, Ms Linder, also referred to the intensity of work and said that she didn't like the daily teaching schedule because:

> 'There are no breaks in the day, not time to correct papers, plan
> . . . You don't get to know the students as individuals . . . I have
> a seating chart.'

Therefore, the unit that is all pre-packaged, ready-to-go and includes few assign-ments to be corrected provides some benefits to teachers whose normal routine is far more labour intensive.

For some teachers, a curriculum that separates conception from execution can sometimes seem to be a benefit, not a loss. In addition to providing some time for teachers, the unit was also seen to provide the pedagogical support and information about computers, interpreted as helpful. Ms Wilson said that the tapes helped her because she learned about computers along with the students and anticipated using the same lessons again, although she would 'branch out' as she became more computer-literate. Teaching a unit for which she was unprepared was intimidating, and she welcomed the prepared unit where she could turn on the tape recorder and use worksheets. When asked about how she viewed the content of the unit she said, 'I think it covered the important things . . . but I really don't know much about computers you know . . .'[26] Ms Wilson, in general, was positive in her assessment of the unit.

Even though all the teachers had equally intensive schedules, they did not all interpret the form of the CLU in terms of benefits. For example, Ms Linder was more than a little distressed by the form of the unit as well as some of the content. Her main objection was that she preferred to plan her own curriculum. She said:

> 'You didn't have to be a teacher to teach this unit. Just turn on and off tapes . . . I would have done things a little different. I have enough computer background to have done some things differently if I had had time to prepare it . . . I was dependent on their plan, tapes and worksheets . . . I kept asking to see the unit, but it wasn't done and I was told, "Don't worry, there isn't much to do, just tapes". But I didn't like those two weeks at all, I knew when I was out those days, the sub would be able to do it, she just had to turn on the tape recorder.'

These comments are echoed in other places and by other teachers, though perhaps not as strongly. To varying degrees, most felt something was being lost by relying too heavily on the 'curriculum on a cart'. Yet by and large, the teachers accepted these two weeks as they were originally planned and did not markedly alter the standardized curriculum. How can we understand this?

GENDER AND THE INTENSIFICATION OF TEACHING

The rhetoric of computer literacy often turns out to be largely that — rhetoric. Even given the meritorious aims of the staff and the school district and the extensive amount of work put in by teachers, the curriculum is reduced once again to worksheets, an impersonal pre-packaged style and fact-based tests.

A good deal of this can only be fully understood if we place these attempts at curriculum reform back into what we have called the fiscal crisis of the state. School systems are often caught between two competing goals — accumulation and legitimation. They must both support an economy, especially when it is in crisis, and at the same time maintain their legitimacy with a wide range of different groups. The fiscal crisis makes it nearly impossible for schools to have sufficient resources to meet all of the goals they say they will meet; yet not at least to try to meet a multitude of varied goals means that an educational system will lose its legitimacy in the eyes of the 'public'. Given this, many goals will simply be symbolic. They will serve as a political rhetoric to communicate to the public that schools are in fact doing what concerned groups want them to do.

Yet they will not be totally rhetorical. Many teachers will be committed to the goals, believing that they are worth meeting and worth spending the exceptional amounts of additional time trying to take them seriously. These teachers will exploit themselves, working even harder in underfunded and intensified conditions to overcome the contradictory pressures they will be under. At the same time, however, the additional workload will create a situation in which fully meeting these goals will be impossible.

This school developed a Computer Literacy Unit under the same conditions and with the same intentions that many schools are currently developing similar curricula. Computer knowledgeable teachers, ample computers and adequate time, and scheduling flexibility are more like wishes than realities in most school districts. Mr Nelson and Mr Miller worked intensively for over a month to develop a curriculum that would provide introductory experiences for all the seventh graders. The CLU they developed was significant because it exemplified how the process of transforming a very general goal like computer literacy into a specific curriculum was mediated by the 'given' organizational factors and resources — both human and material — typifying the school, and by the gender divisions that organized it, a point to which we shall return in a moment.

It was apparent that the structure of the Unit and its implementation schedule, as well as the heavy load of teaching and paperwork that these teachers had, made it difficult for teachers to contribute more to the unit than brief and occasional additions and clarifications. A 'canned' or pre-packaged curriculum did emerge. Yet it was valued by some teachers as a practical and sensible solution to the problem of curriculum time, resources, and skills.

Certainly the major condition here was that of curriculum planning time, both in the immediate and long-term sense. In this school, only the two male teachers were technically prepared to teach the unit. Because the unit had to be completed within the first ten weeks of school, the other teachers did not have time to prepare themselves to develop the new curriculum for their classes. Paying two teachers to develop the unit for the department was the district's way of compensating individual teachers for their lack of curriculum preparation time. However, lack of comprehensive curriculum planning time is characteristic of the structure of most schools. Thus the 'curriculum on a cart' solution tends to be a generalized response to the demands of new curriculum projects in many schools, especially since other responses would require more money, something we cannot expect in times of the fiscal crisis of the state.

This practice compensates teachers for their lack of time by providing them with pre-packaged curricula rather than changing the basic conditions under which inadequate preparation time exists. In the immediate context, some teachers may interpret this as helpful and appreciate it as a resource. But in the broader context, it deprives teachers of a vital component of the curriculum process. Over time, these short-term compensatory practices function as deprivations because they limit the intellectual and emotional scope of teachers' work. This deprivation was specifically recognized and articulated by Ms Linder in her quote at the end of the previous section. As an experienced teacher who was very anxious to resume her full responsibilities, she expressed her feelings of alienation and unimportance when she said, 'You don't have to be a teacher to teach the unit', and went on to say that she wasn't worried when she was absent and a substitute had to teach her seventh-grade class during the unit. Her skills and curriculum responsibilities had been usurped and this angered her. Thus while in the immediate context the availability of the 'curriculum on a cart' was positively interpreted by some teachers, in the long term this form of curriculum functions to compensate for and not to alleviate the problem for which it was viewed as a solution: that of time and expertise.

The condition of time must be examined in *gender* terms here. It was the women teachers, not the men, in the Maths Department who were seen as less prepared to teach about computers and they were the ones most dependent on the availability of the unit. Typically, the source of computer literacy for inservice teachers is either through college and university courses, school district courses or independent study, all options that take considerable time outside of school. Both Mr Miller and Mr Nelson had taken a substantial number of university courses on computers in education. Given the gendered specificities of domestic labour, many women, such as those with childcare and household responsibilities like Ms Linder or women who are single parents, may have considerably less out-of-school time to take additional course work and prepare new curricula. Therefore, when a new curriculum such as computer literacy is required, women teachers may be more dependent on using the ready-made curriculum materials than most men teachers. Intensification here does lead to an increasing reliance on outside experts. An understanding of the larger structuring of patriarchal relations, then, is essential if we are fully to comprehend both why the curriculum was produced the way it was and what its effects actually were.

It is absolutely crucial to say, however, that at the same time the commitments to environments that embody an ethic of caring and connectedness — commitments that as Gilligan and others have shown are so much a part of women's daily experiences and are so critical in an education worthy of its name — may actually provide the resources for countering such rationalized curricular models.[27] The sense of loss, of an absence of community, the struggle to personalize and reduce anonymity all enable one to restore the collective memory of difference. The women teachers here may have some of the most important resources for resistance in the long run.

These points about the gendered realities of the women teachers are significant in another way. It would be all too easy to blame them for basically following the 'curriculum on a cart' and hence ultimately participating in the degradation of their own labour and a reductive 'that'-based curriculum. This, we believe, would be a major error.

As a number of commentators have suggested, the real lives of many women teachers, when seen close up, are complicated by the fact that they often return home exhausted after being in the intensified setting of the classroom, only then to face the emotional and physical demands of housework, cooking, childcare, and so on. Since many women teachers are already doing two jobs, their caution and 'lack of enthusiasm' towards taking on additional work is anything but a simplistic response to 'innovation'. Rather it is a realistic strategy for dealing with the complications in the objective reality that they face daily.[28]

We need to remember that doing nothing is a form of action itself. Though it is not always the result of a set of conscious decisions, it can have serious consequences.[29] Women teachers, like all workers, may overtly resist intensification and the loss of their autonomy and skills. At other times, from the outside it may seem that they are passively accepting a separation of conception from execution or the de-skilling of their jobs. However, as we know from an immense amount of research, most individuals will attempt to take even the most alienating experiences and turn them to their own advantage, if only to maintain control over their own labour and simply to keep from being alienated and bored,[30] or as in this case to solve other equally real problems brought about by the conditions of fiscal scarcity, overwork, bureaucratic realities, and external constraints. Teachers are never dupes, never simply the passive puppets that structural models would have us believe. Their agency and actions in concrete situations such as these may have contradictory results. They may have elements of 'good sense' and 'bad sense' in tension as they construct their responses to a crisis in the economy, in authority relations, and in education. Yet the fact that they *do* construct these responses once again shows the very possibility of difference. In a time when the right would like to commodify education[31] and once again to turn our schools into factories, that possibility is of no small importance. These constructions are *not* preordained. They can be reconstructed in ways that will allow us to join with teachers to challenge the redefinitions of skills and power that are currently going on. Too much is at stake if we don't.

NOTES AND REFERENCES

1. See Apple, Michael W., *Teachers and Texts: A Political Economy of Class and Gender Relations in Education*. New York: Routledge, 1986, and Apple, Michael W., 'Redefining equality: authoritarian populism and the conservative restoration'. *Teachers College Record*, 90, pp. 167–84, Winter 1988.

2. Apple, Michael W., *Education and Power*. New York: Routledge, ARK Edition, 1985.

3. Ball, Stephen, 'Staff relations during the teachers' industrial action: context, conflict and proletarianization'. *British Journal of Sociology of Education*, 9 (3), p. 290, 1988.

4. Apple, *Teachers and Texts*, op. cit., note 1.

5. The issue of the 'proletarianization' of teachers is a complicated one. For further discussion, see Apple, op. cit., note 2, and Apple, *Teachers and Texts*, op. cit., note 1. Some of the complexities are nicely articulated in Ozga, Jenny and Lawn, Martin, 'Schoolwork: interpreting the labour process of teaching'. *British Journal of Sociology of Education*, 9 (3), 1988, pp. 289–306. Much of the next section is based on Apple, Michael W. and Teitelbaum, Kenneth, 'Are teachers losing control of their skills and curriculum?', *Journal of Curriculum Studies*, 18 (2), pp. 177–84, 1986.

6. Apple, op. cit., note 2, and Apple, *Teachers and Texts*, op. cit., note 1.

7. Tayloristic strategies have a long history of use in education. For further discussion, see Kliebard, Herbert, *The Struggle for the American Curriculum*. New York: Routledge, 1986; Apple, Michael W., *Ideology and Curriculum*. Boston: Routledge, 1979; and Apple, op. cit., note 2.

8. Ibid.

9. Apple, *Teachers and Texts*, op. cit., note 1.

10. Ibid.

11. Stedman, Lawrence and Smith, Marshall, 'Recent reform proposals for American education'. *Contemporary Education Review*, 2, Autumn pp. 85–104, 1983, and Apple, *Teachers and Texts*, op. cit., note 1.

12. The negative impact of such testing and reductive objectives-based curriculum and evaluation strategies is a major problem. It is nicely documented in Gitlin, Andrew, 'School structure and teachers' work' in Apple, Michael W. and Weis, Lois (eds.), *Ideology and Practice in Schooling*. Philadelphia: Temple University Press, 1983, pp. 193–212. See also McNeil, Linda, *Contradictions of Control*. New York: Routledge, 1986.

13. Apple, *Teachers and Texts*, op. cit., note 1.

14. Ibid. We are, of course, here making a 'functional' argument, not necessarily an 'intentional' one. Managers, policy experts, and others need not consciously plan to specifically control the work of women for it to have this effect.

15. Apple, op. cit., note 2.

16. The economics and politics of textbook publishing are analysed in much greater depth in Apple, *Teachers and Texts*, op. cit., note 1, especially

Chapter 4. The history of some of the socio/economic conditions that led to such adoption policies is investigated in Apple, Michael W., 'Regulating the text: the socio-historical roots of state control', *Educational Policy*, forthcoming.

17. See, for example, Edward, Richard, *Contested Terrain*. New York: Basic Books, 1979, and Gordon, David, Edwards, Richard and Reich, Michael, *Segmented Work, Divided Workers*. New York: Cambridge University Press, 1982.

18. Ibid. and Apple, op. cit., note 2.

19. Some of these data are reviewed in Danziger, Sheldon and Weinberg, Daniel (eds), *Fighting Poverty*. Cambridge MA: Harvard University Press, 1986; Wright, Erik Olin, *Classes*. New York: Verso, 1985; and Apple, Michael W., 'American realities: poverty, economy and education', in Weis, Lois (ed.), *Dropouts from School*. Albany: State University of New York Press, 1989.

20. For a more detailed elaboration of the process and results of intensification, see Apple, *Teachers and Texts*, op. cit., note 1, especially Chapter 2.

21. Gitlin, 'School structure and teachers' work', op. cit., note 12.

22. Ozga and Lawn, 'Schoolwork: interpreting the labour process of teaching', op. cit., note 5, p. 333.

23. Whether such 'literacy' is in fact necessary in the way its proponents propose and the possible educational, social, and economic effects of such technology, are examined in greater depth in Apple, *Teachers and Texts*, op. cit., note 1.

24. Most of the material in this section is taken from Jungck, Susan, 'Doing computer literacy', unpublished PhD thesis, University of Wisconsin, Madison, 1985.

25. See Apple, *Teachers and Texts*, op. cit., note 1 for further discussion of and references on this important point.

26. This response, with all its contradictions, is historically similar to the calls by teachers in the later part of the nineteenth century for the provision of standardized textbooks. Many teachers, especially young women, rightly felt exploited by low pay, poor working conditions, and an expanding curriculum for which they felt either ill-prepared to teach or, more usually, had insufficient time to prepare quality lessons for. The standardized text was one way to solve parts of this dilemma, even though it may actually have undercut some of their emerging autonomy at the same time. Some elements of this story are told in Danylewycz, Marta and

Prentice, Alison, 'Teachers, gender, and bureaucratizing school systems in nineteenth-century Montreal and Toronto', *History of Education Quarterly*, 24, pp. 75–100, Spring 1984.

27. See, for example, Gilligan, Carol, *In a Different Voice*. Cambridge: Harvard University Press, 1982. For a general discussion of the issue of gender and experience, see Connell, R. W., *Gender and Power*. Stanford: Stanford University Press, 1987, and Roman, Leslie, Christian-Smith, Linda and Ellsworth, Elizabeth (eds.), *Becoming Feminine*. Philadelphia: Falmer Press, 1988.

28. Acker, Sandra, 'Teachers, gender and resistance', *British Journal of Sociology of Education*, 9 (3), p. 314, 1988. See also Apple, *Teachers and Texts*, op. cit., note 1.

29. Acker, 'Teachers, gender and resistance', op. cit., note 28, p. 307.

30. For a review of some of this literature see Apple, op. cit., note 2, and Kessler-Harris, Alice, *Out to Work*. New York: Oxford University Press, 1982.

31. Apple, *Teachers and Texts*, op. cit., note 1, and Apple, 'Redefining equality', op. cit., note 1. For a more general theoretical discussion of the process of commodification and what conceptual resources might be necessary to understand it in all its complexity, see the dense but important book by Wexler, Philip, *Social Analysis and Education*. New York: Routledge, 1988.

Chapter 3

Teacher Development and Gender Equity

Heather-jane Robertson

INTRODUCTION

Within educational debate, gender issues and teacher development are almost always dealt with as mutually exclusive spheres of enquiry. This chapter explores the nature and impact of this estrangement, and challenges the posture of gender neutrality assumed by staff development theorists. It will be argued that such an artificial neutrality perpetuates androcentrism, or male-centredness, and that gender-sensitive approaches are essential if the goals of staff development are to be achieved. A critical analysis of a representative staff development model will be used to develop this thesis. I will argue that gender sensitivity requires the recognition and integration of what is known about the differences between males and females within the conceptualization, design and delivery of staff development programmes.

Our education systems teach, reflect and are sustained by androcentrism, which imposes a particular paradigm; a cultural filter with three characteristics.[1] Androcentrism first requires us to see the world from the male point of view, and to assume and assert that this is not a selective or limited perception. Androcentrism also requires the valuing of that which is associated with the male, including men, men's work, men's experiences, and stereotypically masculine characteristics and values, more than that which is associated with the female. Finally, androcentrism elevates male experience to universal experience, and simultaneously renders this process invisible. Schools are compelled to maintain each element of this paradigm.

Androcentrism requires the world to be viewed and understood within a particular framework. It obliges us to reduce the world to some enduring and familiar themes: competition, hierarchical power, dominance, conflict. Additional characteristics of the masculine paradigm include declarations of certainty even in complex and changing circumstances; an over-confident reliance on the power of rationality to predict accurately effect from cause (and vice versa); a tendency to elevate what is quantifiable and objective over what is valued and subjective; and a preference for the instrumental and rational rather than the affective and intuitive.[2] It is these characteristics that can be found in abundance among the guiding principles and practices of staff development.

43

Androcentrism persists despite the apparent efforts of schools to react to the mainstreaming of demands for 'sex equity'. Schools have responded to a growing awareness of gender bias by mandating an obligatory gender neutrality. To redress bias, many school systems have undertaken measures to encourage equal access to all programmes, and have instructed their teachers to treat male and female students in precisely the same manner. The system's, school's and teacher's stated objective becomes one of gender neutrality. Although a superficial equality of access may be achieved in this way, such measures rarely result in equality of outcome, for mandated gender neutrality ignores the need to address the deeply embedded and often non-conscious beliefs and behaviours of teachers, parents and students themselves which reinforce dependency, low expectations, passivity and lack of self-confidence in female students. Gender neutrality obliges its adherents to ignore the substantial body of research which confirms gender-linked differences, and fails to address any of the substantive aspects of gender difference or gender bias. The facile egalitarianism of the objective 'treat all students similarly' serves only to hide the underlying biases embedded in the system. Unfortunately, when this strategy fails to produce results, the argument focuses on whether neutrality was achieved rather than whether gender neutrality was ever an appropriate means of transforming a biased system.

Despite its ineffectiveness, gender neutrality persists as the strategy of choice partly because our institutions and professions have avoided or dismissed analyses and research which identify systemic bias. This avoidance is best understood as the utilization of the prerogative of every dominant class, which has been called 'the right to not know'. Those who aspire to being accepted by the dominant class, but do not belong to it by virtue of birth, may mimic this state of perpetual naïveté, which I call 'the advantage of not knowing'. Some dismiss gender-related criticism of schools because they choose to find it unbelievable. Those unable to claim either ignorance or disbelief often excuse their lack of action by focusing on the need to develop a general 'awareness', as if by admitting the existence of a problem it has somehow been addressed. Of course, if the impact of gender bias is limited, the justifications for inactivity are unnecessary. Androcentrism can be and is denied; indeed, some argue that since the recognition and redress of sexism would require the wholesale redistribution of power, wealth and authority, the voice of privilege must insist that sexism is a false analysis persuasive only to a hostile and suspicious psyche. A less class-based explanation reminds us that each of us has an intrinsic investment in maintaining a world view consistent with our organizing principles, and that static gender roles are fundamental to these principles. Examining the merits of these competing explanations of the marginalization of gender-related topics in educational debate is an important undertaking, for a world view which relegates androcentrism to a subordinate issue guarantees its perpetuation and its permeation of public and personal spheres.

Whether we are born male or female, the masculine paradigm dominates our cultural interpretation of reality. As instruments of society, schools are intrinsically androcentric, even though — particularly at the elementary level — they have been described as domains of the feminine, presumably because they are inhabited by women and children. Whether this description presents a fair characterization is questionable, but it is true that many of the criticisms levelled at schools are directed towards those characteristics associated with the feminine sphere. If current school reform efforts succeed in making the teaching profession more competitive, cerebral, efficient and focused on instrumentalism, its values will more closely resemble those of masculinism; its ethic will stray further from 'the ethic of care' identified by Carol Gilligan as associated with the feminine paradigm.[3]

Many of these school reform initiatives are designed to be achieved through teacher and staff development. Such efforts should be scrutinized to determine not only the principles supporting proposed educational models, but also the degree to which the models challenge or perpetuate existing cultural biases. An attempt to critique the orientation, objectives and processes of staff development from a gender-sensitive perspective is a reasonable task only if there is relative consistency and homogeneity within the content and approach of the major theorists and practitioners in the staff development field. Setting aside those who violate all generally accepted principles of pedagogy and androgogy, there exists a sufficiently shared understanding of desirable characteristics of staff development that criticism directed towards a specific source cannot be dismissed as irrelevant to other models. In addition, it is useful to identify a particular source and model so that the critique can be grounded in specifics. For these purposes, I have chosen to discuss Bruce Joyce and Beverly Showers and their book *Student Achievement through Staff Development*.[4]

I have chosen Joyce and Showers not because they are misogynistic dinosaurs, but because they are both influential and representative of theory-into-practice advocates. With Marsha Weil, Bruce Joyce wrote the first edition of the innovative *Models of Teaching* in 1972. Together, Joyce and Showers appear as the authors of more than a hundred books and articles published since 1966 on peer coaching, models of teaching, school organization and supervision. They are in great demand as resource people, and in particular are seen as sympathetic to administration-directed change. Given the scope of their influence, it is particularly regrettable that these well-respected authors seem so committed to gender neutrality, and thus to the further entrenchment of androcentricity.

Certain topics recur in any discussion of staff development. The overall purposes of staff development, the nature of staff members as learners and teachers, the content for professional study, the requirements of leadership, the choice of targets, and the implementation of staff development processes are familiar themes. These general headings will be used to present Joyce and Showers's staff development model.

THE PURPOSES OF STAFF DEVELOPMENT

It is often possible to infer a philosophy of education from what is said about the goals of staff development. In this case, Joyce and Showers view the best staff development as providing teachers and students with a 'competitive edge'; staff development is not valued as an end in itself, but because it can be instrumental in enhancing student achievement. In the introduction to their text, the authors argue that the goal of the teacher must be 'to compete with the student and the society by increasing the talents of learning . . . the purpose of staff development is to increase the ability of teachers to engage in that competition'.[5] As well as presenting a rather shocking example of educational jingoism, this statement provides a compelling example of a masculinist view of the world in which life is a battle, there are winners and losers, and even the classroom is a playing field in which competition is to be the core value and activity for teachers as well as students.

After Joyce and Showers promote staff development as providing teachers with the competitive edge required to win, they provide their team with a pep talk. Not only is the profession to become more competitive, it is to acquire mastery of the skills needed to give teachers a strategic advantage. One can hear a stereotypically masculine over-confidence when the authors quote Ron Edmonds in their introduction: 'We can, whenever and wherever we want, successfully teach all children whose schooling is of interest to us. We already know more than we need to do that'.[6] Such certainty and predictability are familiar aspects of a masculine view of reality, as is the dependency on external rather than internal knowing. The 'we' to whom Edmonds is referring is assuredly not classroom teachers; this claim for the power of knowledge and instrumentalism refers only to those whose expertise is validated within hierarchical systems. The authors give no indication that they believe teachers might already know enough to teach more children better, but rather that experts can train teachers in observable and tested behaviours which will produce predicted results. It is not connected learning but new learning which is to be emphasized in both content and process.

THE NATURE OF STAFF MEMBERS AS LEARNERS AND TEACHERS

Joyce and Showers go on to claim that 'knowledge exists to engineer staff development programs'.[7] Apparently, however, not all teachers are equally amenable to boarding the train thus engineered, so the authors advance a classification system to help planners identify and deal with reluctant participants. Joyce and Showers believe that enthusiasm for staff development primarily reflects a teacher's self-concept and conceptual strengths, factors which can be determined by measuring how personally and professionally 'active' each teacher is revealed to be through responses to a standardized questionnaire. The authors describe their use of a variety of questionnaires intended to measure 'the dynamic of individual interaction with the environment of both the personal and professional realms'.[8] Varying levels of activity are thus judged to be products of individual disposition, rather than individual or collective circumstance. Joyce and Showers contend that teachers' tractability for staff development falls along a continuum, and they describe three prototypical staff members falling at either end and in the middle of this continuum. They label those most eager to participate in staff development activities 'omnivores', described as mature, high-activity people who have learned to 'successfully exploit the environment'. Omnivores are professionally voracious, spend time in informal interaction with peers, and have ample time to experiment with the school computer. In their personal lives, they are enthusiastically involved in sports, hobbies and games. They are keen to participate in all kinds of professional development.[9] Omnivores are ideal candidates for staff development because in addition to being active, they show initiative, exert influence, mentor and are mentored, and excel at identifying high pay-off opportunities.

At the other end of this continuum fall the 'reticent consumers' who represent protypical problem teachers from a staff development perspective because they have 'developed an orientation of reluctance to interact positively with their cultural environment. We can observe this dynamic in both professional and domestic settings'.[10] The application of 'activity levels', 'positivity', and 'keenness' reveals an infuriating ignorance of the relationship between gender and constructs such as assertiveness, power and influence, mentoring and even distribution of leisure time. The compounding effects of gender stereotypes, gender-linked characteristics, unequal distribution of family and domestic responsibilities, and differential valuing of the skills and abilities of men and women will result in perpetuating a masculinist system in which those who 'exploit' the environment are valued more than those who cope with, shape or respond to the world around them.

Joyce and Showers attribute the 'reluctance' of reticent consumers to personality variables and individual inclinations rather than to situational responses. How might the authors have reframed their continuum by considering that reluctance might be a sane response to a hostile environment? Calabrese and Anderson confirm that women teachers experience more stress than male teachers, and that this stress is the product of powerlessness, isolation and meaninglessness.[11] They conclude that the male orientation of curriculum, administration and the school environment are contributing to a growing sense of disenfranchisement among women teachers. There is evidence of ample opportunity for women's professional frustration; Heilman and Kram found that women tend to expect their colleagues to assign them more responsibility for failure and less for success in a shared undertaking. Women expect to be evaluated more harshly and more negatively than their male counterparts.[12] This perception may contribute to a verbal reticence which may well be labelled 'reluctance': a recent study of problems facing professional women cited by

Sadker and Sadker found that 43 per cent of respondents identified their own failure to speak up in mixed groups as their greatest liability. Another 22 per cent said that their greatest problem in group meetings was interruptions by males.[13]

Perhaps the greatest injustice inherent in using an 'activity index' as a teacher evaluation tool is its denial and dismissal of the multiple roles of contemporary women. Like women everywhere, women teachers and administrators continue to bear disproportionate responsibility for home and childcare, and at the median age of 40 are affected increasingly by the responsibility of caring for ageing parents.[14] No one who has held a role greater than 'helper' in the complex exercise of family management could see failure to sign up for voluntary weekend inservice or a reluctance to attend after-hours staff meetings as evidence of inactivity, or of personality deviation. To be assumed to be uninterested rather than overextended is grossly unfair, but this reaction is typical of those who see male priorities as setting the standard to be met. At a time when there is a growing awareness of increasing conflict between work and family, such standards are completely inappropriate. In fairness to Joyce and Showers, it should be noted that virtually all personnel assessment models implicitly value those who are not impaired by conflicting responsibilities. Biklen points out the frustrations of the tightrope. Women teachers are often seen as lacking career commitment because typically they express disinterest in vertical mobility, and are intensely classroom focused.[15] Although there is increasing public and private acceptance of women holding jobs, the same cannot be said of women pursuing careers, for a career is what you have if your work competes with family life. To the extent that the career wins, one is said to have a career commitment. As Biklen observes, the status of a field or profession is based in part on its ability to induce its members to do the job no matter how long it takes[16] (or, presumably, at what cost to private endeavours). It should be noted that as men increase their participation in family life, such an antiquated definition of career becomes ill-suited to them as well. The difference, however, is that men will be supported in arguing for a rethink of our concept of 'career'. There is growing sympathy (and considerable media attention) available to men who admit to mixed feelings about neglecting home in favour of career, or who make public choices which favour their families. Some have become the cultural heroes known as 'new men'. Equivalent support for women, tangible in either contractual form or in public sympathy, is sadly lacking.

It is inappropriate to ignore significant culturally induced differences in any human resource model; it is particularly inappropriate in a model which grounds itself in interpersonal influence, use of time, and leisure interests. An organizational model which was designed to accommodate a variety of life experiences, as well as a variety of ways of experiencing life, would consider how to respond to role differences synergistically. Instead, Joyce and Showers clearly establish their preference for the male-centred orientation, and set out to create more 'omnivores' because of their assumed intrinsic worth to education. 'The goal of human resource development', they state, is to 'ensure that the children are in contact with more active, seeking personalities.'[17]

In setting this goal in the context they have developed, androcentrism becomes more deeply entrenched. As Gilligan explains, 'The failure to see the different reality of women's lives and to hear the differences in their voices stems in part from the assumption that there is a single mode of social experience and interpretation'.[18] Indeed, the failure to see and hear is present, but the right to not know is invoked when the differences are seen and heard yet wilfully ignored. An omnivoric model, to coin a phrase, perpetuates and validates the right to not know and contributes to the silencing of other voices.

THE CONTENT FOR PROFESSIONAL STUDY

Although in their model Joyce and Showers move well beyond providing information to teachers, they still rely on the power of expert information to motivate change in teacher behaviour. Expert dependency implicitly supports the message, not unfamiliar to teachers, that student achievement is not what it should be because practitioners do not know enough, or do not know the right things. This stereotype of the teaching profession as intellectually and cognitively deficient may reflect a more generalized contempt for women's competence, since the profession is widely viewed as feminine in its characteristics. (Whatever criticisms are levelled at male-dominated professions, they rarely focus on the lack of personal knowledge of practitioners.) As Acker notes, in times when more overt gender bias was considered to be socially acceptable, women teachers were portrayed in the literature as 'damaging, deficient, distracted and sometimes dim'.[19] Although Joyce and Showers confidently claim that 'teachers have lots of learning ability', there is no similarly unqualified statement regarding what teachers already know.

What teachers are to learn is to be drawn from expert sources, designed to impart expert knowledge and to make out-of-context and objective knowledge more familiar to learners. As with most expert-dependent systems, this can often be accomplished only at the expense of personal and subjective knowledge. In *Women's Ways of Knowing*, Mary Field Belenky and her colleagues argue that this approach is masculinist and has impaired women's education, for in our culture, expert, validated knowledge is male knowledge. 'Along with other academic feminists, we believe that the conception of knowledge and truth as they are accepted and articulated today have been shaped throughout history by the male-dominated majority culture.'[20] Because such knowledge and truth neither reflect nor respect women's experience, 'expert opinion' is often in contradiction with women's subjective realities.

Exploring these contradictions has been a central theme of feminist scholarship seeking to identify those facts and theories projected as gender neutral or gender inclusive, but which have been biased through the male-centredness of approach or research. Best known of these critiques is Carol Gilligan's analysis of the work of Lawrence Kohlberg, whose theories of moral development have shaped many values education curricula. Gilligan noted that although Kohlberg's research was based in its entirety on males, it has been generalized without reservation to apply equally to both males and females. In explaining why women rarely attained the higher levels of moral development on Kohlberg's scale, many suggested that women might well be morally inferior. Gilligan, in revisiting the original research while conducting new work, posited that the ethic of rights to which men adhere does not correspond with women's values, and that women tend to practise an ethic of care grounded in responsibility and the guiding principle of 'doing no harm'.[21] Rather than demonstrating moral inferiority, women were describing a different moral system.

Gilligan's concept of a 'different voice' has guided many researchers who find the absence of women in the practice of research to be grounds to question the legitimacy of what passes for objective, gender-neutral knowledge. Women's absence in educational research is not difficult to document. Shakeshaft and Nanson reviewed ten issues of the *Educational Administration Quarterly* and found 'that androcentric bias was evident in all phases of the research ... in problem selection and formulation, review of previous research, selection of samples, data collection, procedures, and interpretation of results. All-male samples generalized to both genders and instruments that measured male viewpoints were consistent practices ...'.[22] Many theories of adult development and career stages are based on research conducted only with men, and include barely a passing reference to the possibility that not all observations may be applied to women. Unfortunately, this kind of footnote is too often an afterthought and is too easily forgotten in a climate of mandated gender neutrality. There is little doubt that this kind of work is being generalized to include women, without reference to these inherent limitations.

The mainstream sources of the 'objective' knowledge presented to teachers are at best silent about women's points of view, and at worst contradict women's realities. Some women resolve this contradiction by silencing their inner voices, and by attending only to knowledge gained from 'objective' sources. For others, it is the 'objective' voice in its entirety which is rejected, and only the subjective and intuitive which can be heard. Such forced choices limit knowing and learning. Belenky *et al.* argue for education which is consciously connectivist, which engages multiple ways of knowing, and which respects intuitive as well as scientific knowledge.[23] Key characteristics of a connectivist approach are an eschewal of ideological certainty and a revaluing of the tentative. Connectivist learning takes exception to masculine assertion and voice of authority, and acknowledges 'the uncertainties implicit in an approach which values the personal'.[24] Yet Joyce and Showers reject the intuitive and the tentative, and insist on an 'objective' grounding for teacher actions. 'All the yield from research', they assert, 'shares the attribute of intentionality ... doing something because it is believed that it will make a difference. Professional skill involves more than doing something because it is customary or feels right. Customs and intuitions may work, but they are not based on shared and examined professional knowledge.'[25] Nothing remotely connectivist can be found in this assertion. A position which creates a false dichotomy between what is professional and what feels right devalues both the art and skill of teaching, particularly for those individuals, primarily women, who by virtue of the age of their students or personal inclination are child-focused rather than role-focused.

THE REQUIREMENTS OF LEADERSHIP

The staff development model proposed by Joyce and Showers is not unique in its fealty to objective knowledge, nor does it deviate from accepted notions of the role of the hierarchy in managing and supervising change.

Neither the existing hierarchical structure nor the training and inclinations of hierarchical leaders are called into question by the authors, who, in concert with most of their colleagues, view the role of the designated leader as pivotal to the success of staff development efforts. Joyce and Showers remind principals that not only are they to be instructional leaders, they must also create the collegial climate in which omnivores may thrive. The general (and genial) characteristics of principals of effective schools are by now quite familiar: effective principals are people-orientated, negotiate solutions to problems, use collegial management styles, take risks, and so on.[26] They are warm and caring individuals with low personal control needs, able to juggle multiple priorities, and committed to putting relationships first.

The pool from which these leaders among leaders are to be chosen is overwhelmingly male; in 1986–7 across Canada (excluding Quebec) one quarter of male teachers were principals, vice-principals or department heads; the corresponding figure for women was six per cent.[27] The characteristics of 'effective principals' are not necessarily those of typical principals; there are many teachers who do not describe their principals as particularly relationship-orientated or collegial. There is extraordinarily little mainstream analysing of whether the nature of the pool has any impact on the nature of individuals drawn from it; indeed an enforced gender neutrality precludes such an inquiry. By insisting that gender is irrelevant we impair our schools, for, according to researchers such as Charol Shakeshaft, when feminine values and behaviours are allowed to flourish in schools, teachers, administrators and students benefit.[28] Females appear to practise feminine values. Overviews of the research on American women administrators conclude that in schools and districts with female administrators achievement scores in reading and maths are higher, there is less violence, and student and staff morale is higher. Men and women administer differently; women tend to put relationships with others in the centre, spend more time with people, promote communication, motivate others more effectively and receive greater community support. Teachers working with women administrators tend

51

to be more productive, to experience higher morale and to have a greater sense of community with their colleagues. Women principals have been found to exhibit a more participatory style of leadership than their male colleagues, and to lead schools in which staff members are more committed to the goals of learning and professional growth. Their schools are more co-operative than competitive, and are much more likely to address the whole child. Academic achievement is higher, overall, in schools of which women are principals.[29]

Such assertions would appear to invite exploration and investigation of the most rigorous kind; multi-purpose interventions are rare gems in complex fields. Unfortunately, findings such as these appear to be subject to 'the right to not know'; most of those who presume to comment on educational administration or school effectiveness do not incorporate this body of knowledge into their private or professional views. Such an exclusion is inexplicable unless ideological forces have been engaged. Instead of welcoming the opportunity to learn about women's styles of leadership, or to investigate these outcomes more comprehensively, we have perpetuated the male dominance of school leadership. There are now 14 per cent fewer women administrators in Canadian schools than there were a decade ago.[30] Under the guise of gender neutrality our institutions pretend to have adequately addressed women's exclusion from administration by self-consciously using neuter pronouns when referring to principals, and by dropping the coaching of football from explicitly required pre-administrative experiences. Such superficial accommodations have had no impact on women's experience; being female is still perceived as being the main obstacle facing women teachers who seek career advancement.

In addition to losses resulting from residual and intentional sex bias in promotions, there is also a growing reluctance among women to assume a role increasingly associated with autocratic school leadership and ruthless, product-orientated management.[31] Following a decade during which women who aspired to leadership were expected to demonstrate how well they could fill existing roles, there is a shift towards avoiding administration unless roles can be reshaped instead of women themselves. Shakeshaft notes that women prefer to view the key responsibilities of principals and superintendents as master teachers and educational leaders, while men tend to view the same positions from a managerial and industrial perspective.[32]

Those few women who lead schools appear to attempt to implement this vision. Women's leadership styles are expressed through communication patterns which are more typical of collegial than autocratic endeavours. Women's language patterns appear to create a consensual and participative atmosphere for decision-making. Joyce and Showers are not alone in describing this kind of communication as the key to successfully guiding change through staff development, nor are they alone in ignoring gender and sex-role orientation as relevant variables to be considered in discussing leadership and administration. Fullan, for example, in his widely praised and supportive articles on the principalship, has not discussed, to my knowledge, gender-related issues.[33] This oversight precludes discussions which would provide an opportunity to reconsider the wisdom of shaping our schools in the image of the masculine paradigm. A redefinition of educational leadership which includes women's perspectives is necessary if we are to promote the growth of more humane and intelligent schools. Unfortunately, to be subsumed by the masculine paradigm is to be oblivious to the existence and validity of other realities; voices raised will not necessarily be voices heard.

CHOOSING TARGETS FOR PROFESSIONAL GROWTH

Following their discussion of desirable leadership behaviours, Joyce and Showers address the nature of the content for staff development. They emphasize the advantage of choosing as targets those innovations and strategies demonstrated to enhance student achievement. The authors identify pertinent research and suggest targets falling under the three categories of teacher practices, dimensions of effective schools and curriculum revision. Each target proposed is justified by introducing the concept of 'effect size',[34] and by claiming that each strategy has been discussed extensively in the literature. The authors elaborate on the use of advance organizers, mnemonics, and several models for the teaching of thinking skills. An extensive section of the book is devoted to descriptions of the behaviours of effective teachers. In their discussion of these topics, the authors are scrupulously gender neutral, and avoid any suggestion that there may be gender differences to be found within the effects they describe. Only once do they admit that every student group may not derive equal benefit: 'We need to be careful that we do not advocate practices that appear to raise the average but which actually disadvantage certain categories of students.'[35] This caution refers to high and low achievers rather than to those who differ by race or gender.

The inference that gender is irrelevant to student response to curriculum and instruction is fallacious; such differences are broadly established and deserve thorough discussion. Because of the marginalization of gender-based debate, few recognize that we have shaped our schools to respond to the needs and characteristics of male learners. Although females mature earlier, and are ready for maths and verbal skills before boys, the curriculum for the early elementary grades reflects and is geared to the developmental pattern of boys. Primary curricula reflect an emphasis on interpersonal skills, receptive and expressive language and development of fine motor co-ordination. These skills are sufficiently mastered by most six-year-old girls that a higher level of abstraction could be required. It is not just the primary schools which favour boys; at more senior levels, there is considerable evidence that girls' achievement improves in same-sex environments, but since the opposite is true for boys we have established mixed-sex schools.

If the school structure favours boys, so does instruction. In the classroom, male students receive more attention than female students: teachers allow boys more opportunities to respond to questions, to express their opinions, and to participate actively in class projects. Boys talk more, receive more teacher time, and have more opportunity to learn. They are more often praised and more often told they have ability. Boys are also more likely than girls to be reprimanded.[36] While this would appear, at first glance, to provide evidence of the classroom being more hospitable to girls, others argue that in coping with reproval, boys learn to live with criticism and to become less dependent on approval from authority figures.

In contrast, the average female is ignored; she is neither reprimanded nor praised. Girls come to believe it is because they are lucky or work hard that they succeed at school; they rarely attribute good results to their innate abilities. Boys are more likely to credit their personal ability in explaining school success; failure is most often attributed to 'bad luck'. Gender neutrality obliges educators to ignore male/female differences in learning styles. Research which demonstrated that female students learn better in co-operative rather than competitive settings, which reports that assignment to mixed-sex work groups in the classroom often stalls young women's initiative, and which suggests that girls require a different kind of reinforcement as compared with males, must also be ignored.[37] Differences which might bear directly on student achievement cannot be accommodated in gender neutral classrooms.

Gender bias persists in curriculum materials despite the comparative attention it has received. Where gender bias has been excised from texts, a false gender neutrality that is every bit as deceitful as Dick and Jane fills each page. Women are 'given' the vote; the most significant enfranchisement movement in history is often relegated to reprinting the vicious humour of cartoonists of the day. Teacher language and textbook language reinforces the 'otherness' of females; student language and behaviour that is hostile to women is permitted in ways that racist language and behaviour would not be.

The effects on achievement of classroom sexism begin to appear by late elementary grades. Using American data, Harvey reports consistent differences in achievement by gender and by subjects, and adds that recently girls have relinquished their achievement advantages even in verbal areas. Boys outperform girls on standardized tests, although girls outperform boys on teacher evaluations of student work. Any general move to standardized evaluation will penalize girls. Harvey notes that during this period of heightened educational reform 'when there is evidence of an achievement decline, the scores of females have tended to decline more than those of males, and when there is evidence of a gain, males have generally exhibited greater gains than females'.[38] Girls' disadvantage is cumulative. What other group, ask Sadker and Sadker, 'starts out ahead and twelve years later finds itself behind?'.[39] Surely a reference to these effects in a book which explicitly sets out to improve student achievement would be in order.

The absence of discourse about gender and achievement encourages the myth that elementary classrooms tend to be hostile towards boys and hospitable towards girls. Gender, when it is discussed, is often introduced as a factor associated with learning disabilities. Boys dominate this category, some say, because the typical learning environment is unresponsive to boys' learning styles. A countering view claims that what is described as unresponsive may in fact reflect a heightened sensitivity to boys which is reflected in the early identification of their needs. Harvey notes that only 33 per cent of American students identified as needing special education services are female, and that when girls are referred for such services, they are older, further behind in their work, and are experiencing more pronounced problems than the typical male referral.[40]

It seems reasonable that exploring the remediation of one or more of these differences might be a worthy target for staff development activities, particularly when enhanced student achievement is the expressed goal. Surely when a factor such as distribution of teacher time is receiving so much attention, the pervasive skewing of teacher time to male students would be noteworthy. It is unconscionable to spend so much time sharpening the ability to ask higher-order questions while ignoring to whom these questions are being posed. In the 48 pages Joyce and Showers devote to surveying possible content and targets for staff development, there is not one reference to gender differences. To refuse to admit that gender might be relevant to what goes on in schools is to elevate ignorance to the level of ideology. It is not hard to understand why Shakeshaft concludes, in her comments about similar silences in *A Nation at Risk*, that 'maybe the writers were influenced by the reality that gender does limit the educational and life choices of females and that many people are satisfied with that situation'.[41]

STAFF DEVELOPMENT PROCESSES

The processes to be employed in the implementation of Joyce and Showers's model rest on two principles. The first principle is designed to increase the transferability of new knowledge and skills to the classroom and requires an increased emphasis on practice, feedback and coaching. The second principle is the engagement of every staff member in diads, triads and study groups, some of which assume responsibility for interpreting the opinions of colleagues and for meeting identified needs. Quite elaborate co-ordination structures are suggested, and a general climate of interpersonal trust, risk-taking and collegiality is seen as both an outcome and a precondition of success.

The assumptions underlying these processes, and in some cases the processes themselves, would seem to be problematic for women. For example, Joyce and Showers advise a needs assessment phase which requires considerable expert input, since the authors contend that teachers cannot be expected to choose strategies with which they are unfamiliar. As the process unfolds, it becomes clear that any felt and expressed needs which cannot be matched with expert solutions will be dropped in favour of those which can be more succinctly addressed.

Joyce and Showers provide an anecdotal example of how effective planning for staff development might take place. A collaborative governance structure is developed from an existing curriculum committee which represents all high school departments. With the principal and his administrative staff, this committee chooses a staff development focus for the next two years.[42] Since such a committee's recommendations would require external support, their choices must reflect sensitivity to political as well as pedagogical concerns if they are to be approved, and final decisions will serve many masters. Few school staffs are empowered to make their own substantive staff development decisions; the kinds of intensive staff development that produce change do not receive final approval in the staffroom. It should be noted that the further a decision is obtained from the classroom teacher, the less likely it is that women will participate in that decision. If this planning activity was taking place in a typical Canadian school, the authors' hypothetical committee comprising administrative and departmental leadership would have little or no female participation, given that in 1986 women held only six per cent of secondary principalships, 12 per cent of the vice-principalships and an estimated 20 per cent of departmental headships. Beyond the school level, women with authority are even more rare; Canadian female superintendents can be counted on two hands.[43] Joyce and Showers's model of decision-making makes it very likely that it will be exclusively or predominantly men who will decide the focus of staff development. This is not to say that every proposed project would be inappropriate because it would be chosen by men, but rather that it is unlikely that the unaltered opinions women express from their unique experiences and needs could withstand translation by committee, the tests of political criteria, and the need for validation by men who experience their schools and their lives differently.

In the proposed model, this same planning committee now guides implementation. The implementation model proposed by Joyce and Showers is grounded in interpersonal communication, but the gender-related aspects of interpersonal communication are ignored.

Interpersonal communication is not gender neutral; gender-related differences in communication styles and behaviour in groups are well documented. For example, substantial numbers of women recognize and feel guilty about their own reluctance to speak out in mixed-sex groups. Many report themselves to be victims of bias in professional as well as personal conversations. Contrary to their garrulous stereotype, women in mixed groups talk far less than their fair share of the time. Men tend to emerge as group leaders, and are more successful at influencing groups to accept new ideas. Men interrupt more often, and exert influence by answering questions which are not addressed to them. Women tend to withdraw when interrupted, to provide conversational maintenance, and to ask questions.[44]

Belenky and her colleagues emphasize that many women, including those with extensive professional training, live with the conviction that they are not capable of intelligent thought.[45] Such a confluence of negative experiences and an insecure internal state does not suggest that women are predisposed to easy and positive professional relationships. Most women will resonate with Sadker and Sadker's findings that males exhibit more powerful behaviours than females in group settings. Sadker and Sadker go on to point out that men are more likely to influence group discussions, and that women's comments are more likely than those of men to be ignored. This gender gap in communications, they contend, puts women teachers and administrators at a disadvantage in having their ideas heard and implemented.[46]

Often, women are simply not present when professional topics are raised; women's absence is often seen as evidence of professional uninterest. Joyce and Showers make much of the need for a warm and casual collegiality; they emphasize their desire to rid teaching of professional isolation, and show no sympathy for those who must schedule every minute of the day in an attempt to fill personal as well as professional roles. Multiple-role teachers often find what passes for professional collegiality to be a frustrating waste of time rather than an empowering experience. Isolation is sometimes solace; Biklen suggests that isolation has played an important role in sustaining many excellent women teachers in what they experience as a hostile environment.[47]

Thus to the extent that the content and nature of staff development rely on decisions reached by mixed-sex groups, and to the extent that these groups use typical communications patterns, women will be separated from their own thoughts and opinions and from those of their female colleagues. Women's voices will not be heard. If what is chosen by such groups reflects women's needs and interests, it will result from good luck rather than good management. Another group is much more likely to influence outcomes: the authors suggest a judicious placement of omnivores to ensure that work groups choose suitable topics for study.

In addition to the work group, Joyce and Showers propose to support implementation through peer coaching. In this context, peer coaching in a stable diad is to take place over an extended period; its effective implementation will require varying levels of time, trust, objectivity and willingness to give and receive feedback. Those who have worked with collegial improvement efforts will not need to be reminded of the potential of this strategy, nor to be convinced that diads are effective only if considerable attention is paid to the establishment and maintenance of a trusting relationship between partners. This is not always easy to accomplish, particularly if gender is ignored. Several gender-related variables can interfere with pair effectiveness. In particular, women are not accustomed to receiving professional feedback.[48] It may be difficult to set aside the cultural distribution of power between men and women within a male–female pair. Men's culturally bestowed right to judge women on both personal and professional criteria tends to interfere with the attainment of non-judgemental collegiality. Heilman and Kram remind us that women expect to be evaluated more harshly and negatively than their male counterparts,[49] while even the most capable women live with extraordinarily low self-concepts.[50] Gilligan's model of the ethic of care suggests that women are reluctant to give feedback if they believe it will be hurtful.[51] Finally, there are suggestions that individuals are more likely to trust same-sex colleagues than those of the opposite sex.[52] Without attention to these considerations, the coaching pairs may never attain their potential. Unfortunately, such attention is not possible if the mask of gender neutrality is to be maintained.

CONCLUSION

This paper has argued that gender neutrality masks the androcentrism which dominates all forms of cultural thought and action. It encourages the validation of an unexamined, masculinist paradigm of education and the values which coexist with androcentrism. It prevents us from acknowledging uncertainty, the validity of experiential knowledge, and from considering alternatives to our current goals and strategies. It teaches us to evaluate our colleagues and ourselves on a male-biased continuum, and to practise victim analysis if we fall short of an external standard. It prevents us from acknowledging or addressing the particular needs of women as knowers, learners, teachers and students. It sanctifies and then generalizes knowledge about one part of the population, passed on by that same part of the population. It requires us to choose our leaders from those who are socialized to be uncomfortable with the kind of leadership we say we want and need. It requires us to ignore what being male or female means to each child in our classrooms. Gender neutrality robs us of the ability to fully understand and learn from our colleagues. It creates a silence which promotes gender bias while superficially adopting the mannerisms of impartiality. Staff development which ignores gender bias becomes a vehicle for its perpetuation.

If Joyce and Showers were unique, this paper would not be necessary. Unfortunately, they appear to fit comfortably among the vast majority of their peers, complicit in promoting an ideology which insists that these matters are tangential to the real business of improving schools. If this ideology is to be challenged successfully, every researcher, policy analyst, staff developer and teacher must feel obliged to contribute to what is known about gender and education and to incorporate this knowledge into her or his work. Equity in education will not be achieved until this work is done.

NOTES AND REFERENCES

1. It should be made clear that 'masculinism', the masculine paradigm, 'androcentric', and so forth, are not synonymous with the noun 'males'.

Although males are more likely to hold a masculinist paradigm and to be more androcentric than females, it could hardly be otherwise given the ruthlessness and effectiveness of an engenderation system which teaches those born male and female to become masculine and feminine. To a greater or lesser extent, each of us experiences the world and behaves in androgynous ways. Unfortunately, personal androgyny is no guarantor of cultural androgyny, and it is culture rather than personal inclination which shapes our institutions.

2. Schaef, Anne Wilson, *Women's Reality: An Emerging Female System in a White Male Society*. Silver Spring, MD: Winston Press, 1985.

3. Gilligan, C., *In a Different Voice: Psychological Theory and Women's Development*. Cambridge, MA: Harvard University Press, 1982.

4. Joyce, B. and Showers, B., *Student Achievement through Staff Development*. New York: Longman, p. 188, 1988.

5. Ibid, pp. xi–xii.

6. Edmonds, R., 'Some schools work and more can'. *Social Policy*, 9 (5), pp. 28–32, 1979.

7. Joyce and Showers, op. cit., note 4, p. 8.

8. Ibid., p. 131.

9. Ibid., p. 133.

10. Ibid., p. 136.

11. Calabrese, R. L. and Anderson, R. E., 'The public school: a source of stress and alienation among female teachers'. *Urban Education*, 21 (1), April 1986.

12. Heilman, M. E. and Kram, K. E., 'Male and female assumptions about colleagues' views of their competence'. *Psychology of Women Quarterly*, 7 (4), Summer 1983.

13. Shockley, P. and Staley, C., cited by Sadker, M. and Sadker, D., 'Sexism in the classroom: from grade school to graduate school'. *Phi Delta Kappan*, March 1986.

14. MacLeod, L., *Progress as Paradox: A Profile of Women Teachers*. Ottawa: Canadian Teachers' Federation, November 1988.

15. Biklen, S. K., 'I have always worked: elementary schoolteaching as a career'. *Phi Delta Kappan*, March 1986.

16. Biklen, S. K., 'Can elementary schoolteaching be a career? a search for new ways of understanding women's work'. *Issues in Education*, 3 (3), Winter 1985.

17. Joyce and Showers, op. cit., note 4, p. 133.

18. Gilligan, op. cit., note 3, p. 173.

19. Acker, S., 'Women and teaching: a semi-detached sociology of a semi-profession'. In Walker, S. and Barton, L. (eds), *Gender, Class and Education*. Sussex: Falmer Press, 1983.

20. Belenky, M. F., Clinchey, B. M., Goldberger, N. R. and Tarula, J. M. *Women's Ways of Knowing: The Development of Self, Voice and Mind*. New York: Basic Books, p. 5, 1986.

21. Gilligan, op. cit., note 3.

22. Shakeshaft, C. and Hanson, M., 'Androcentric bias in the *Educational Administration Quarterly*'. *Educational Administration Quarterly*, 22 (1), Winter 1986.

23. Belenky *et al.*, op. cit., note 20.

24. Ibid., p. 221.

25. Joyce and Showers, op. cit., note 4, p. 96.

26. See, for example, Fullan, M. G., *What's Worth Fighting for in the Principalship*. Toronto: Ontario Public School Teachers' Federation, p. 23, 1988.

27. Statistics Canada, *Education in Canada, A Statistical Review for 1986–87*. Toronto Ministry of Supply and Services, 1987.

28. Shakeshaft, C., 'A gender at risk'. *Phi Delta Kappan*, March 1986.

29. For an extensive discussion of this research see Shakeshaft, C., *Women in Educational Administration*. Beverly Hills, CA: Sage, 1987.

30. MacLeod, op. cit., note 14.

31. MacLeod, L., Presentation made at Women Building Tomorrow, the 10th Annual Conference on Women and Education, Ottawa, Canadian Teachers' Federation, November 1988.

32. Shakeshaft, C., 'Female organizational culture'. *Educational Horizons*, 64 (3), Spring 1986.

33. Fullan, M., *What's Worth Fighting for in the Principalship*. Toronto: Ontario Public School Teachers' Federation, 1988.

34. Joyce and Showers, op. cit., note 4, p. 38.

35. Ibid., p. 56.

36. See Shakeshaft, op. cit., note 28, for a summary of research and discussion of these statements.

37. MacLeod, L., *The Idea Book: A Resource for Improving the Participation and Success of Female Students in Math, Science and Technology*. Canadian Teachers' Federation, November 1988.

38. Harvey, G., 'Finding reality among the myths: why what you thought about sex equity in education isn't so'. *Phi Delta Kappan*, March 1986.

39. Sadker, M. and Sadker, D., 'Sexism in the classroom: from grade school to graduate school'. *Phi Delta Kappan*, March 1986.

40. Harvey, op. cit., note 38.

41. Shakeshaft, op. cit., note 28.

42. Joyce and Showers, op. cit., note 4, p. 45.

43. MacLeod, op. cit., note 14.

44. See Shockley and Staley, op. cit., note 13, for a discussion of communications and gender.

45. Belenky *et al.*, op. cit., note 20.

46. Shockley and Staley, op. cit., note 13.

47. Biklen, op. cit., note 15.

48. Belenky *et al.*, op. cit., note 20.

49. Heilman, Kram, op. cit., note 12.

50. Belenky *et al.*, op. cit., note 20.

51. Gilligan, op. cit., note 3.

52. Scott, D., 'Trust differences between men and women in superior-subordinate relationships'. *Group and Organization Studies*, 8 (3), September 1983.

Chapter 4

Helping Teachers Develop

Philip W. Jackson

I

A joke that has become a favourite of mine over the years goes like this: This fellow named Johnson played double bass for the Metropolitan Opera company for thirty years without ever taking an evening off. One night he was forced to take the night off because of a new union rule, and like the proverbial busman he decided to go to the opera, where they were playing *Carmen*. Our hero sat in a choice seat and beamed with pleasure throughout the performance. When it was finished he rushed backstage and grabbed the conductor by the hand. 'Maestro, maestro,' he said, 'what a performance! And I learned so very much tonight.' The conductor looked at him, rather puzzled. 'But Johnson,' he said, 'you've been playing double bass in *Carmen* for thirty years. What could you possibly have learned tonight?' 'Well, sir,' Johnson replied, 'You know in the second act where the double bass has the melody that goes Zum, zum, Zum, zum? You know what the violins are doing? They're going Tum-tum-ti-tum-tum, Tum-ti-tum-ti-tum,' as he hummed a few bars of The Toreador Song.

That old gag popped into my mind once again as I began to prepare my contribution to this volume. I didn't understand why it did so at first, but then I realized that Johnson's belated insight into the musical complexity of *Carmen* was a good example of a certain kind of professional development, a kind that I would like to discuss in this chapter. To make the connection clear, I must start with some general remarks about teacher development and then move to the question of how those of us who want to help teachers might act upon our desire. To answer that question I shall introduce a system of categorizing the different ways of helping teachers that I have found to be useful and that I trust others will as well. The system contains four categories, one of which — the one most often overlooked I fear — covers experiences much like that of our musically naïve bass player.

II

First, a word about what the expression 'teacher development' stands for. The phrase suffers from ambiguity as double nouns are apt to do. It could refer to how individual teachers develop in the process of their careers or it could also apply to how the teaching profession as a whole has developed over the years. I shall assume that we are chiefly concerned with the former rather than the latter meaning and will so restrict the focus of my remarks.[1]

To locate our topic within a broader context we need to distinguish between development and change. Teachers change in countless ways during the process of their careers. That much is obvious. They become more experienced, at least in the sense of having taught for a longer time. They often learn new skills. They do things better. They become more knowledgeable. They sometimes grow in power, control and authority. They earn more money. They change fields, transfer from one grade level to another, from school to school. They sometimes become more patient, compassionate, wise, and witty. Some of them, however, become discouraged, fatigued, 'burnt out', cynical, lazy. A few of them go dotty. Some lose their enthusiasm for teaching. Not a few lose their teeth. They all grow older. They get grey, bald, wrinkled, forgetful, full of memories, sometimes full of sleep. Some quit teaching long before they reach retirement age. They become school administrators, college professors, textbook writers, educational researchers. Others stay to reap the rewards of a lifetime spent doing what they love.

Many of these changes are inevitable. Certainly all those having to do with ageing are. Some changes happen to some teachers but not to others. Not all teachers grow increasingly cynical, for example, but some do. Some of these changes we may want to include under the rubric of 'development', but surely not all of them. Those deserving of the term are drawn from that subclass of changes that are desirable and positive in quality as opposed to negative. Thus increases in ability, skill, power, strength, wisdom, insight, virtue, happiness and so forth would certainly qualify as development, whereas changes that we might wish would not happen, such as a decline in enthusiasm or an increased sense of discouragement, would clearly not qualify. This too strikes me as being fairly obvious.

III

We turn next to the relationship between teacher development and the work of those of us who are not teachers, at least not classroom teachers, but would like to be of help to those who are. For the sake of discussion let us call ourselves teachers' helpers, or teachers' aides if you prefer, remembering that many of us are also teachers ourselves. Our task is to aid and abet teacher development. How is that done?

As the various chapters of this book make evident, there are a variety of ways to help teachers develop. Moreover, varied as the programme offerings are, the list of approaches they include is by no means exhaustive. No one, for example, is scheduled to talk about ways teachers might plan better bulletin boards, yet for some teachers that might be just the set of skills they are seeking to develop. In any event, my interest at this point is less with the comprehensiveness of the presentations yet to come than with the question of how all such efforts might be classified. To that end I propose a classification system containing four categories. The first three are fairly easy to explain. The fourth proves more difficult, as will soon be evident.

1. Surely the most obvious way to contribute to teacher development is to tell teachers how to teach or, if they already know how, by telling them how to teach better than they are presently doing. I shall call this *the way of know-how*. I was initially going to call it *the way of technique*, but a researcher friend of mine talked me out of it. He said that the word 'technique' is not much in favour among teachers these days. It apparently sounds too mechanistic. He recommended the word 'principle'. What he is trying to do in his own work, he explained, is to identify principles of teaching that might guide practitioners in their work. To avoid taking a stand on whether the search should be for techniques or principles I have chosen the more colloquial term 'know-how', which seems to me to embrace both the narrower and broader conceptions of what teachers might need to know.

In any event, help of this kind takes the form of advice that basically says 'Do this' or 'Don't do that' or 'Do this rather than that'. The advice need not be expressed dogmatically of course. It could be softened to expressions like 'Try this' or 'Consider these alternatives', or even 'Why not for a change, if you've got nothing else to do, think about doing it this way?' Moreover, not all of it need focus on how teachers behave when their pupils are before them. Advice about how to plan, how to evaluate, how to organize the physical space of the classroom, how to group students, even how to make better bulletin boards all falls within this general category. All such advice belongs to the same strategy of teacher development.

The bulk of what is usually called research on teaching is designed to contribute to this way of helping teachers. However, a lot of good advice comes from teachers themselves with little or no help from the research community. Much of it takes the form of tips or suggestions that experienced teachers pass along to novices. When teacher centres were popular they specialized in this kind of exchange. A lot of professional magazines, such as *Instructor*, still do.

2. A second way of helping teachers is to improve the conditions under which they work. This would include reducing their teaching load, giving them more time for planning, fewer students, more aides, and so forth. A special category of this form of help, one that has become prominent of late, includes efforts to increase teachers' power and authority in matters such as choosing textbooks, scheduling classes, establishing the curriculum, overseeing their own evaluation procedures, and so on. In short, it involves giving teachers a greater hand in

controlling their own destinies. I shall call this collection of efforts *the way of independence.*

Here too I have some trouble with terminology. Among teachers there is a lot of talk these days about something called *empowerment*, and within certain circles the word *emancipation* is also enjoying renewed popularity after a century or so of relative neglect. I have chosen to avoid both terms, principally because each has become a buzz word and I have no wish to be identified with those who use them in that way, which is to say mindlessly. *Independence* is perhaps not much better than either of the more popular terms, but at least it avoids the patois of the cult while capturing the general notion of freeing teachers to function as relatively autonomous professionals.

Those who want to help teachers in this way commonly focus on a group of some kind, such as all of the teachers in a school building or a district or even a state, though the individual remains the beneficiary of the majority of such efforts. There is some research going on about how best to accomplish the goal of increased independence (e.g., the experiments with self-governance now taking place in some Florida schools) but a lot of such efforts are straightforward political manoeuvring whose goal is to wrest power and authority from school administrators, school boards, certifying agencies, the taxpaying public, and so forth.

3. A third way of helping teachers develop is by relieving them of psychological discomfort of one kind or another and, in general, by helping them come to terms with the demands of their work. I shall call this *the way of role accommodation.* It involves giving teachers encouragement, support, sympathy, respect, and in the extreme case, some form of therapy. Its goal is to help teachers handle the psychological stresses of their work.

Some years back there was a move afoot to encourage all teachers to undergo psychological therapy of one form or another. A few prominent figures, such as Anna Freud and Arthur T. Jersild, went so far as to recommend that all teachers be psychoanalyzed. Today there is a renewed interest in helping teachers come to terms with the demands of their work, but the emphasis seems to be on finding ways for them to do it more or less on their own rather than recommending that they lie down on the analyst's couch. The use of journals, autobiographies, and diaries figure prominently in these more recent efforts, as do so-called 'support groups' within schools and the kind of 'buddy' system that pairs up experienced and novice teachers as a way of inducting the latter into the guild.

These three ways of seeking to contribute to teacher development — the way of know-how, the way of independence, and the way of role accommodation — have been around for a long time. Each is a legitimate endeavour. Each has obvious pay-offs for both teacher helpers and teachers or it would not have lasted for as long as it has. It is important to emphasize the legitimacy of all three strategies because from time to time one hears it said that one or other of them is *infra dig*. For example, as I have already intimated there is a tendency among some educators to look down their noses at the practice of offering specific advice to teachers on the grounds that such advice is ultimately belittling to those at whom it is directed. Complaints have arisen with respect to the other two strategies as well. Without bothering to examine such complaints and leaving aside the question of the relative merits of the three strategies of intervention I have described, I wish only at this point to insist that there is plenty of room for all three.

4. I turn now to the fourth category promised earlier. Again, the question of what to call it proves troublesome. I initially wanted to call it *the way of art* but that turned out to be quite misleading once I had settled upon the range of activities the category was to cover. I next thought of calling it *the way of wonder* but that sounded too sentimental, even though it does come close to naming what lies at the heart of this mode of development. My next choice was *the way of altered sensibility* but that too I finally discarded because it reminded me of 'altered states of consciousness', a phrase I associate for some reason with Shirley MacLaine. In the end I decided not to call it anything — at least not at the start — but instead to go ahead and describe what it's about and then see whether some word or phrase contained in the description might prove adequate.

The reason *the way of art* came to mind first when I was casting about for a label is that the mode of development covered by this fourth category is closely analogous to what happens when someone encounters a work of art and is deeply affected by it. We have no clear and unequivocal language for describing that process. As a consequence we resort to metaphor. We also speak of what happens in a variety of different ways. Yet common elements recur in the figures of speech we employ.

We use a lot of visual imagery to speak about such events, even when the object of our concern is not something that can be physically seen. We say things like, 'Oh, now I see', or 'I see now what he is getting at', or 'I now look at it differently'. In short, we speak as though our vision has been altered in some fundamental way. Moreover, what undergoes change is usually not our vision in general, at least not consciously. Rather, it is our perception of the object or the work we are considering. We see *it* differently.

We also use language that reflects a distinction between surface and depth, a verticality of our perception. We speak of becoming aware of the *deeper* significance of the work. We grasp the meaning that lies at its core. We speak of penetrating it with our understanding, of looking into it, of seeing behind its glossy or its dull appearance. We immerse ourselves in our investigation of the piece. It is as though the work was a three-dimensional object whose interior we could explore.

Sometimes our spatial imagery takes on a horizontal dimension as well. When that happens it is usually ourselves, rather than the art object, that we are talking about. We say that our horizons have been broadened, that our awareness has been extended. We see *more* than we did.

We speak too of changes in the value we attach to the work. We say it *means more* to us now. We come to appreciate it, even to treasure it. We recommend it to our friends. 'You should see . . .,' we say, or, 'Wait till you read . . .'. Often we seek to own the work ourselves, or at least a replica of it. We hang it on our wall or display it in our bookcase or record cabinet. We become attached to it. We might even go so far as to say it has now become a part of us. If someone borrows the work and fails to return it for a long time we feel bereft. We *miss* it, we say. When we do get it back we receive it eagerly and with pleasure. We handle it fondly.

I would maintain that these kinds of experiences are not limited to our encounters with works of art, even though the latter may be exemplary of the broader category. I believe that a similar thing happens when we read a stimulating scientific article or listen to a provocative lecture. It can also happen when we look closely and reflect upon the world around us. And it need not be the grandeur of the world we reflect upon. '[T]he meanest flower that blows can give/Thoughts that do often lie too deep for tears', Wordsworth reminds us. To the patient observer, the lowly, the mundane and the familiar can also be revealing.

What does all this have to do with teacher development? Just this: there are countless ways in which we who teach might come to a deeper, broader and richer understanding of what we do. Some of these ways entail looking at teaching differently, seeing it in a new light, coming to appreciate its complexity more than we have done as yet. Such transformations of our vision may not leave us changed in ways that others can readily see. We may not *look* like better teachers, at least not to the naked eye. In fact we might even look worse. We might possibly develop a more hesitant manner, a kind of pedagogical stammer, as a result of our reflection and our newly won insight. We also may not *feel* any better as teacher either. Again, we might actually feel worse, at least temporarily: more doubt-ridden, puzzled, sadder perhaps. After all, sadness and wisdom are not incompatible. That too the poets teach. Recall the wedding guest as he bids adieu to the ancient mariner.

And yet might we not from time to time want to say that the sadder, wiser, more puzzled teacher has undergone a positive change, a change worthy of being described as development? I certainly would. In fact I would go further than that. I would say that once we have mastered the most rudimentary pedagogical skills, the indispensable skills that keep us from being booed and jeered at by our students or run out of town by the local school superintendent or college dean, the really important changes that we undergo through the years are of the kind I am trying to describe here. I shall not pursue the point, but I thought it only fair to keep my strong bias out in the open.

By now it should be clearer why I had trouble finding a label for this category of developmental changes, and also why I entertained the alternative I did, the ones I decided to discard. We are still no closer than before, I fear, to finding a satisfactory name for our fourth way of helping teachers to develop, so I shall once more abandon the effort for now and move on.

IV

In my opinion, what is needed at this point is an example of some kind to drive my point home, a work of art or its equivalent drawn from our unnamed category and presented in such a way that its power to contribute to a teacher's development would be blatantly evident. But as soon as one tries to do that one runs into trouble. The problem is that there is no reliable way to predict in advance the transformative impact a text or a lecture or a planned observation might have. So much depends on the fit between what is chosen and its audience. Every teacher who has worked with such material already knows this, of course, which is why so many of us who routinely engage in that kind of teaching mentally cross our fingers each time we open the classroom door. Yet we do manage to open the door and cross the threshold in the face of that uncertainty, and so must I here.

But there is still the question of what *kind* of material to choose, for if I am right those experiences that have what might be called 'a developmental impact' on us as teachers can be triggered in countless ways, which means by many different kinds of material, including some that — at least superficially — have nothing to do with teaching at all. Nonetheless, it does seem reasonable to expect that material whose content explicitly referred to teaching would in the long run have a greater chance of having such an impact than would material that had nothing to do with teaching at all. That restricts our search somewhat, but it still leaves a lot to choose from. We might select something from our own experience as teachers or as observers of teachers, or even from our experience as students, for the latter will inevitably have to do with teaching as well. Alternatively we might choose something that someone else has written about teaching, a research study perhaps, or a story or an anecdote, or even a poem. Items from this second set of alternatives have the advantage of being ready-made, which makes them especially suitable for my purpose here.

With that in mind I selected four books containing anecdotes, essays and poems about teaching. These were: *Going to School*, edited by Abraham H. Lass and Norma L. Tasman,[2] *Unseen Harvests*, edited by Claude M. Fuess and Emory S. Basford,[3] *Great Teachers*, edited by Houston Peterson,[4] and *An Apple for My Teacher*, edited by Louis D. Rubin.[5] I leafed through each of them quickly. They contained more than enough material to draw upon, but I still faced the question of what to use.

It was then that I said to myself that it almost doesn't matter; that virtually anything about teaching can provide sufficiently rich material for reflection if we stay with it long enough. In his novel *Roger's Version* one of John Updike's[6] characters observes: 'there are so few things which, contemplated, do not like flimsy trapdoors open under the weight of our attention into the bottomless pit below'. I believe in the truth of that observation and I think it works as well for material connected with teaching as it does for everything else. The trouble is that there is not enough space for examples here, so I searched for ones whose trapdoors seemed to me flimsier than most.

What I came up with was a pair of documents from which I shall draw excerpts for our perusal, all done of course with fingers crossed. The first describes a teacher's last day of teaching. The teacher is George Lyman Kittredge, who taught Shakespeare to Harvard's undergraduates for close to fifty years. The author of the anecdote is Heywood Broun, New York columnist and reporter, who was one of Kittredge's students and who, along with three hundred others who had shared the great man's tutelage, attended 'Kitty's' last class. Here are portions of Broun's description:

> Somewhere in *Julius Caesar* Brutus and Cassius sit down in a tent and talk together very quietly . . .

> That would be the mood of Professor Kittredge's farewell. The high and florid tradition of Shakespeare was revised into the swaggering underemphasis of New England.

> Professor Kittredge has a long white beard but insufficient showmanship to swing it, and so when he came to the river's brink he made no oration but set up his tent and placed upon it the sign 'Business as Usual'. In addition to the pupils in his course some three hundred other students had gathered to hear 'Kitty' take off. If any expected him to weep or sing *The Last Round-Up* they were disappointed. He did fetch Shakespeare out and saddle the old word painter for a final foray, but it was done without benefit of bugle calls. The absent-minded professor gave no indication of noticing the studio audience. He addressed his remarks solely to those enrolled in English 2.

> The class was at work on . . . *A Winter's Tale*. Where they had left off on the previous occasion they took up again. No hint was given by the preceptor that this was an occasion having anything of unusual significance. It was just a segment of that same old course . . .

> A little before his hour was up he informed the class that he would not be able to finish the play at that morning session. He suggested that they might use the printed notes in the book, although he added that they were hardly as good as he could furnish. And then quite casually, too casually I fear, he said, 'We'll stop here'.

> Perhaps he may be pardoned for departing at the end a little from
> the honored tradition of Harvard. He did not, as he might have
> done, step directly toward the door and so out into the yard and
> through the gate and home from Harvard. He blew himself for a
> full minute to the privilege of behaving like a leading man or a
> Yale professor in the department of English. He stood poised at
> the edge of the platform and took his full sixty seconds of
> applause from the three hundred . . .
>
> But precisely at the end of a minute the Professor indicated with
> his hand that he wanted the side aisle cleared.
>
> It used to be a cloak he wore, if I remember. But in any case he
> threw something over his shoulders and without another word he
> left fifty years of teaching behind him.[7]

What I find intriguing about this description is the contrast between the deeply symbolic significance of Kittredge's last lesson and his insistence on 'business as usual'. Consider what must have been going on in his mind. He must of course have known, as did everyone else present, that that morning's class was very special indeed and could hardly be looked upon as ordinary by anyone there, including himself. Picture him entering the room. Did he anticipate the crowd? I suspect he did. After all, word of the event must have been circulating around the campus for weeks. How else could we explain such a turnout? *Three hundred* spectators? As a matter of fact, if the room was large enough to hold that many visitors it couldn't have been just a classroom. It must have been a vast hall. Might the class's regular meeting place have been switched for this last lesson? The account doesn't say so but I should not be surprised to learn that some kind of special arrangements had been made.

What about the manner of his entrance? Do you think he strode in, eyes forward, looking neither to right nor left? That seems unlikely. After all, he must have recognized many of his visitors. He had probably taught most of them. I imagine him nodding and smiling as he walked down the aisle, perhaps even discreetly returning a wave from a former student seated in the far corner of the room. By the time he reached the front and turned round the room must have been alive with chatter. But now came the silence of anticipation. What the audience was about to witness was going to be a very special event indeed.

So why the business-as-usual attitude? Why did he proceed to teach just as though this was an ordinary day and the three hundred spectators were not there? Could it have been for dramatic effect? It certainly must have made a powerful impression on those present. It still does on those of us who can only read about it. Here is the last day of a dedicated teacher's professional life, and what does he do? Just what he has always done, no more nor less. A little talk of Shakespeare, a few questions and answers, a closing apology for not being able to finish the text. What an admirable lack of sentimentality!

What oblivion to the spectators in the gallery!

Kittredge must have been conscious of the effect his sticking to the lesson would have, but exactly *how* conscious was he, do you think? Do you imagine he thought about it much in advance? Would it matter if he had? It seems to me it would. If we thought that Kittredge had stayed awake the night before, planning how to wring the last drop of drama from his pedagogical swan-song, we would have a very different attitude toward his performance than the one the audience expressed with its applause at the end of the lesson. The power of his actions depends, in other words, on our believing them to be consonant with his character rather than contrived. 'That's just the way old Kittredge was', we want to say.

But was he? Listen to how another pupil described 'Kitty' at work — Stuart P. Sherman — who later, like Broun, went on to become a New York journalist. The lesson he describes is clearly not the one Broun witnessed, though the subject is still Shakespeare.

> A pretty abrupt hush follows his rapid footsteps up the aisle,
> deepens as he seats himself sidewise, and menaces us thunderously
> from behind the formidable blue glasses, becomes painfully
> intense as he rises to stride to and fro the length of the platform
> in a kind of tiger tred, and the blackboard pointer, overstrained
> by his nervous fingers, breaks with an electrifying snap. We are
> about to enjoy a bad quarter of an hour. 'Mr. A! How does a play
> begin?' 'With dialogue,' hazards Mr. A. 'Mr. B! How does a play
> begin?' 'With the introduction of the characters,' stammers Mr.
> B. anxiously. 'Mr. C! How does a play begin?' Mr. C, who is from
> the Gold Coast, quietly mumbles, 'I don't know'. The hunt is
> afoot. The next dozen men go down amid derisive snickers — no
> one dares to laugh aloud — like clay pipes before a crack marks -
> man. Panic spreads. Half of us refuse to answer our names. The
> other half, in desperate agitation between an attempt to conjure
> up any sort of reply and a passionate desire to sink through the
> floor, shudderingly wait for the next victim, till the pursuer, at
> last weary of the sport, cries out, 'A play begins in *mediis rebus*!'
> Then we turn to the text.[8]

Good old Kittredge is it? How much is any teacher like the person we see in the classroom? Who sees? On which day? What does it mean to be oneself as a teacher? Can one ever do that? Don't we all put on a public demeanour the minute we open the classroom door? Isn't it a good thing we do? Who would want to have seen old 'Kitty' blubber like a walrus on that final morning of his career?

Such are the questions that come most quickly to mind in response to these two quite different images of a well-known and highly respected teacher. You may well have thought of others. If we had time to discuss the two readings in a rather more leisurely manner I have no doubt that we would come up with additional questions. We would almost surely have other reactions as well. In fact when I related these two episodes to my jogging partner on an early morning run she reacted with great animation to Sherman's account. 'Oh, I had a teacher just like that in high school', she said. 'Her name was Margaret Fisher and she taught Latin'. There followed a spirited account of my friend's experience with her old Latin teacher, complete with a story about how she and a group of her classmates would meet in the cafeteria before class each morning to be coached in the daily translations of Cicero by the most brilliant student in the class. Even then she feared the ordeal to follow, although she confessed to learning a lot of Latin in the process. She also told me how, many years later, she thought of writing to her former teacher, who by then had been retired for a long time, but wound up not doing so because she was still uncertain about how she felt about dear old Margaret Fisher, the scourge of Westfield High, and she therefore did not know what to say to her.

Back to the Kittredge episodes. What impact does the reading of fragmentary texts like these have? Have I been changed forever by virtue of having chanced upon them while preparing this chapter? I confess I don't feel as though I have, but who knows? I am left with two sharp and contrasting images of a teacher at work, each lodged firmly in my memory, at least for the time being. What use I shall make of those images in the future I cannot begin to tell. Nor can I assess what subtle adjustments, if any, they have already forced me to make in my understanding of how teachers can or should act, nor even in how I myself shall act on that fateful day when I stand before my last class.

And what of my readers? What effect has my relating of these episodes had on you? Perhaps some of you found them boring and skimmed through them quickly or perhaps you even skipped them entirely. 'No effect at all', would be your answer. Others, I suspect, would reply more or less as I have. You simply have no way of telling what the impact of your reading has been. Fortunately, I need not worry too much about the long-term effect of my comments, for my sole purpose in relating these brief anecdotes is to use them as examples of my fourth category of ways to help teachers develop. I never contended that every such effort has to work.

However, let me make it clear what I *am* contending. I am not just saying that it is often interesting or entertaining to talk and think about teaching in ways that have nothing to do with know-how or independence or psychological comfort. I am claiming that there *is* no other way, chancy though the process may be, to further the development of teachers along lines that lead to a deepened and intensified appreciation of the social and cultural complexities of their work. There are other forms of teacher development, as we have seen, but none substitutes for the kind of enriched understanding that only prolonged reflection on teaching, from a variety of different perspectives, can ultimately give.

At this point I cannot resist inserting a methodological note, even though there is little space left for its development. One obvious way of moving in on an object of reflection, whether it be a story or a poem or a fragment of our own experience, is by seeking to locate it within some larger setting. By so doing we give the object background, either literally or figuratively, which has the dual effect of creating an illusion of depth while at the same time pushing the object into the foreground of our perception. Expressed formulaically the goal is to *articulate the context*, a phrase I borrow from Charles Wegener, a colleague at my university.

We can seek to accomplish this goal in a variety of ways. In the Kittredge example I began to do so, very superficially of course, by imagining what he might have been thinking that morning in preparation for his last class. I also tried to supply some of the circumstances that might have preceded the event — the word circulating around the campus, the switch of rooms to accommodate the large audience. Whether in such a short time I succeeded in deepening and broadening our understanding of the event Broun described remains very questionable. However, I am confident I was moving in the right direction, and so would anyone else be who sought to work within this fourth mode to teacher development. The rule to follow is the one I have just named: one begins by seeking to *articulate the context*.

All of which brings us back to Johnson, the famous bass violist mentioned at the beginning of this chapter. As I said, I have been relating his experience for years but it wasn't until I began to prepare this chapter that I realized that what happened to Johnson is analogous to what we hope will happen frequently (with or without our help) to the teachers with whom we work (and to ourselves too far that matter). Johnson certainly returned from his night off a changed man. Moreover, the change was accomplished by following the principle I have just introduced. What the experience did for Johnson was to articulate and broaden the context. No longer will he ever hear his heavy melody (Zum, zum, Zum, zum) without those airy 'grace notes' behind it going: Tum, tum, ti, tum, tum, Tum, ti, tum, ti, tum.

But fortunately there is more to his experience than that. I say fortunately because it seems that his insight might have affected his spirits in either of two ways. As it turns out, he apparently reacted with delight to his busman's holiday. He was thrilled to learn what the violins were doing while he sawed away on his two notes. Even after the event he clung to the idea that his part was the melody. That too seems a healthy reaction, though a bit deluded perhaps.

But he might have gone the other way. He could have left the opera house in a depressed state, having just discovered that what he thought all along was the melody was actually nothing but two rasping bass notes played in the corner of the stage. Had that been the case, he might even have quit the orchestra for good. Then I would have had no joke to begin this chapter and you would never have heard of Johnson. His good fortune is therefore also mine (and yours as well

I hope); but it does point to something else, which is that we can never be sure how our efforts to deepen and broaden the insights of teachers (and ourselves for that matter) will ultimately turn out. All we can do is what teachers have done for ages, which is to choose materials and arrange experiences as wisely as possible and hope for the best.

Finally, what *shall* we call our unnamed strategy of teacher development? Sad to say, I still don't know. The perfect title continues to elude me. Even a good one that refers to the goal of the process fails to come to mind. So until I come across something better I'll just have to refer to it as *the fourth way* and leave it at that. If this label makes some of you think of Buddha, as it did a friend of mine on whom I tried it out, so be it. There are worse names and worse associations, as I trust these remarks have helped to make clear.

NOTES AND REFERENCES

1. I wish to thank Robert Boostrom, Diane Bowers and David Hansen for their helpful comments on an earlier draft. I am also grateful to Jennifer Gates and Andrew Porter for their reactions to parts of the chapter.

2. Lass, A. H. and Tasman, N. L. (eds), *Going to School*. New York: New American Library, 1980.

3. Fuess, C. M. and Basford, E. S. (eds), *Unseen Harvests*. New York: Macmillan, 1947.

4. Peterson, H. (ed.), *Great Teachers*. New York: Vintage Books, 1946.

5. Rubin, L. D., Jr. (ed.), *An Apple For My Teacher*. Chapel Hill, NC: Algonquin Books, 1987.

6. Updike, J., *Roger's Version*. New York: Knopf, 1986.

7. Lass, op. cit., note 2, pp. 171–3.

8. Peterson, op. cit., note 4, p. 255.

Chapter 5

Teachers as Designers in Self-directed Professional Development

Christopher M. Clark

In some quarters the phrase 'professional development of teachers' carries a great deal of negative undertones. It implies a process done to teachers; that teachers need to be forced into developing; that teachers have deficits in knowledge and skill that can be fixed by training; and that teachers are pretty much alike. Now, as a teacher, how eager would you feel about co-operating in a process in which you are presumed to be passive, resistant, deficient, and one of a faceless, homogeneous herd? This is hardly an ideal set of conditions for adult learning, support and development.

The good news is that teachers are not passive, needy, deficient and homogeneous. We know this from personal experience and from research. Research on teacher thinking, which began in earnest in 1976, supports and describes the experienced professional teacher as a complex individual doing very complicated work in a sometimes stressful, sometimes rewarding, always uncertain and dynamic variety of settings.

Research on teacher thinking is only one source of information about the nature of teaching, and it is the source that I will draw on most heavily here. My simple message has three parts: (1) there is much more to teaching than meets the eye; (2) the enriched image of teachers as reflective professionals is a good place to start in rethinking professional development; and (3) experienced teachers can become designers of their own personal programmes of self-directed professional development. First, let us examine what researchers on teacher thinking have discovered and concluded about teachers and teaching in the last decade.

A comprehensive review and summary of research on teacher thinking appeared recently as a chapter in the third edition of the *Handbook of Research on Teaching*.[1] This review, of which I was co-author,[2] summarized about ten years of research on topics such as teacher planning, interactive decision-making, judgement, and implicit theories. The extent of the literature is relatively small, perhaps 35–40 studies in all, but this work broke new ground in that, for the first time, educational researchers chose to rely on teachers to think aloud, describe their thoughts and decision processes, and make the invisible aspects of teaching visible. In short, teachers were taken seriously as professionals as a starting condition for this research. Teachers rose to this long overdue occasion. The image of the teacher that emerges from this research is far more flattering and complex than was the case ten or twelve years ago. The following quote from the concluding section of the literature review illustrates this:

> First, the research shows that thinking plays an important part in teaching, and that the image of a teacher as a reflective professional . . . is not farfetched. Teachers do plan in a rich variety of ways, and these plans have real consequences in the classroom. Teachers do have thoughts and make decisions frequently . . . during interactive teaching. Teachers do have theories and belief systems that influence their perceptions, plans, and actions. This literature has given us an opportunity to broaden our appreciation for what teaching is by adding rich descriptions of the mental activities of teachers to the existing body of work that describes the visible behavior of teachers . . .
>
> The emerging picture of the teacher as a reflective professional is a developmental one that begins during undergraduate teacher education . . . and continues to grow and change with professional experience. The teacher education majors who would become professional in this sense are firmly grounded in the disciplines and subject matters that they will teach. Their study of subject matter focuses on both content and on the cognitive organization of that content in ways useful to themselves and their future students. They have had both supervised practice in using the behavioral skills and strategies of teaching and have also been initiated into the less visible aspects of teaching, including the full variety of types of planning and interactive decision making. The maturing professional teacher is one who has taken some steps toward making explicit his or her implicit theories and beliefs about learners, curriculum, subject matter, and the teacher's role. This teacher has developed a style of planning for instruction that includes several interrelated types of planning and that has become more streamlined and automatic with experience. Much of this teacher's interactive teaching consists of routines familiar to the students, thus decreasing the collective information-processing load. During teaching, the teacher attends to and intently processes academic and nonacademic . . . events and cues. These experienced teachers have developed the confidence to be appropriate. They reflect on and analyze the results of these reflections to their future plans and actions. In short, they have become researchers on their own teaching effectiveness.[3]

In sum, research on teacher thinking supports the position that teachers are more active than passive, more ready to learn than resistant, more wise and knowledgeable than deficient, and more diverse and unique than they are homogeneous. This is a flattering and optimistic picture, and it is not true of all teachers in all situations. But it is true often enough to be taken seriously, as a point of departure for asking 'What can we do to make professional development programmes work for professional teachers?' The answer is deceptively simple: we must give the responsibility for professional development to teachers themselves. This is what I mean by 'Self-directed professional development'.

Why should teachers, individually and collectively, take charge of their own professional development? Why is this a good idea? First, we need to recognize that adult development is voluntary — no one can force a person to learn, change or grow. When adults feel that they are in control of a process of change that they have voluntarily chosen, they are much more likely to realize full value from it than when coerced into training situations in which they have little say about the timing, the process or the goals. Second, because each teacher is unique in important ways, it is impossible to create a single, centrally administered and planned programme of professional development that will meet everyone's needs and desires. Why not let the individual be in charge of asking and answering the timeless questions: 'Who am I? What do I need? How can I get help?'. Third, I advocate self-directed professional development because I think that is the way that the best teachers already operate.

Wouldn't it be good for all teachers to have support and encouragement in following an approach to lifelong learning that is pursued now only by a few crusty and inspiring veterans? I think so.

To summarize the argument to this point: there is more to teaching than meets the eye, and responsibility for teachers' professional development ought to be placed in the hands of professional teachers. Building on these two propositions, there is one more level of detail to address about the idea of self-directed professional development. To carry off the concept of self-directed professional development, we, as teachers, must begin to think of ourselves as designers. To develop ourselves as professionals we must plan, select, sketch, make errors, and rearrange the familiar furniture of the mind. We must design ourselves, and continue to revise, redesign, and learn from experience. We must conspire with the world to make for ourselves a heaven or purgatory of our own designing.

The idea of teachers as designers of their own professional development is a metaphor that can become real. To form a picture of what it means to be a designer, think of the different examples of design professions that you already know something about: interior design, architecture, consumer product design, urban planning, film-making, advertising, sculpture, photography, music composition, and cosmetology, to name a few. You can add others to this list, to persuade yourself that you already know a considerable amount about design in its many varieties, and that you are already acting as a designer in some domains. The question is not whether teachers have what it takes to be designers of their own professional development. They do. The question is, 'How can we help with the process?' My tentative answer is to offer and illustrate a list of seven principles of design that I hope will help those teachers who choose to take on this responsibility.

PRINCIPLES OF DESIGN

Write Your Own Credo of Teaching

What a teacher knows and believes about teaching, about learning, about curriculum, and about herself and her students are quite important to professional development. Our beliefs and personal theories set boundaries or frames around what we see and how we interpret experience. Our attention is selective: we cannot attend to everything. And our beliefs and theories define what is foreground and what is background; what to attend to and what to ignore.

By itself, this process of seeing the world through our own theoretical lenses is no problem; it is simply the way that people deal with complex situations. But it can become a problem for a professional teacher when this interpretive process and the beliefs and theories that underlie it remain completely unconscious. In this instance we become mechanical, reactionary, bored and frustrated. The implicit theories that were once tools for thoughtful interpretation become tyrants, manipulating us in painfully familiar patterns.

Teachers' implicit theories are more than private matters of personal taste and opinion. They can have dramatic consequences. For example, consider a study of kindergarten teachers published just recently.[4] Researchers Mary Lee Smith and Lorrie Shepard were commissioned to help the administration in a school district to understand the causes and consequences of radically different patterns of retaining children; that is, having children repeat the kindergarten year. They interviewed 40 of the 44 teachers of kindergarten in the district to find out, among other things, what each teacher believed about children and how they develop, learn, and adapt to the changing demands of schooling. The researchers found two broad belief patterns in the teachers' responses: a 'nativist' belief system, in which only the passage of time can enable child development, and three 'non-nativist' theories, in which child development is believed to be effected by teaching, encouragement, family support, and other factors in addition to maturation. In short, the researchers found that both sides of the classic 'nature versus nurture' debate are represented among contemporary kindergarten teachers.

Now, if this were all that Smith and Shepard had discovered — if they had stopped at a description of two kinds of implicit theories held by teachers — I would be interested but not alarmed. But the researchers went further, to correlate beliefs with actions, and found that the nativist teachers retained children for a second year of kindergarten much more frequently than did teachers who held non-nativist positions. Retention rates varied from a low of 1 per cent to a high of 25 per cent. In other words, a child's chance of spending two years in kindergarten depend, to a significant degree, on a teacher's implicit theory of child development. Implicit theories can make a difference. Implicit beliefs have consequences.

Returning to the first principle of design, what I am advocating here is that we resolve to wake up, to take our own beliefs and implicit theories seriously and to make them more explicit and visible, at least to ourselves. Beliefs and theories that remain unconscious and implicit will not grow or become elaborated, or evolve in response to critical analysis. For our beliefs and theories to develop, we must get them out on the table where we can see them. I therefore recommend that you write down what you know and believe about teaching once a year. Do it in the spring, or on a summer holiday, or on your birthday. You'll be surprised at some of what you write, and gratified by the ways in which your story changes over the years. And seeing your own statement of belief, your own credo of teaching, will alert you to topics and questions helpful in designing your own course of professional development.

Start with Your Strengths

One reason that traditional professional development has negative overtones is that most of the time it is designed to focus on and compound our weaknesses. It is grounded in a disease model. Professional developers promise a quick fix for our deficits, if only we will co-operate in our humiliation and redemption. The problem with this, of course, is that professionals are not interested in being humiliated as a prerequisite to learning and development. That approach simply doesn't work.

Even seasoned and gifted teachers can fall into deficit model-thinking. Recently I was privileged to attend an English department faculty meeting at an outstanding high school in California. The agenda was to plan professional development activities for members of the department. They had a generous budget; they were free to bring in outside experts in their field; and there were no administrators present. It appeared that all the conditions were in place for a wonderful, positive exercise in self-directed professional development. But the meeting got into a downward spiral from the start. All the suggestions for consultants and activities were tied to perceived weaknesses in their programme. Enthusiasm tailed off. If this was what professional development was going to mean this year, no one wanted a part in it.

After listening to this for thirty minutes, I made the suggestion that the faculty should list the things that they did particularly well and were proud of in their English programme, and proud of about their students. Then we reframed the planning problem as 'How can we build on, show off, and celebrate the many things we already do well?' I am happy to report that this changed the whole tone of the meeting for the better. Now everyone had ideas for inviting experts, organizing conferences, and for involving their students, colleagues from other departments, and the faculty from a nearby university in their professional development plan. There was a real charge in the air when the bell rang — no one wanted the meeting to end. Here was a group of teachers excited about shaping their own professional development.

So what might we conclude from this experience? Professional teachers need to abandon the idea that they have a responsibility to become excellent at everything. Instead, make an inventory of the ways of teaching that you do well and that are close to your heart. Then choose professional development activities that help you celebrate, improve and show off the things that you love to do. Give yourself permission to lead with your strengths.

Make a Five-Year Plan

You've heard it said many times: 'If you don't know where you are going, you'll never get there.' I prefer the Arabic version, which goes: 'To the traveller with no destination, one road is as good as another.' The reason that I prefer this second version of wisdom is that it warns me of a trap. A life, a career or a journey full of motion can still be aimless and empty. Meaning and a sense of direction and progress don't come automatically from activity, even apparently competent activity. A professional career made up of doing what we believe other people expect of us can lead to a painful and sometimes tragic mid-career crisis.

To some extent, a mid-career reassessment is part of normal human development. Adults tend to ask different questions of themselves and their work at different ages. Remember your first year or two of teaching? The big questions were: 'Will I make it? Can I survive? Was this a big mistake?' Later, you came to believe that you finally knew something and were doing quite well. For me, this stage lasted about six weeks. Then I turned 40. I began to ask 'Is this all there is? Is this as good as it gets? Have I painted myself into a corner, using paint that takes 25 years to dry?'

Especially at this mid-career time, taking charge of your own plan for professional development can be very useful. When the world itself and the structure of the profession cease to give a sense of growth and progress, you can begin to provide that for yourself. Outline the ways in which you hope to be different four or five years from now, and some of the possible means to those changes. Recognize that some of the most important developmental changes involve doing less (e.g. less yelling, less testing, less worrying), rather than always adding more knowledge, skill or activity.

Of course, this five-year plan should not be allowed to dominate completely our lives and choices. In studying the instructional planning of teachers, I have learned at least two things: that it is important to have a plan, and that it is important to feel free to depart from the plan when reality does not match our predictions. A plan can give us direction, a way to begin, a feeling of control and a basis for evaluating our choices. But a plan is not a script.

Look in Your Own Backyard

One of the facts of life for teachers is that, no matter how enlightened your school district may be about professional development, you will spend between 170 and 190 days of the school year in your own classroom. This is not likely to change in the foreseeable future, except in the direction of a longer school year. Moreover, that is acceptable to most teachers — the classroom is where we belong. The challenge of this fourth principle of design is to figure out ways to make a virtue of the fact that teachers can rarely go elsewhere in search of professional development support. How can we continue to nurture our own professional development in our own backyards?

Anthropologists who study teaching and learning have coined an expression that may be helpful with this challenge. They say that, in order to appreciate the richness and complexity of familiar everyday situations, we must 'make the familiar strange'. This involves at least two steps: first, to believe that interesting, exciting, amazing things are happening all around us all the time; and second, to question the traditional ways, reasons and explanations that we usually take for granted. Try to see this through the eyes of a novice teacher or of a Martian. Experiment by reversing the order in which you do things (e.g. give the final exam at the beginning of a unit, or on Tuesday instead of Friday). Exchange roles and make your students act as teachers while you become the student. Meanwhile, pay attention to what you are learning about yourself, your students, about subject matter, and about the ways that your usual classroom organization works to make some things possible and others difficult. This approach can be a powerful antidote to the feeling of being trapped in a boring and completely predictable job.

One example of discovering the amazing within the apparently ordinary happened to me in October 1987. I was working as a teacher's aide in a second-grade classroom as part of my role as Professor-In-Residence at Whitehills Elementary School. The teacher and the children were making apple sauce that afternoon and also writing about the process. I helped by supervising the apple peeling and cutting, the clearing up, and the tasting. I also wrote a short piece describing that afternoon and attempting to answer the question, 'What can you learn from making apple sauce?'[5] I was surprised and gratified to discover that there is a great deal that can be learned from making apple sauce. The answers came tumbling over one another as soon as the question was put. And this is the point: if we ask real questions about the everyday events of our ordinary lives, we will more often than not be amazed and delighted by what we learn.

Ask for Support

On the one hand, each teacher's path and pattern of development is a solitary journey. I have been advocating here that we accept this, take responsibility for our own development, and make the most of it. On the other hand, there is no rule that requires us to pursue this solitary journey without any outside help. The paradox is that becoming a fully developed, autonomous individual is a process that we cannot make happen alone.

Asking for help is often difficult for us teachers, for most of us have succeeded by being rugged individualists, by keeping our eyes on our own papers, and by choosing to try only those activities in which we are quite confident of immediate success. We want to look good all of the time. Asking for help makes us feel vulnerable — vulnerable to being discovered as imposters who don't know as much as we pretend to know. The words 'I have a problem' become 'I am a problem'.

But the simple truth is that we all need help and support. Most educators love to give help, if only we would ask. A friend of mine who teaches third grade was in real difficulties last autumn. She agreed to the installation of two microcomputer systems in her classroom. But she did not have a clue about how to make use of them, nor did she have any inclination to become a computer expert herself. But there was the hardware, staring back at her and the third graders. And there were parental and administration expectations to deal with. She solved her problem in an elegant way, by asking for help from fourth graders. The teacher realized that some students in the school already had more expertise than most adults in the use of microcomputers. Risky as it felt to turn over a measure of control to the children, she did so. Beyond solving an immediate practical problem for the teacher, this sequence of events opened her eyes to other ways in which seeing 'kids as experts' could change the whole learning environment for the better.

Other forms of help include time, money, equipment, ideas, encouragement, and appreciation. Asking for help does not guarantee that it will be forthcoming. But not asking for help virtually guarantees that you will remain helpless.

Go First Class

As a professional teacher, you deserve respect. And that begins with respecting yourself. If we think and act like second-class citizens, as if we deserve to be treated as doormats, there are plenty of people who will oblige us. And as we begin to treat ourselves with respect, our students, our colleagues, our administrative helpers and the public will do likewise. At the very least, we will begin to teach by example how to treat teachers more respectfully.

Learning to treat oneself with respect can be a life's work. It involves accepting both one's successes and one's failures, one's bright side and one's shadow side. We must believe that we are intrinsically worthwhile and lovable, regardless of whether we have done enough good works to earn love and appreciation. Coming to this position usually takes more than a two-day workshop on building self-esteem.

But there are some relatively direct ways in which we can express our self-respect in support of our own professional development. Read great literature, visit Stratford and see a play, use the most beautiful room available for your conference, buy yourself a beautiful pen, make your professional development into an art. And practise showing sincere respect for others, children and adults alike. For there is a part of the human mind that experiences the way we treat others as directed towards ourselves.

For the past two summers I have been a staff member at a workshop for high-school teachers held at Stanford University. There are many factors that contribute to the success of this ten-day programme. But I want to focus on one: we have met, both summers, in the most handsomely appointed conference room on the campus. The room is located on the top floor of the Aeronautics and Astronautics building, it is very comfortably furnished, and opens on to a big, sunny balcony that overlooks the red tile roofs and palm trees of a beautiful campus. From the first moment of the workshop a message is clear: teachers are important people who ought to be treated in a first-class manner.

Blow Your Own Trumpet

My final suggestion for a principle of design is to blow your own trumpet. Let others know what you are doing on your own behalf and how good you feel about yourself. Learn how to teach about what you are learning. Teach about what excites you. Exaggerate during your annual review. Make a demonstration videotape, or write a paper, or invite a fellow teacher to visit your class, or report once a year at a faculty meeting.

These may sound like difficult things to do for humble, self-effacing teachers like us, and they are. But the real benefits of blowing your own trumpet have nothing to do with taking credit from others or showing off. The real benefits come from confronting and answering difficult questions like: 'What have I been doing lately that is worthwhile and interesting? What ideas and insights have I had that might be useful to others? How do I want to frame and remember the positive side of this year?' Blowing your own trumpet means making coherent and public the ways in which your professional development is developing.

---

1. Write Your Own Credo of Teaching

2. Start with Your Strengths

3. Make a Five-Year Plan

4. Look in Your Own Backyard

5. Ask for Support

6. Go First Class

7. Blow Your Own Trumpet

Figure 5.1. Self-Directed Professional Development Principles of Design.

CONCLUSION

In conclusion, I hope that this line of argument, moving from research on teacher thinking to self-directed professional development, to principles of design, has provoked your thinking. This has been the story of how I am trying to organize and make sense of my own professional development as a teacher. Every reader will have made her own sense of this story. If my words have confirmed what you already know and are doing, have puzzled you, enraged you, and have started the germ of an idea, then I have succeeded, and so have you. May you all continue to develop as professionals, each in your own way.

NOTES AND REFERENCES

1. Wittrock, M. (ed.), *Handbook of Research on Teaching* (3rd edn). New York: Macmillan, 1986.

2. Clark, C. M. and Peterson, P. L., 'Teachers' thought processes'. In Wittrock, note 1, pp. 255–96, 1986.

3. Ibid., pp. 292–3.

4. Smith, M. L. and Shepard, L. A., 'Kindergarten readiness and retention: a qualitative study of teachers' beliefs and practices', *American Educational Research Journal*, 25, pp. 307–33, 1988.

5. Clark, C. M. 'What you can learn from apple sauce: a case of qualitative inquiry in use'. Paper presented at the Conference on Qualitative Inquiry in Education, Stanford University, Stanford, CA, 26 June 1988.

Chapter 6

Classroom-based Teacher Development

Dennis Thiessen

INTRODUCTION

Recent approaches to teacher development have centred more in schools and involved teachers more directly in decisions which shape these approaches. These changes are introduced cautiously, however. Genuine efforts to transfer the balance of power to teachers and their colleagues and students or to embed teacher development in the classroom are infrequent. Classroom-based teacher development (CBTD) is an orientation which situates the professional growth of teachers within the daily realities of classroom life.

This chapter elaborates the conditions of CBTD — focus, power, environment, reference points and action — and reviews possible approaches to CBTD. Teachers can work in three modes — alone, with other teachers and with their students — to adapt, study and transform classroom practices. Their development is intrinsically connected with the classroom experiences they share with students.

Despite some significant improvements in teacher development, many teachers continue to endure limited and often problematic efforts to enhance their development. Frequently, programmes operate with simplistic notions of how teachers learn professionally. Seldom are teachers involved in decisions about the content and structure of the workshops they have to attend. They are expected to change their practices after only brief demonstrations of what is required, with few opportunities to compare their ideas with other teachers, and little substantial follow-up. Scant consideration is given to how teachers' work circumstances help or hinder the complex process of altering what they do. Yet, as if part of a benevolent 'factory recall', teachers are none the less expected to seize the chance to remedy their defects. Understandably some choose to ignore, co-opt, or even subvert the attempts to develop them.[1]

Ultimately, I want to argue, teachers should develop themselves. It should be less a matter of determining what to do 'to' them or 'on their behalf', and more a matter of teachers inventing what to do 'with' others or 'by themselves'. To some extent, recent school-focused strategies such as peer coaching, action research and teacher centres have encouraged independent and collaborative teacher development experiences of this sort. However, these strategies have often not been sustained and have occasionally drifted back into the old problems of being developed according to the agendas, structures and strategies of others. In response to the often imperceptible erosion of teachers' influence on their own development, I propose classroom-based teacher development (CBTD) as an alternative approach. CBTD is an orientation which both reconceptualizes how teachers improve their professional effectiveness in the work place and builds on the relationships that matter most to teachers in their development: their relationships with their students.

CBTD is guided by a framework of five conditions which focus on learning, shared power, experiences in the classroom, an interrelated set of personal, educational, and social reference points and constructive and critical actions. There is no simple form of CBTD. Within CBTD, teachers can work alone, with other teachers, or with students. Its mode, in this sense, can vary. In each case, however, teachers commonly emphasize adapting, studying or changing their classroom practices. In this chapter, I want to outline the conditions of CBTD, describe some of the modes it can take and suggest approaches which make it possible for teacher development to involve enriching, studying or changing classroom practices.

CONDITIONS OF CBTD

Viewing the classroom as not only a place of work but also a source of professional development requires a considerable shift in perspective for some teachers. In CBTD, doing one's job should involve simultaneously developing one's practices. Teachers should work alongside their students as co-learners. They should engage their students as partners in action creating both experiences and classroom norms which are mutually beneficial for their personal, educational, and social growth. The following five conditions provide a lens for teachers to guide their efforts in such classroom-based teacher development. Each section briefly outlines the present practices associated with the condition and then argues how CBTD should re-orientate the meaning, importance, and experience of this condition.

Focus: CBTD Centres on Improving the Quality of Learning for Students *and* Teachers

Student learning is the 'bottom line' for many teacher development programmes. Training teachers in new practices is only considered important if the implementation of these practices results in significant gains in student achievement. Some approaches in clinical supervision[2] and some models of staff development[3] endorse this instrumental responsibility of teachers. According to this view, the classroom is not a source of learning for teachers but a context for the application and modification of practices developed, supported and learned elsewhere. Development here occurs prior to actual classroom use or in later reflections about its effectiveness for student learning.

In CBTD, however, improving the quality of learning should involve every classroom participant. Teachers and students alike are learners whose mutual development depends on the intersection of their experiences. For example, when primary teachers try to introduce activity-based learning, they should not only concentrate on manipulative materials and inductive tasks but also examine and evaluate the changes expected of students. As they adapt their approaches in response to comments from and observations of their students, teachers should consider how their efforts to improve their practices interact with students' efforts to learn from these activity-based opportunities. Improvement of classroom learning can only happen by attending directly to the interdependent development of teachers and students. Concentrating on only one of the learners diminishes the possibilities for both. A focus on student learning ignores its intimate relationship to teaching. A focus on teacher learning, especially through training prior to and removed from the classroom, ignores the people and the context in which the new practices are to be developed. CBTD should therefore approach the improvement of classroom learning by focusing on teachers and students together.

Power: CBTD Supports Those Who Have the Most Influence on and Stake in What Happens

In more interventionist, 'outside-in'[4] notions of teacher development, there are numerous stakeholders who attempt to influence, if not control, classroom practice. Other teachers in designated roles such as mentors, advisers, evaluators, or coaches lend their expertise to support the improvement of their colleagues.[5] Principals influence the development of their staff members through disseminating resources, discussing classroom and school concerns, encouraging risk-taking and experimentation, and publicly recognizing important changes in individual and organizational practices.[6] Outside consultants work within the school to organize, negotiate and co-ordinate projects involving change.[7] Parents also have a say in evaluating innovations which affect the classroom experiences of their children.[8] Finally, policy-makers assess changing directions in classroom practices as part of their accountability to various constituent groups within society. These stakeholders have a right and an obligation to help shape classroom realities.

Although they are important, the standpoint of CBTD dictates that these stakeholders and their concerns should not displace the primary protagonists on the classroom stage: teachers and students. Teachers and students have the most direct influence on and the most at stake in what happens in the classroom. Consequently, they should retain control of decisions to improve learning but negotiate with other stakeholders for structural and political support in their development. In most circumstances, teachers should represent the classroom position to these stakeholders.

Within the classroom, CBTD should also redefine the power relationships between teachers and students. Students can influence the professional socialization of new teachers,[9] shape the course of curriculum practices[10] and classroom improvement,[11] and take charge of community-orientated projects.[12] Decisions which directly affect what happens in the classroom should be shared between teachers and students. The political presence of students as acknowledged junior partners is essential to the direction, magnitude and authenticity of how CBTD should occur. The strength of this joint relationship between teachers and students should give them controlling shares in decisions about classroom development.

Environment: CBTD Occurs in the Complex and Changing Situation of Classroom Life

During the last decade, teacher development approaches have incorporated a range of classroom-focused activities. Some workshops and training modules concentrate on demonstrations which simulate factors relevant to classroom use.[13] Frequently, inservice courses require teachers to test innovative practices with their own students. Support groups compare classroom trials of new teaching methods and discuss ways to overcome obstacles to effective implementation.[14] Coaching strategies insist on peer feedback and ongoing dialogue about observed applications of particular techniques and models.[15] In these approaches, teacher development anticipates the results of classroom changes and takes new methods into the classroom to stimulate what Joyce and Showers call the transfer of training to the classroom setting.[16] In these approaches to teacher development and educational change, the classroom is the endpoint in mind for developers and also the final point of application.

In contrast, CBTD should view the classroom as the *culture* in which teachers and students form, make sense of and adapt their development experiences. The classroom is where teachers and students learn. It is where they have the most influence and where most is at stake. It is where they set up the physical, procedural and interactive conditions which frame their practices. It is where they deliberate, where they negotiate meaning, and where they evaluate possibilities. It is where they define their unique working relationships and, over time, create and re-create their own cultural world. The classroom is both the means and the end to teacher and student development.

As an example of the cultural importance of the classroom to teacher development, consider the introduction of enquiry teaching into a secondary school history programme. It may disrupt the norms of interaction and control in the existing traditional classroom. Here, cultural dissonance may arise, prompting teachers and students either to assimilate enquiry within their present patterns of teaching and learning, or to struggle through the dilemmas of altering existing traditions to embrace the change.[17] The classroom, then, is more than a dependent variable patiently waiting to obstruct or welcome the passage of independent variables, such as enquiry, into its midst. Its unique routines and demands give meaning to and establish the possibilities for new instructional techniques. Developments in instruction cannot usefully be made without development in the context and culture of the classroom. The classroom in CBTD should therefore constitute the primary setting for changes in practice.

Reference Points: CBTD Combines Personally Meaningful, Educationally Defensible and Socially Justifiable Practices

'Does it work?' is the key question in most teacher development initiatives. When asked by teachers, it is a question of compatibility (Is it similar to what we do now?), procedure (How is it done?), efficacy (Will we be able to learn how to do it with the same level of effectiveness as we currently experience?), support (Will there be time, money, people, and resources available to assist our development?) and impact (Will the students benefit from this change?). These concerns attend to the practical, instrumental implications of innovations.[18] The key reference point for numerous teacher development approaches, then, is one of pragmatic feasibility.

In CBTD, what works in the practical, instrumental sense is not dealt with on its own, but is incorporated into the broader question of what teacher development experiences are of most value.[19] This question of value is addressed through three reference points: personal meaningfulness, educational defensibility and social justifiability. CBTD relies on these reference points to elaborate how teacher development efforts, both educationally and morally, connect the world of the classroom with society.

The first reference point of *meaningfulness* acknowledges the personal nature of development. Teachers and students must discover why certain changes are personally worth the time and psychological energy to pursue. Are the changes important to each person in the classroom? Are they likely to enrich the ways in which teachers and students work together? Practical feasibility without personal engagement is insufficient. Teachers and students should believe that their participation in a teacher development experience is not only instrumentally possible but will also make a difference that matters to their personal and interpersonal development in the classroom.

The second reference point is *educational defensibility*. This recognizes the challenge of conceptual and empirical rigour in teacher development and school improvement. Existing propositional, practical and experiential knowledge in these areas provides a source for comparison with personal preferences in the classroom. Previewing alternatives involves neither a hunt for a theory to rationalize what is already occurring nor a search for *the* answer to the teacher development question. Comparisons, rather, permit teachers and — where possible — students, to locate, criticize and either enhance or reframe their development experiences in relation to the options available in the literature. Judgements about classroom practice and CBTD should be based on personal meaningfulness, but they should also be open to the influence of educators whose work has relevance to the teachers and students involved in CBTD.

The final reference point is *social justifiability*. This relates personal and educational responsibility to the values of the community and society. How does any proposed development or change within the classroom become part of a long-term agenda for improving the world outside it? Teachers and students can address this question in terms of relevance, discussing how the proposed development or change is important to their present and future experiences in life. They can then examine the congruence between the cultural norms of their classroom and school, the norms within their community, and those implied in any proposed development experiences. Teachers and students in CBTD should remain conscious of these micro–macro connections and avoid the possible myopia of attending only to concerns in the immediate operation of the classroom, as if they were somehow self-contained.

No one reference point should govern decisions about CBTD. A good illustration can be seen in efforts to develop greater classroom democracy. Here, while teachers and students may want to have a more democratic classroom with students having more choice within the curriculum and more influence in discussions, previous case studies have revealed how difficult such a change can be.[20] Yet some of the difficulties can be overcome if teachers and students explicitly address the structural and political constraints on the sharing of power. If such constraints are not ignored or idealistically overlooked and if they are acknowledged as a serious reference point for development, it may be possible to surmount the immediate obstacles. For instance, teachers and students may choose to persist with their democratic project so as to test the limits of equity in the school and beyond, working towards a more active yet politically realistic role for students in their daily lives.

These personal, educational and social reference points, and the inter-relationships between them, are important catalysts for teacher development.

Action: CBTD Engages in Reflective, Interactive and Transformative Experiences

Current approaches to teacher development tend to be sequential and programmed in their formats, intense in their delivery, responsive to immediate concerns for support, and concentrated on specific and incremental adjustments.[21] Networks exist with colleagues, resource people and administrators for troubleshooting, assistance and co-ordination. In these approaches the actions of teacher development constitute small, instrumental and systematic steps forward. Over time, it is hoped, these steps escalate into a significant change.

The previous four conditions of CBTD suggest a very different model for teacher development. In CBTD, teachers and students should reflect *on* and *in* the actions of their classrooms,[22] focusing on the improvement of themselves as learners and evaluating the personal, educational, and social implications of their changing practices. According to this view, change initiatives attend to teachers' and students' respective rights to control their individual and mutual development. Teachers and students involved in CBTD learn primarily within the interactions of the classroom, using their evolving relationships to promote reflection, to understand their circumstances, and to alter their patterns of work. The actions of teacher development become intertwined with the actions of the classroom itself. Changes in classroom practices, then, also entail adaptations in teacher–student interactions and in classroom culture. In CBTD, seemingly minor modifications, such as the introduction of a new textbook, can result in an open and shared enquiry in which teachers and students critically examine the place of this and other resources in their learning. Innovation in whatever form and magnitude, therefore, has a ripple effect, creating successive waves of change in the ways that teachers and students work together in the classroom. CBTD should foster this dynamic process of informed debate, experimentation and transformation.

Summary

In this section, I have contrasted CBTD with traditional approaches to teacher development. This contrast has exposed the limiting and largely unsubstantiated assumptions about teachers that are implicit in many of those more traditional approaches. Among the most prominent of these assumptions are that teachers are:

- not learners in their own classrooms;
- incapable of determining what and how they should develop;
- in need of special training only available through organized sessions outside the workplace;
- responsive to changes which are broken down into easily applied steps, and work efficiently and immediately;
- best served with instruction that requires initiation into something new, uncomplicated procedures, and immediate reinforcement and reward.

By contrast, the conditions of CBTD recognize that teachers are co-learners in their own classrooms. In CBTD, teachers root their development in the classroom. They pursue changes which are practical but which also have personal, educational and social priority. And they participate in reflective and collaborative experiences which ultimately empower and transform how teachers and students interact. The five conditions of CBTD that I have outlined provide a framework to guide how CBTD should operate in practice. I shall now review, adapt and enrich these examples to demonstrate the forms that teacher development now take when it is grounded in the conditions of CBTD as I have described them.

MODES OF CBTD

Three modes of CBTD are possible: teachers on their own, teachers with teachers, and teachers and students. For each mode, I outline approaches which emphasize building from, studying or changing existing classroom practices. Numerous references already exist which describe how teachers work alone or with others in teacher development[23] and I briefly review some of these through the lens of CBTD. There are comparatively fewer examples of teacher–student approaches however. Yet directly engaging teachers and students together in teacher development realizes the conditions of CBTD most thoroughly and extensively. I therefore devote greater space to these. Ultimately, though, all three modes of CBTD are necessary and mutually supportive.

Teachers on Their Own

Probably the most enduring mode of teacher development occurs on the job as teachers diligently work alone in their classrooms searching for, trying out and modifying strategies that best respond to the needs of their students. In early career, teacher development centres on the basic goal of survival in a lonely and often professionally isolated occupation. Teachers learn their trade in the 'school of hard knocks' through repeated trial-and-error cycles. Classroom experimentation with new practices by experienced teachers is a self-directed programme that teachers initiate to improve their learning environment.

Self-improvement projects should be more than instructional adjustments, however. When CBTD is undertaken by teachers without direct influence from colleagues or students, they should also learn about themselves and the implications of their practices for their classrooms.[24] Self-understanding is not, or need not be, egocentric or narcissistic. It can also inform teachers about the experiences of their students. As Connelly and Clandinin state,

> if you understand what makes up the curriculum of the person
> most important to you, namely, yourself, you will better
> understand the difficulties, whys, and wherefores of the
> curriculum of your students. There is no better way to study
> curriculum than to study ourselves.[25]

Working alone in CBTD should directly engage all five of the conditions described earlier, but the extent to which the environment, power, and action conditions are implemented varies. Approaches where teachers write their own journals do not directly address how students and teachers share control (power), are not situated in the classroom (environment) and are not interactive or normally transformative (action). Yet these conditions can be incorported indirectly into journal writing if teachers frame their written reflection in terms of decisions, relationships and norms in their own classrooms. For example, teachers may write about incidents which describe their struggle to work effectively with reluctant or disruptive students. In these journal entries, teachers may think about tests of control (power) in the classroom (environment) and possible solutions (action) to the problem. Figure 6.1 introduces classroom based-teacher development approaches which teachers can carry out alone.

I. Constructing Classroom Routines

1. *Organizing Curriculum 'Artefacts'*: Each teacher determines her lesson plans, units of study, resources, desk arrangements, and displayed materials. She co-ordinates and analyses the use of these 'artefacts' in ways which support her curriculum priorities.[26]

2. *Managing the Environment*: Each teacher compares what she does and anticipates doing to maintain the efficiency and order of classroom activities. In particular, she focuses on how the implicit and explicit rules regulate her actions and those of her students.[27]

II. Documenting One's Actions

3. *Maintaining Journals*: Each teacher describes and comments on the significant people, situations, forces, or events that permeate past and present classroom experiences. The translation of experience into written or audio-taped journal entries generates insights about everyday occurrences.[28]

4. *Engaging in Self-Evaluation*: Each teacher becomes a self-monitor, systematically describing a teaching episode, analysing it from different points of view, evaluating the underlying assumptions and values, and acting on any perceived contradictions, problems or dilemmas. It is a cyclic process of constructive and critical review.[29]

III. Adapting Teaching and Learning Strategies

5. *Self-Directed Development*: Each teacher initiates changes in how teaching and learning occur in the classroom. She considers and experiments with different strategies, examines the intended and unintended consequences of available alternatives, and adopts those which improve the quality of teacher and student interaction.[30]

Figure 6.1. Independent teacher development experiences.

I. Constructing classroom routines These involve teachers developing a more critical awareness of everyday classroom operations. In CBTD teachers do not only clarify the consistencies and inconsistencies of their taken-for-granted classroom norms, the roles they insist on, or the way they do

things. They also act to remove obstacles to or gaps in their preferred curriculum. Teacher development is part of this constant attention to the
mundane.

II. Documenting one's actions Here, teachers are educational critics of their
own practices. They transform their spontaneous sense of instrumental
effectiveness or practicality into a thoughtful and rigorous review of some
fundamental theme in classroom learning. Various forms of recording, journal
keeping and self-evaluation provide teachers with ways to track, judge and
reconsider their experiences. In this approach, teachers develop from the
informed interrogation of themselves.

III. Adapting Teaching and Learning Strategies In these adjustments,
teachers alter their pedagogical actions in the classroom. They are independent,
one-teacher versions of action research. With these approaches, teachers use
their initiatives as change agents to facilitate their own development.

Teachers with Teachers

Teachers learn much from each other. They cite fellow teachers as the most
valuable source of professional development.[31] In recent years, teacher development approaches which build on collegial and collaborative work among teachers
have become prominent in the discourse on school improvement and educational change.[32] Peer coaching,[33] advising teachers,[34] co-operative professional
development[35] and mentoring[36] are all examples of this mode of teacher
development.

Not all teacher-to-teacher development approaches meet the conditions of
CBTD, however. For example, some coaching approaches are part of a more comprehensive training model[37] which use teaching models or results from previous
studies to direct what teachers should learn and how they should work together.
Cadres of expert and peer coaches often guide and support the process. Coaching
systems become vehicles for transfer training, driving paired teachers to the efficient, effective and congruent uses of desired teaching models. These coaching
approaches generally focus on learning and, at times, occur in the classroom; but,
as Robertson indicates in this volume, they do not address the CBTD conditions
of power, action and reference points.[38] Though they are interactive, the limited
enquiry of much peer coaching is neither reflective nor transformative.

In this mode, CBTD should actively engage all five conditions, but the
environment and power conditions are not always emphasized directly. Without
direct involvement of students, the power condition becomes a reflective component, with teachers talking among themselves about the extent to which they
share control with their students. Similarly, when teachers work together in
planning or support groups, they discuss the implications of changes for their
classrooms but do not necessarily extend their joint efforts to classroom applications. Figure 6.2 outlines six teacher-to-teacher development approaches.

I. Building Joint Endeavours In CBTD partnerships, teachers extend how they presently work together in schools. This entails more than redistributing labour or capitalizing on the knowledge of others. Rather, teachers consciously attend to the relationship between their planning and their teaching. They deliberate about preferred practices. They search for possibilities and alternatives. And in all this, they learn from their ongoing interactions.

I. Building Joint Endeavours

1. *Exchanging Expertise*: Two teachers combine their classes in a unit of study. One teacher is the 'expert' organizing the unit activities while the other teacher is the 'assistant' learning from the 'expert' how the unit should be implemented. In a subsequent unit, the team teaching roles are reversed.[39]

2. *Planning Co-operatively*: Two or more teachers work together to plan for classroom instruction. They pool strategies and resources, compare ideas, determine the structure and emphasis in topics and approaches, and evaluate the success, merit and worth of their products.[40]

II. Probing for Meaning

3. *Comparing Vignettes*: Teachers create stories, describe situations, or develop memos and cases of important classroom experiences. Through conversation or written communication, they react to each others' accounts.[41]

4. *Learning through Participation*: Teachers become 'insiders' in each others' classrooms. They are active observers participating as team teachers, support people or students to discover the unique and complex realities of what happens.[42]

III. Promoting Collaborative Development

5. *Elaborating Practical Theories*: Teachers counsel each other in ways which make explicit the basis of decisions and actions in the classroom. They examine the relationship (and tension) between their espoused theories and their theories-in-use to define and direct their separate and shared improvement.[43]

6. *Enhancing Professional Dialogue*: Teachers form partnerships to generate critical insights into and improvements of classroom practices. The 'supervised' teacher determines the focus of observation but negotiates with the partner how the observations are gathered, interpreted and used.[44]

Figure 6.2. Teacher-to-teacher development experiences.

II. Probing for Meaning   In this set of approaches, teachers apply strategies which require them to research into each other's practices. Such 'research' or enquiry emphasizes portrayals, interactions and interpretations more than measurements, detached observations or statistical analyses. These CBTD approaches range from reflective reviews about classroom experiences to participant observations in the classroom. In them, teachers get beneath the surface meanings of classroom events to make sense of their efforts to facilitate and share responsibility for learning. In each case, teachers develop from the informed insight of and exchange with colleagues.

III. Promoting Collaborative Development   Here, teachers co-operate to change their classroom practices. Approaches such as peer coaching or clinical supervision become genuinely reciprocal in CBTD. Teachers generate and sustain the energy for change within their evolving relationship. They learn from monitoring each other's implementation of an innovation and reviewing the changing patterns of their partnership.

Teachers and Students

Of the three modes of CBTD, approaches which involve teachers and students are the least discussed and practised, yet the ones that have the greatest potential. This is the only mode that readily engages all five conditions. In particular, it is the only mode that directly applies the power condition, requiring teachers and students to act as partners in teacher development. In CBTD, the nature of the partnership in any teacher–student development experience should incorporate the following three principles:

1. Teachers *and* students are active participants in all aspects of classroom life.

2. The different positions of teachers and students in the classroom limit the extent to which they work as equal partners.

3. The symmetrical dimensions of teacher–student relationships sustain and extend the partnership.

Teachers and students are the main characters on the classroom stage. Traditionally, students are less involved in 'behind-the-scene' actions that frame what happens in the classroom. In CBTD, however, students participate with teachers in the determination, planning, adaptation, and evaluation of teacher development initiatives.

In terms of qualifications and formal responsibilities, the position of teachers is quite different from that of students. Teachers are older, have more formal education, know more about the content and process of teaching, and probably rely on a broader and more diversified range of experiences. Teachers have more status, with more official responsibility for the curriculum as intended and practised. In most cases, they are expected to stimulate student learning, create an efficient and effective learning environment, and establish and manage the

I. Sharing Teaching and Learning

1. *Negotiating the Curriculum*: Teachers involve their students in decisions about the purposes, organization, content, approaches and evaluation of learning.[45]

2. *Forming Teaching Teams*: Students not only become cross-age or peer tutors for other students but also join with teachers to develop and extend their collective understanding of approaches to teaching.[46]

3. *Problem-Posing*: Students in concert with teachers investigate, discuss and act on issues relevant to their lives in the school and the community. Teachers and students combine reflection and action to take charge of their own learning.[47]

II. Examining Classroom Phenomena

4. *Creating Investigative Clubs*: Students work as a research unit which initially advises teachers about the focus and direction of a classroom research project. As the study evolves, students and teachers together collect, interpret and triangulate data.[48]

5. *Inquiring into Student Learning*: Teachers combine enquiry and teaching in ways that probe the nature of learning in the classroom. In-depth accounts emerge from intensive and varied interactions with students.[49]

6. *Evaluating Teaching*: Teachers engage students in a critique of teaching, exploring what constitutes effective teaching and how various teaching strategies influence what happens in the classroom.[50]

III. Improving What Happens

7. *Transforming Teacher–Student Interaction*: With the aid of videotapes, students and teachers analyse their mutual efforts to implement innovative practices. In particular, they focus on ways to change the form, substance and orientation of their working relationship.[51]

8. *Altering the Curriculum in Use*: Teachers, consultants, and students form action research groups to enhance their capacity to bring about meaningful changes. A critical comparison of the curriculum intended by teachers and the curriculum construed by students reveals what and how classroom and school realities should change.[52]

9. *Culture-Making*: In innovations, students and teachers develop alternative strategies to establish new norms and conditions in the culture of the classroom. They come to a mutual understanding of what matters in their new 'world'.[53]

Figure 6.3. Teacher-student development experiences.

direction, appropriateness and standards of what students do. They are neither colleagues nor peers with students. The roles of teachers and students in these areas are not reciprocal. When teacher development approaches need the expertise of qualification or the voice of authority, teachers dominate the relationship with students.

Yet there are areas of symmetry in teacher–student relationships that should not be overlooked. Teachers and students live in the classroom and in relation to each other with similar *definition*, *agency* and *rights*. Both are learners, developing from their common situation and evolving relationships. Within the context of the classroom, teachers and students mutually *define* what and how CBTD happens.

In terms of *agency*, teachers and students construct their own meaning and actions in the classroom. Each teacher or student is the expert on his or her own past, present or future experiences. Previous classroom situations, reactions to present circumstances and anticipations of future realities influence how each teacher or student views and shapes his or her opportunities as a learner. Teachers and students have to respect, understand and work with each other's agency in any CBTD activity.

Another area of symmetry is the human *rights* which underpin teacher–student relationships. Both teachers and students have rights to fair treatment and participation. Such rights compel one party to inform, consult, and deliberate with the other party about judgements and actions which affect the relationship. The rights shared by teachers and students in the classroom are the foundation upon which CBTD builds.

The symmetrical dimensions of definition, agency and rights give a form of equality to teacher–student relationships. Students have the same expectation and obligation as teachers to influence classroom experiences. Though the symmetry cannot alter the inequalities of qualification and experience, it can modify the ways in which teachers use their formal responsibilities. Some inequalities persist: students remain as significant but junior partners. Nevertheless, when the symmetry of the partnership dominates, the active engagement of both partners becomes the dynamic force in CBTD.

Figure 6.3 lists nine examples of teacher–student development approaches organized into three groups: sharing teaching and learning, examining classroom phenomena and improving what happens. For the three approaches in each group, I elaborate one approach and discuss the adaptations of the other two within the CBTD framework.

I. Sharing Teaching and Learning Experiences in this approach are constructed to enhance the ways in which teachers and students already work together. This might include, but will also go beyond, matters of determining student interests and encouraging active learning. Students are also part of those decisions which determine classroom structures and activities.[54] Both teachers and students 'seek to question each other's ideas, to reinterpret them, to adapt them and even to reject them, but not to discount them'.[55] In CBTD, as I have defined it, the distinction between teachers and students blurs and melds into a partnership. Teacher development in this view should involve joint efforts which extend the scope and mutuality of teacher–student interactions.

In Australia, Boomer established a network of teachers committed to negotiating the curriculum with students.[56] Students in elementary and secondary schools were empowered to construct, in collaboration with their teacher, the unfolding conditions and priorities of their own learning. The students and the teacher discussed proposed units of study, examining their feasibility, appropriateness, relevance and surrounding constraints. Co-operatively, the intentions of, approaches to and structures for the unit were planned. The negotiated frameworks of such units are open to constant scrutiny and revision as students and their teachers live through the practical implications of their negotiations. The curriculum here remains problematic, with students and their teachers in a process of 'constructive struggling'[57] to build meaningful and valued curriculum experiences. The work of Boomer illuminates the increase in experimentation, deliberation and institutional literacy that develops as students participate within the classroom decision-making process. The power of students is acknowledged and integrated into the organization and improvement of classroom learning. Some of the teachers in Boomer's network reduced student involvement to input on decisions about content or methods. In CBTD, however, students should negotiate as many decisions as possible with their teachers.

Two other forms of sharing teaching and learning — forming teaching teams and problem-posing — involve modified versions of cross-age or peer tutoring[58] along with the dialogical pedagogy of Freire[59] to emphasize the partnership of teachers and students. Cross-age or peer tutoring becomes CBTD when teachers teach all students about teaching and then work with them in small groups as rotating teaching teams for the rest of the class. Problem-posing requires a critical examination of 'generative themes', personally and socially relevant issues which have the potential to enhance learning. In this endeavour, repeated cycles of reflection and action enable teachers and students to develop within and beyond their initial partnership.

II. Examining Classroom Phenomena Here, CBTD occurs through joint efforts by teachers and students to conceptualize, implement and interpret the study and evaluation of classroom practices. Such investigations lead to more than mere appreciation of the insights of students[60] or improvements in teachers' abilities to enquire into the world of their students.[61] In CBTD, rather, students should be not simply research subjects but research associates, perhaps even co-investigators and co-evaluators. Teacher development results from the discoveries made during collaborative classroom research.

Pollard[62] enlisted a group of 11- or 12-year-old students to help him study the social world of the elementary school. The group, formally known as the Moorside Investigations Department, interviewed each other and peers in their school, advised Pollard about the content and tactics in his study, and reviewed his interpretations of their world. If Pollard was to understand the culture of students from their vantage point, he needed their help. He commented:

> They helped me to decide who was likely to be available for interview next, operated recorders, initiated discussions, labelled and catalogued the cassettes and helped me considerably by discussing my analysis as it unfolded. I offered them the role of 'experts' — which in many senses they were. What was familiar to them was relatively strange to me. I played the role of the naïve adult so that whilst I was there to 'learn', they, perhaps a little flattered and entertained by my interest, agreed to 'teach'.[63]

Creating investigative clubs legitimizes the knowledge which students possess about their classroom experiences. For CBTD, teachers should recognize that understanding the experiences of students is a metaphor for understanding and consequently developing the experiences of teachers.

Enquiring into student learning involves an ongoing case study of how the interaction of teachers with each of their students facilitates learning.[64] In a third approach — evaluating teaching — students are included in an interactive review of what teachers do.[65] In this CBTD experience, students should formatively evaluate teaching acts to improve classroom learning.

III. Improving What Happens This approach commits teachers and students to justified changes in their classroom world. Students are not just beneficiaries of change or objects of training.[66] They are not only strategic agents in innovations planned by others.[67] They are also the authors of change, partners with teachers in the improvement of classroom life. Teacher development in this approach should occur within deliberate and sustained attempts to change the interdependent curriculum experience of teachers and students.

A variation of this approach involves transforming the very nature of the interaction between teachers and their students. In this respect, Hull[68] has conducted interesting work with students as teacher educators. In his work with secondary school teachers in England, Hull made videotapes of lessons. From the tapes, Hull's teachers selected those sections which they felt would promote reflection and discussion with students. During the next meeting of the class, the students observed and reviewed what the tape revealed. Initial tendencies to react to the novelty of viewing their peers and themselves, combined with hesitancy about commenting on the practices of their teacher, gave way to a form of 'constructive critical discourse' between students and teacher. Through extended dialogue and evaluation, students and teachers worked as 'fellow conspirators or collaborative colleagues' to define and improve their interaction. Hull concluded:

> Teacher educators should take urgent steps to promote the view of teacher education as an ongoing enterprise in which teachers

and pupils work together through the principles of research to refine classroom practice. Teacher education is not separate from the education of pupils, any more than understanding the processes of education is separate from 'getting educated'.[69]

In CBTD, students should increase their participation in this teacher — student partnership by being involved in recording, editing and production decisions about video- or audio-tapes of practice.

Another approach — altering the curriculum in use — continuously compares teachers' and students' images of their present and anticipated learning opportunities.[70] Enquiry, in this form of CBTD, should uncover the differences between teacher and student perspectives and use these discrepancies to assess and stimulate curriculum change. Culture-making should approach innovations as occasions for teachers and students to reconsider and, where necessary, reconstruct life in the classroom. The imaginative energy of teacher–student partnerships should guide this community-building enterprise.[71]

CONCLUSION

The improvement of teacher development is not fundamentally about increased input from teachers, consistent time for consultation and follow-up, greater availability for human and financial resources, more sophisticated training strategies, or adaptive organizational structures. These changes are only important if they are part of a reconceptualization of teacher development, which begins with teachers as the primary agents of their own development and builds from the relationships they form with students in the classroom. CBTD works within a set of conditions that makes this reconceptualization possible.

Ultimately, the bottom-line justification for CBTD is that it should generate informed and justified improvements in classroom practices. CBTD focuses on student and teacher learning; gives control to teachers in concert with key stakeholders (especially colleagues and students); is situated within the cultural realities of the classroom; consciously combines personal, educational and social reference points, and pursues significant changes in classroom practices through considered and collaborative actions. In CBTD teachers can work alone or in concert with their colleagues and students. Development is stimulated by more deliberate considerations of daily experiences, intensive examinations of fundamental classroom processes, or committed efforts to changing how the classroom works.

Figure 6.4 portrays how the major modes and emphases of CBTD interact. The categories of Figures 6.1, 6.2, and 6.3 are distributed within the cells. The dotted lines indicate that the categories can overlap. For example, attending to ongoing experiences may reveal either areas for further study or directions and strategies for change. Or an action research project introduced by an individual teacher may expand to include other teachers and students.

EMPHASIS

MODE		Attending to ongoing experiences	Studying areas of importance	Implementing new practices
	Teacher-Student	Sharing teaching and learning	Examining classroom phenomena	Improving what happens
	Teacher-Teacher	Building joint endeavours	Probing for meaning	Promoting collaborative development
	Teacher Alone	Constructing classroom routines	Documenting one's actions	Adapting teaching and learning strategies

Figure 6.4. Interaction of modes and emphases.

The figure itself is offered as an organizer for teachers in planning, implementing and evaluating their CBTD activities. Each cell presents a conceptual strategy for the creation of activities based on who is to be involved in CBTD (the mode) and what kinds of activity are going to be involved (the emphasis). Taken together, the nine cells act as an *aide-mémoire* to the range of CBTD possibilities.

The use of the figure as an organizer for CBTD, however, is only valuable if the chosen activities meet the five conditions that make this orientation to teacher development distinct. Careful consideration and inclusion of each condition is necessary for CBTD, as I have defined it.

In most emphases and modes, CBTD directly:

1. Centres on improving the quality of learning for students and teachers (focus);

2. Combines personally meaningful, educationally defensible and socially justifiable practices (reference points);

3. Engages in reflective, interactive and transformative experiences (action).

The intent of these three conditions, however, is not always realized. For example, the focus can easily concentrate on developing teachers and assume an impact on student learning as a consequence of changes in teaching practices, or it can concentrate on developing students while ignoring the complex connections with teacher learning. Reference points can also respond to the most immediate and visible demands and avoid the social implications of teacher development strategies. Similarly, actions can easily shift to instrumental modifications and consequently limit considerably the nature of interaction, scope of reflection and depth of transformation.[72] Rigorous efforts are necessary to resist compromises in these three conditions.

For the most part, CBTD only indirectly:

4. Occurs in the complex and changing situation of classroom life (environment);

5. Supports those who have the most influence on and stake in what happens (power).

Under their present circumstances, teachers frequently situate their development outside the classroom. For example, they plan and train for later classroom applications or think back to earlier experiences to re-examine their practices. Such prospective or retrospective strategies attend to, but do not occur within, the classroom. When the environment condition is only indirectly applied, CBTD loses the opportunity to embed improvement within the dynamic cultural realities which teachers and students share and create.

The least prevalent condition, power, is only actively present in the least prevalent mode — that of teachers and students. It is not common for teachers to share control of classroom activities and decisions with their students. Until teachers infuse their development experiences with a genuine search for partnership with students, CBTD will remain hollow and incomplete.

CBTD is not simply a change in venue from more traditional workshop or conference settings. It is not simply a shift in time, method or person. It is an alternative orientation, one which uses the five conditions I have specified to create a dynamic, contextually rich and meaningful learning environment for everyone. In particular, CBTD proposes to re-establish the importance of the classroom as the key cultural and contextual force for teacher development and teachers, in collaboration with their students, as the primary agents in that process.

NOTES AND REFERENCES

1. Thiessen, D., 'Alternative perspectives on teacher development'. *Journal of Education Policy*, 4 (3), pp. 289–95, 1989.

2. Hunter, M., 'Knowing, teaching and supervising'. In Hosford, P. (ed.), *Using What We Know about Teaching*. Alexandria, VA: Association for Supervision and Curriculum Development, 1984.

3. Wood, F., 'Organizing and managing school-based staff development'. In DeJarnette, Caldwell, S. (ed.), *Staff Development: A Handbook of Effective Practices*. Oxford, OH: National Staff Development Council, 1989.

4. Hunt, D., *Beginning with Ourselves: In Practice, Theory, and Human Affairs*. Toronto: OISE Press, 1987.

5. Little, J., 'Teachers as colleagues'. In Richardson-Koehler, V. (ed.), *Educators' Handbook: A Research Perspective*. New York: Longman, pp. 491–518, 1987.

6. McEvoy, B., 'Everyday acts: how principals influence development of their staffs'. *Educational Leadership*, 44 (5), pp. 73–7, 1987.

7. Miles, M., Saxl, E. and Lieberman, A., 'What skills do educational "change agents" need?: an empirical view'. *Curriculum Inquiry*, 18 (2), pp. 157–94, 1988.

8. Seeley, D., 'A new paradigm for parent involvement'. *Educational Leadership*, 47 (2), pp. 46–49, 1989.

9. Wildman, T., Niles, J., Magliaro, S. and McLaughlin, R., 'Teaching and learning to teach: the two roles of beginning teachers'. *Elementary School Journal*, 89 (4), pp. 471–93, 1989.

10. Boomer, G. (ed.), *Negotiating the Curriculum: A Teacher–Student Partnership*. Sydney: Ashton Scholastic, 1982.

11. Hull, C., 'Pupils as teacher educators'. *Cambridge Journal of Education*, 15 (1), pp. 1–8, 1985.

12. Wigginton, E., 'Foxfire grows up'. *Harvard Educational Review*, 59 (1), pp. 24–49, 1989.

13. Joyce, B. and Showers, B., *Student Achievement Through Staff Development*. New York: Longman, 1988.

14. Pacquette, M., 'Voluntary collegial support groups for teachers'. *Educational Leadership*, 45 (3), pp. 36–9, 1987.

15. Showers, B., *Peer Coaching: A Strategy for Facilitating Transfer of Training*. Eugene, OR: Center for Educational Policy and Management, 1984.

16. Joyce and Showers, op. cit., note 13.

17. See Olson, J., 'Classroom knowledge and curriculum change: an introduction'. In Olson, J. (ed.), *Innovation in the Science Curriculum*. London: Croom Helm, 1982, and Olson, J., 'Changing our ideas about change'. *Canadian Journal of Education*, 10 (3), pp. 294–308, 1985.

18. See Doyle, W. and Ponder, G. A., 'The practicality ethic in teacher decision-making'. *Interchange*, 8 (3), 1977–78, pp. 1–12, and Fuller, F., 'Concerns of teachers: a developmental characterization'. *American Educational Research Journal*, 6, pp. 207–26, 1969.

19. Thiessen, D., 'Teachers and their curriculum-change orientations'. In

Milburn, G., Goodson, I. and Clark, R. (eds), *Re-interpreting Curriculum Research: Images and Arguments*. London: Falmer Press and Althouse Press, p. 137, 1989.

20. Day, C., 'Classroom based in-service teacher education: the development and evaluation of a client-centred model'. Occasional Paper 9, Falmer: Education Area, University of Sussex, 1981.

21. Caldwell, S. (ed.), *Staff Development: A Handbook of Effective Practices*. Oxford, OH: National Staff Development Council, 1989.

22. See Schon, D., *The Reflective Practitioner*. New York: Basic Books, 1983, and Schon, D., *Educating the Reflective Practitioner*. San Francisco: Jossey-Bass, 1987.

23. Connelly, F. M. and Clandinin, D. J., *Teachers as Curriculum Planners: Narratives of Experience*. Toronto and New York: OISE Press and Teachers College Press, 1988; Chapters 4 and 5 offer numerous 'tools for reflection' that teachers can use on their own or with others to better understand themselves as practitioners.

24. Many resources are available for teachers who want to guide their own development: Connelly and Clandinin, op. cit., note 23; Handal, G. and Lauvas, P., *Promoting Effective Teaching: Supervision in Action*. Milton Keynes: Society for Research into Higher Education and the Open University, 1987; Haysom, J., *Inquiring into the Teaching Process: Towards Self-Evaluation and Professional Development*. Toronto: OISE Press, 1985; Hunt, op. cit., note 4; and Pollard, A. and Tann, S., *Reflective Teaching in the Primary School: A Handbook for the Classroom*. London: Cassell, 1987, provide teachers with strategies and frameworks to enquire into, reflect about, and reform their practices.

25. Connelly and Clandinin, op. cit., note 23.

26. Burgess, R., *In the Field: An Introduction to Field Research*. London: George Allen & Unwin, 1984; Connelly and Clandinin, op. cit., note 23.

27. Pollard and Tann, op. cit., note 24.

28. Holly, M., *Keeping a Personal–Professional Journal*. Seelong: Deakin University Press, 1984; Tripp, D., 'Teachers' journals: an illustrated rationale for teacher/researcher partnership in curriculum research', a paper presented at the annual meeting of the American Educational Research Association, San Francisco, CA, 1986; Tripp, D., 'Teachers, journals and collaborative research'. In Smyth, J. (ed.), *Educating Teachers: Changing the Nature of Pedagogical Knowledge*. London: Falmer Press, pp. 179–92, 1987.

29. Oberg, A., 'Professional development through self-evaluation'. In

Holborn, P., Wideen, M. and Andrews, T. (eds), *Becoming a Teacher*. Toronto: Kajan & Woo, 1988.

30. Loucks-Horsley, S., Harding, C., Arbuckle, M., Murray, L., Dubea, C. and Williams, M., *Continuing to Learn: A Guidebook for Teacher Development*. Andover and Oxford: Regional Laboratory for Educational Improvement of the Northeast and Islands, and National Staff Development Council, 1987; Iwanicki, E. and McEachern, L., 'Teacher self-improvement: a promising approach to professional development and school improvement'. *Journal of Staff Development*, 4 (1), pp. 62–77, 1983.

31. Flanders, T., 'Teachers' realities, needs and professional development'. In Butt, R., Olson, J. and Daignault, J. (eds), *Insiders' Realities, Outsiders' Dreams: Prospects for Curriculum Change*. Curriculum Canada IV, Vancouver: Centre for the Study of Curriculum and Instruction, University of British Columbia, 1983.

32. See Fullan, M., 'Change processes and strategies at the local level'. *Elementary School Journal*, 85 (3), pp. 391–421, 1985; and Wideen, M. and Andrews, I. (eds), *Staff Development for School Improvement: A Focus on the Teacher*. London: Falmer Press, 1987.

33. See Seller, W., 'A coaching model for professional development'. Paper presented at a meeting of the American Educational Research Association, San Francisco, CA, 1986; and Showers, B., 'Teachers coaching teachers', *Educational Leadership*, 42, pp. 43–8, 1985.

34. Mai, R., 'The advisory approach as a form of professional growth'. In Honey, K., Bents, R. and Corrigan, D. (eds), *School-Focussed Inservice: Descriptions and Discussions*. Reston, VA: Association for Teacher Educators, 1981.

35. See Glatthorn, A., *Differentiated Supervision*. Alexandria, VA: Association for Supervision and Curriculum Development, 1984; and Glatthorn, A., 'Cooperative professional development: peer-centred options for teacher growth', *Educational Leadership*, 45, pp. 31–5, 1987.

36. Galvaz-Hjornevik, C., 'Mentoring among teachers: a review of the literature'. *Journal of Teacher Education*, 37, pp. 6–11, 1986.

37. Joyce and Showers, op. cit., note 13.

38. See also Hargreaves, A. and Dawe, R., 'Paths of professional development: contrived collegiality and the case of peer coaching'. *Teaching and Teacher Education*, 4 (3), 1990.

39. Taylor, M. (ed.), *Team Teaching Experiments*. London: NFER Publishing Company, 1974.

40. Little, op. cit., note 5; Little, J. and Long, C., *Portraits of School-Based Collegial Teams*. San Francisco: Far West Laboratory, 1985.

41. Connelly and Clandinin, op. cit., note 23; Lieberman, A., 'Documenting professional practice: the vignette as a qualitative tool'. Paper presented at the annual meeting of the American Educational Research Association, Washington, DC, 1987; Miles, M., 'Innovative methods for collecting and analyzing qualitative data: vignettes and pre-structured cases'. Paper presented at the annual meeting of the American Educational Research Association, Washington, DC, 1987.

42. Day, op. cit., note 20; Woods, P., *Inside Schools: Ethnography in Educational Research*. London: Routledge & Kegan Paul, 1986.

43. Handal and Lauvas, op. cit., note 24.

44. Ruddock, J., 'Partnership supervision as a basis for the professional development of new and experienced teachers'. In Wideen, M. and Andrews, I. (eds), *Staff Development for School Improvement: A Focus on the Teacher*. London: Falmer Press, 1987, pp. 129–41.

45. Boomer, op. cit., note 10; Boomer, G., 'Students and the means of production: negotiating the curriculum'. In Schostak, J. and Logan, T. (eds), *Pupil Experience*. London: Croom Helm, pp. 231–51, 1984.

46. Hedin, D., 'Students as Teachers: A Tool for Improving School'. *Social Policy*, 17 (3), pp. 42–47, 1987.

47. Wallerstein, N., 'Problem-posing education: Freire's method for transformation'. In Shor, T. (ed.), *Freire for the Classroom: A Sourcebook for Liberatory Teaching*, 1987. Portsmouth, NH: Heinemann, 1987.

48. Pollard, A., 'Studying children's perspectives — a collaborative approach'. In Walford, G. (ed.), *Doing Sociology of Education*. London: Falmer Press, pp. 95–118, 1987.

49. Rowland, S., *The Inquiring Classroom: An Introduction to Children's Learning*. London: Falmer Press, 1984.

50. McKelvey, J. and Kyriacou, C., 'Research on pupils: a teacher evaluation'. *Educational Studies*, 11 (1), pp. 25–31, 1985.

51. Hull, op. cit., note 11.

52. Oldroyd, D. and Tiller, T., 'Change from within: an account of school-based collaborative action research in an English secondary school'. *Journal of Education for Teaching*, 12 (3), 1987, pp. 13–27; Kemmis, E. and McTaggart, R. (eds), *The Action Research Planner*, 3rd edn. Geelong: Deakin University Press, 1988.

53. Rudduck, J., 'Introducing innovation to pupils'. In Hopkins, D. and

Wideen, M. (eds), *Alternative Perspectives on School Improvement*. London: Falmer Press, pp. 53–66, 1984; Ruddock, J., 'Curriculum change: management or meaning?'. *School Organization*, 6 (1), pp. 107–14, 1986.

54. Skilbeck, M., *School-Based Curriculum Development*. London: Harper & Row, 1984.

55. Rowland, op. cit., note 49, p. 1.

56. Boomer, op. cit., note 10, and Boomer, op. cit., note 45.

57. Boomer, 'Students and the means of production', op. cit., note 45.

58. Hedin, op. cit., note 46.

59. Wallerstein, op. cit., note 47.

60. See Allen, J., 'Classroom management: students' perspectives, goals, and strategies'. *American Educational Research Journal*, 23, pp. 437–59, 1987; and Hammersley, M. and Woods, P. (eds), *Life in School: The Sociology of Pupil Culture*. Milton Keynes: Open University Press, 1984.

61. See Ball, S., 'Participant observation with pupils'. In Burgess, R. (ed.), *Strategies of Educational Research: Qualitative Methods*. London: Falmer Press, 1985; Fine, G. and Sandstrom, K., *Knowing Children: Participant Observation with Minors*. Newburg Park, CA: Sage Publications, 1988; Hook, S., *Studying Classrooms*. Geelong: Deakin University Press, 1981; Simmons, H., 'Conversation piece: the practice of interviewing in case study research'. In Adelman, C. (ed.), *Uttering, Muttering, Collecting, Using and Reporting Talk for Social and Educational Research*. London: Grant McIntyre, 1981; and Walker, R., *Doing Research: A Handbook for Teachers*. Cambridge: Cambridge University Press, 1985.

62. Pollard, op. cit., note 48.

63. Ibid., p. 108.

64. Rowland, op. cit., note 49.

65. McKelvey and Kyriacou, op. cit., note 50.

66. Joyce and Showers, op. cit., note 13.

67. Furtwengler, W., 'Reading success through involvement — implementation strategy for creating and maintaining effective schools'. Paper presented at a meeting of the American Educational Research Association, San Francisco, CA, 1986.

68. Hull, op. cit., note 11.

69. Ibid., p. 8.

70. Oldroyd and Tiller, op. cit., note 52.

71. See Rudduck, 'Introducing innovation to pupils', op. cit., note 53; Rudduck, 'Curriculum change', op. cit., note 53.

72. Miller, J., 'Atomism, pragmatism, and holism'. *Journal of Curriculum and Supervision*, 1 (3), pp. 175–96, 1986.

Chapter 7

Sponsoring the Teacher's Voice: Teachers' Lives and Teacher Development*

Ivor F. Goodson

Some time ago, I became convinced that the study of teachers' lives was central to the study of curriculum and schooling. In reflecting on the development of my conviction two episodes stand out. Were this merely a reminiscence of personal conversion it would be of little interest, but the two episodes do address a number of salient issues in the argument for greatly extended study of teachers' lives.

The first episode took place in the year of post-graduate certification when I was training to be a teacher. I returned to spend the day with a teacher at my secondary school who had been a major inspiration to me, a mentor. He was a radical Welshman. Academically brilliant, he had a BSc in economics and a PhD in history. He was open, humorous, engaging, stimulating — a superb and popular teacher.

But he faced me with a paradox, because when the school changed from a grammar school to a comprehensive it was he who opposed all the curriculum reforms which sought to broaden the educational appeal of the school for wider social groups. He was implacably conservative and traditionalist on this, and as far as I know only this, issue. But he, it should be remembered, was a man who had personally visited the factory to which I had gone after leaving school early at the age of fifteen. He had implored me to return to school. He had spoken then of his commitment to public schooling as an avenue to working-class emancipation. He no doubt saw me, a badly behaved working-class pupil, as some sort of test case. I knew personally then that he was very deeply concerned to keep working-class pupils in school. So why did he oppose all those curriculum reforms which had that objective?

During the day back visiting my old school, I continually probed him on this issue. At first he stonewalled me, giving a series of essentially non-committal responses, but at the end of the day, in the pub over a beer, he opened up. Yes, of course he was mainly concerned with disadvantaged pupils; yes, of course that was why he had come to the factory to persuade me to return to school. Yes, he was politically radical and yes, he had always voted Labour. But, he said,

* An earlier version of this chapter appears in Goodson, I. and Waller, R., *Biography, Identity and Schooling*. Philadelphia: Falmer Press, 1990.

110

'you don't understand my relationship to the school and to teaching. My centre of gravity is not here at all. It's in the community, in the home — that's where I exist, that's where I put my effort now. For me the school is nine to five, I go through the motions.'

In short, he sought to minimize his commitment while at the school and he opposed any reform which would increase his workload. His centre of gravity was elsewhere.

The point I am making is that to understand teacher development and curriculum development, and to tailor it accordingly, we need to know a great deal more about teachers' priorities. We need in short to know more about teachers' lives.

The second episode began in the late 1970s. I was interested in some work on folk music being conducted at the University of Leeds. At the same time, I was exploring some themes for an ethnography conference that was coming up at St Hilda's College in Oxford. The work of a folklorist, Pegg, suddenly opened up again the line of argument which I had been pondering since 1970. Pegg says,

> The right to select lies not with the folklorist ('Sorry old chap, can't have that — it's not a folk song'), but with the singer. Today's collector must have no preconceptions. His job is to record a people's music, whether it is a traditional ballad or a hymn or a musical song or last week's pop hit!

With this basic attitude comes another revelation:

> I began to realise that, for me, the people who sang the songs were more important than the songs themselves. The song is only a small part of the singer's life and the life was usually very fascinating. There was no way I felt I could understand the songs without knowing something about the life of the singer, which does not seem to apply in the case of most folklorists. They are quite happy to find material which fits into a preconceived canon and leave it at that. I had to know what people thought about the songs, what part they played in their lives and in the lives of the community.[1]

A similar point is made by the folk-song collector Robin Morton:

> The opinion grew in me that it was in the singer that the song becomes relevant. Analyzing it in terms of motif, or rhyming structure, or minute variation becomes, in my view, sterile if the one who carries the particular song is forgotten. We have all met the scholar who can talk for hours in a very learned fashion about folksongs and folklore in general, without once mentioning the

singer. Bad enough to forget the social context, but to ignore the individual context castrates the song. As I got to know the singers, so I got to know and understand their songs more fully.[2]

The preoccupation with 'the singer, not the song' needs to be seriously tested in our studies of curriculum and schooling. What Pegg and Morton say about folklorists — and implicitly about the way their research is received by those they research — could also be said about most educational research.

The project I am recommending is essentially one of reconceptualizing educational research so as to assure that 'the teacher's voice' is heard, both loudly and articulately. In this respect the most hopeful way forward is, I think, to build upon notions of the 'self-monitoring teacher', 'the teacher as researcher', the teacher as 'extended professional'. For instance, in the early 1970s at the Centre for Applied Research in Education at the University of East Anglia, a good deal of work was conducted into how to put this concept into operation. Perhaps the most interesting developments were within the Ford Teaching Project conducted by John Elliott and Clem Adelman in the period 1973–5. They sought to rehabilitate the 'action research' mode pioneered by Kurt Lewin in the post-war period. In the interim period, educational action research had fallen into decline. Carr and Kemmis, who have done a good deal to extend and popularize the concept, give a number of reasons for the resurgence of action research:

> First, there was the demand from within an increasingly professionalized teacher force for a research role, based on the notion of the extended professional investigating his or her own practice. Second, there was the perceived irrelevance to the concerns of these practitioners of much contemporary educational research. Third, there had been a revival of intrest in 'the practical' in curriculum, following the work of Schwab[3] and others on 'practical deliberation'. Fourth, action research was assisted by the rise of the 'new wave' methods in educational research and evaluation with their emphasis on participants' perspectives and categories in shaping educational practices and situations. These methods place the practitioners at centre stage in the educational research process and recognize the crucial significance of actors' understandings in shaping educational action. From the role of critical informant helping an 'outsider' researcher, it is but a short step for the practitioner to become a self-critical researcher into her or his own practice. Fifth, the accountability movement galvanized and politicized practitioners. In response to the accountability movement, practitioners have adopted the self-monitoring role as a proper means of justifying practice and generating sensitive critiques of the working conditions in which their practice is conducted. Sixth, there was increasing solidarity in the teaching profession in response to the

public criticism which has accompanied the post-expansion
educational politics of the 1970s and 1980s; this, too, has
prompted the organization of support net-works of concerned
professionals interested in the continuing developments of
education even though the expansionist tide has turned. And,
finally, there is the increased awareness of action research itself,
which is perceived as providing an understandable and workable
approach to the improvement of practice through critical
self-reflection.[4]

The focus on action research has however tended to be very practice-
orientated. In introducing a survey of action research, for instance, Carr and
Kemmis note:

> A range of practices have been studied by educational
> action-researchers and some examples may suffice to show how
> they have used action research to improve their practices, their
> understanding of these practices, and the situations in which they
> work.[5]

Not surprisingly, with the notion of an extended professional in mind, workers
have 'used action research to improve their practice'. Other developments in
teacher education have similarly focused on practice. The work of Connelly and
Clandinin has argued in innovative and interesting ways that would seek to
understand teachers' *personal practical knowledge*.[6] The addition of the personal aspect in this formulation is a welcome move forward, hinting as it does at
the importance of biographical perspectives. But again the personal is being
linked irrevocably to practice. It is as if the teacher *is* his or her practice. For
teacher educators such specificity of focus is understandable, but I wish to argue
that a broader perspective will achieve more: not solely in terms of our understanding but ultimately in ways that feed back into changes in practical knowledge. In short, I am saying that it does not follow logically or psychologically
that to *improve* practice we must initially and immediately *focus* on practice.
Indeed I shall argue the opposite point of view.

Taking the 'teacher as researcher' and 'action research' as expressing defensible value positions and viable starting-points, I want to argue for a broadened
sense of purpose. In particular I am worried about a collaborative mode of
research which seeks to give full equality and stature to the teacher, but which
employs as its initial and predominant focus the practice of the teacher. It is, I
believe, a profoundly unpromising point of entry from which to promote a collaborative enterprise. For the university researcher, aspiring to collaborative
and egalitarian partnership, it may seem quite unproblematic, but for the
teacher it might seem far less so. In fact it may seem to the teacher that the
starting point for collaboration focuses on the maximum point of vulnerability.

We must, I think, constantly remind ourselves how deeply uncertain and anxious most of us are about our work as teachers whether in classrooms or in (far less contested) lecture halls. These are often the arenas of greatest anxiety and insecurity — as well as, occasionally, achievement. Hence I wish to argue that to place teachers' classroom practice at the centre of the action for action researchers is to put the most exposed and problematic aspect of the teacher's world at the centre of scrutiny and negotiation. In terms of strategy, both personally and politically, I think it is a mistake to do this. I say it is a mistake — and this may seem a paradox — particularly if the wish is to ultimately seek reflection about and change in the teacher's practice.

A more valuable and less vulnerable entry point would be to examine teachers' work in the context of the teacher's life. Much of the emerging study in this area indicates that this focus allows a rich flow of dialogue and data. Moreover, the focus may (and I stress may) allow teachers greater authority and control in collaborative research than has often appeared to be the case with practice-orientated study. What I am asserting here is that, particularly in the world of teacher development, the central ingredient so far missing is the *teacher's voice*. Primarily the focus has been on the teacher's practice, almost the teacher *as* practice. What is needed is a focus that listens above all to the person at whom 'development' is aimed. This means that strategies should be developed which facilitate, maximize, and in a real sense legislate, the capturing of the teacher's voice.

Bringing substance and strategy together points us in a new direction for reconceptualizing educational research and development. In the first section I provided two somewhat episodic arguments for seeking to understand teachers' lives as part of the educational research and development enterprise. In the second section I argued that the 'teacher as researcher' and 'action research' modes were productive and generative ways forward, but that the initial and immediate focus on practice was overstated and undesirable. Strategically, a broader focus on life and work is hereby recommended. Hence for substantive and strategic reasons, I would argue for a broadening of focus to allow detailed scrutiny of the teacher's life and work.

BROADENING OUR DATA BASE FOR STUDYING TEACHING

So far I have argued in somewhat anecdotal fashion that data on teachers' lives are an important factor for our educational research studies. I have argued that *strategically* this is desirable so as to involve teachers as researchers and to develop a collaborative mode. But there is also a *substantive* reason. The primary reason is that in my experience, when talking to teachers about issues of curriculum development, subject teaching, school governance and general school organization, they constantly import data on their own lives into the discussion. This I take to be prima facie evidence that teachers themselves judge such issues to be of major importance. One of the reasons that these data have not been much used, however, is that researchers edit such data, viewing them as too 'personal', 'idiosyncratic' or 'soft'. It is, in short, yet another example of the selective use of the 'teacher's voice'. The researcher only hears what he/she wants to hear, and knows will sound well when replayed to the research community.

There may of course be perfectly valid reasons for not employing data on teachers' lives in our educational research studies. But this would require a sequence of reasoning to show why such data were irrelevant or of no importance. The normal research strategy is, however, to simply purge such data. I have not come across any accounts which give reasoned explanations as to why such data are not employed. The most commonsensical explanation seems to be that data on teachers' lives simply do not fit in with existing research paradigms. If this is the case then it is the paradigms that are at fault, not the value and quality of this kind of data.

The arguments for employing data on teachers' lives are substantial, but given the predominance of existing paradigms they should be spelt out:

1. In the research on schools in which I have been involved — covering a wide range of different research foci and conceptual matrixes — the consistency of teachers talking about their own lives in the process of explaining their policy and practice has been striking. Were this only a personal observation it would be worthless, but again and again in talking to other researchers they have echoed their point. To give one example: David Hargreaves, in researching for *Deviance in Classrooms*, noted when talking about the book that teachers had repeatedly imported autobiographical comments into their explanations.[7] He was very concerned in retrospect at the speed with which such data had been excised when writing up the research. The assumption, very much the conventional wisdom, was that such data were too 'personal', too 'idiosyncratic', too 'soft', for a fully fledged piece of social science research.

Of course in the first instance (and in some cases the last instance) it is true that personal data can be irrelevant, eccentric and essentially redundant. But the point that needs to be grasped is that the features are not the inevitable corollary of that which is personal. Moreover, that which is personal at the point of collection may not remain personal. After all, a good deal of social science is concerned with the collection of a range of often personal insights and events and the elucidation of more collective and generalizable profferings and processes.

The respect for the autobiographical, for 'the life', is but one side of a concern to elicit the teacher's voice. In some senses, like the anthropologist, this school of qualitative educational research is concerned to listen to what the teacher says, and to respect and deal seriously with those data which the teacher imports into accounts. This is to invert the balance of proof. Conventionally, those data which do not serve the researcher's interests and foci are disposed of. In this model the data the teacher provides have a more sacred property and are only dispensed with after painstaking proof of irrelevance and redundancy.

Listening to the teacher's voice should teach us that the autobiographical, 'the life', is of substantial concern when teachers talk of their work. And at a commonsensical level I find this essentially unsurprising. What I do find surprising, if not frankly unconscionable, is that for so long researchers have ruled out this part of the teacher's account as irrelevant data.

2. Life experiences and background are obviously key ingredients of the people that we are, of our sense of self. To the degree that we invest our 'self' in our teaching, experience and background therefore shape our practice.

A common feature in many teachers' accounts of their background is the appearance of a favourite teacher who substantially influenced the person as a young pupil. They often report that 'it was this person who first sold me on teaching'; 'I was sitting in her classroom when I first decided I wanted to be a teacher'. In short, such teachers provide a 'role model', and in addition they most probably influence the subsequent vision of desirable pedagogy as well as possibly choice of subject specialization.

Many other ingredients of background are important in the teacher's life and practice. An upbringing in a working-class environment may for instance provide valuable insights and experience when teaching pupils from a similar background. I once observed a teacher with a working-class background teach a class of comprehensive pupils in a school in the East End of London. He taught using the local cockney vernacular, and his affinity was a quite startling aspect of his success as a teacher. In my interview I spoke about his affinity and he noted that it was ' 'coz I come from round 'ere don't I?'. Background and life experience were then a major aspect of his practice. But so they would be in the case of middle-class teachers teaching children from the working class, or teachers of working-class origins teaching middle-class children. Background is an important ingredient in the dynamic of practice.[8]

Of course, class is just one aspect, as are gender or ethnicity. Teachers' backgrounds and life experiences are idiosyncratic and unique and must therefore be explored in their full complexity.[9]

3. The teacher's *lifestyle*, both in and out of school, his or her latent identities and cultures, impact on views of teaching and on practice. Becker and Geer's work on latent identities and cultures provides a valuable theoretical basis.[10] Lifestyle is of course often a characteristic element in certain cohorts; for instance, work on the 1960s generation of teachers would be of great value. In a recent study of one teacher focusing on his lifestyle, Walker and myself stated:

> how the connections between Youth Culture and the curriculum
> reform movement of the sixties is more complex than we first
> thought. For Ron Fisher there definitely is a connection, he
> identifies strongly with youth culture and feels that to be
> important in his teaching. But despite his attraction to rock
> music and teenage life styles it is the school he has become
> committed to, almost against his own sense of direction.

Involvement in innovation, for Ron at least, is not simply a
question of technical involvement, but touches significant facets
of his personal identity. This raises the question for the
curriculum developer, what would a project look like if it
explicitly set out to change the teachers rather than the
curriculum? How would you design a project to appeal to the
teacher-as-person rather than to the teacher-as-educator? What
would be the effects and consequences of implementing such a
design?[11]

This, I think, shows how work in this area begins to force a reconceptualization
of models of teacher development. In short, we move from the teacher-as-
practice to the teacher-as-person as our starting-point for development.

4. Focus on the *life cycle* will therefore generate insights into the unique
elements of teaching. Indeed, so unique a characteristic would seem an obvious
starting-point for reflection about the teachers' world. Yet our research
paradigms face so frankly in other directions that there has been little work in
this area to date.

Fortunately, work in other areas provides a very valuable framework. Some
of Gail Sheehy's somewhat populist work in *Passages* and *Pathfinders*[12] is, I
think, important. So also is the research carried out by Levinson on which some
of her publications are based. His work, while regrettably focused only on men,
does provide some very generative insights into how our perspectives at particular stages in our life crucially affect our professional work.

Take for instance the case study of John Barnes, a university biologist.
Levinson is writing about his 'dream' of himself as a front-rank prize-winning
biological researcher:

Barnes's Dream assumed greater urgency as he approached 40.
He believed that most creative work in science is done before
then. A conversation with his father's lifelong friend around this
time made a lasting impression on him. The older man confided
that he had by now accepted his failure to become a 'legal star'
and was content to be a competent and respected tax lawyer. He
had decided that stardom is not synonymous with the good life; it
was 'perfectly all right to be second best'. At the time, however,
Barnes was not ready to scale down his own ambition. Instead, he
decided to give up the chairmanship and devote himself fully to
his research.

He stepped down from the chairmanship as he approached
41, and his project moved into its final phase. This was a crucial
time for him, the culmination of years of striving. For several
months, one distraction after another claimed his attention and
heightened the suspense. He became the father of a little boy, and

that same week was offered a prestigious chair at Yale. Flattered and excited, he felt that this was his 'last chance for a big offer'. But in the end Barnes said no. He found that he could not make a change at this stage of his work. Also, their ties to family and friends, and their love of place, were now of much greater importance to him and Ann. She said: 'The kudos almost got him, but now we are both glad we stayed'.[13]

In my opinion, this quotation shows how definitions of our professional location and of our career direction can only be arrived at by a detailed understanding of people's lives.

5. Likewise, *career stages* and *career decisions* can be analysed in their own right. Work on teachers' lives and careers is increasingly commanding attention in professional development workshops and courses. For instance, the Open University now uses our *Teachers' Lives and Careers* book as one of its course's set books.[14] This is symptomatic of important changes in the way that professional courses are being reorganized to allow concentration on the perspective of teachers' careers.

Besides the range of career studies in *Teachers' Lives and Careers*, a body of new researchers are beginning to examine this neglected aspect of teachers' professional lives. The work of Sikes, Measor and Woods, and of Michael Huberman (see Chapter 8), has provided valuable new insights into how teachers construct and view their careers in teaching.[15]

6. Moreover, the new work on teachers' careers points to the fact that there are *critical incidents* in teachers' lives and specifically in their work which may crucially affect perception and practice. Certainly, work on novice teachers has highlighted the importance of certain incidents in moulding teachers' styles and practices. Lacey's work has pointed to the effects on teachers' strategies, and the work of Woods, Pollard, Hargreaves and Knowles has further elucidated the relationship to evolving teacher strategies.[16]

Other work on critical incidents in teachers' lives can confront important themes seen in the context of a full life perspective. For instance, Kathleen Casey has employed 'life history narratives' to understand the phenomenon of teacher drop-out, specifically female and activist teacher drop-out.[17] Her work is exceptionally illuminating on this phenomenon, which is currently receiving a great deal of essentially uncritical attention given the problem of teacher shortages. Yet few of the countries at the hard edge of teacher shortages have bothered to fund serious study of teachers' lives to examine and extend our understanding of the phenomenon of teacher drop-outs. I would argue that only such an approach affords the possibility of extending our understanding.

The same principle applies to many other major themes in teachers' work. The question of teacher stress and burn-out would, I believe, be best studied through life history perspectives, as would the issue of effective teaching and the question of the take-up innovations and new managerial initiatives. Above all, in the study of teachers' working conditions, this approach has a great deal to offer.

7. Studies of teachers' lives might allow us to see the individual in relation to the history of his or her time, allowing us to view the intersection of the life history with the history of society and thus illuminating the choices, contingencies and options open to the individual. 'Life histories' of schools, subjects and the teaching profession would provide vital contextual background. The initial focus on the teachers' lives would therefore reconceptualize our studies of schooling and curriculum in quite basic ways.

Essentially, collaborative study of teachers' lives at the levels mentioned constitutes a new way of viewing teacher development; a way which should redirect the power relations underpinning teachers' lives in significant and generative ways.

COLLABORATION AND TEACHER DEVELOPMENT

Strategically, I have argued that to promote the notion of teachers as researchers and to develop an action research modality where collaboration with externally situated researchers was fostered we need to avoid an immediate and predominant focus on practice. I have further argued that this focus on practice should, at least partially, be replaced by a focus on the teacher's life.

What is at issue here seems to me almost anthropological: we are looking for a point for teachers (as researchers) and externally located researchers to 'trade'. Practice promises maximum vulnerability as the 'trading point'. This is a deeply unequal situation in which to begin to 'trade', for it could be argued that the teacher may already feel vulnerable and inferior in the face of a university researcher.

Talking about his or her own life the teacher is, in this specific sense, in a less immediately exposed situation; and the 'exposure' can be more carefully, consciously and personally controlled. (This is not, it should be noted, to argue that once again 'exploitation' might not take place, nor that there are no longer major ethical questions to do with exposure.) But I think this starting-point has substantive as well as strategic advantages. Some have already been listed; however, in terms of the 'trade' between teacher/researcher and external researcher, this focus seems to me to provide advantages.

Much of the research that is emerging into teachers' lives throws up structural insights which locate the teacher's life within the deeply structured and embedded environment of schooling.[18] This provides a prime 'trading point' for the external researcher. For one of the valuable characteristics of a collaboration between teachers as researchers and external researchers is that it is a collaboration between two parties that are differentially located in structural terms. Each party sees the world through a different prism of practice and thought. This valuable difference may provide the external researcher with a possibility to offer back goods in 'the trade'. The teacher/researcher offers data and insights; the external researcher, in pursuing glimpses of structure in different ways, may now also bring data and insights. The terms of trade, in short, look favourable. In such conditions collaboration may at last begin.

I noted earlier that this possible route to collaboration does not suspend issues of ethics and exploitation. This is above all because the collaboration between teacher/researcher and external researcher takes place in an occupational terrain which is itself inequitably structured. In terms of power, the external researcher still holds many advantages. Moreover, the conditions of university careers positively exhort researchers to exploit research data: the requirements of publications and peer review have their own dynamics.

So whatever the favourable aspects of a focus on teachers' lives might be, we must remain deeply watchful. For if the teacher's practice was a vulnerable focus, the teacher's life is a deeply intimate, indeed intensive, focus. Now more than ever before, procedural guidelines are necessary over questions relating to the ownership and publication of the data. These issues themselves must be conceived of in terms of a collaboration in which each party has clear rights, and in this case the teacher's power of veto should be agreed on early and implemented, where necessary, late.

NOTES

1. Pegg, J., quoted in Goodson, I. and Walker, R., *Biography, Identity and Schooling*. New York and London: Falmer Press, forthcoming.

2. Morton, R., quoted, ibid.

3. Schwab, J. J., 'The practical: a language for curriculum'. *School Review*, 78, pp. 1–24, 1969.

4. Carr, W. and Kemmis, S., *Becoming Critical: Education Knowledge and Action Research*. London and Philadelphia: Falmer Press, pp. 166–7, 1986.

5. Ibid.

6. See, for example, Connelly, F. M. and Clandinin, D. Jean, *Teachers as Curriculum Planners: Narratives of Experience*. Toronto and New York: OISE Press and Teachers College Press, 1988.

7. Hargreaves, D. H., Hester, S. and Meller, D., *Deviance in Classrooms*. London: Routledge & Kegan Paul, 1975.

8. Lortie, D., *Schoolteacher*. Chicago: University of Chicago Press, 1975; and Hargreaves, A., *Two Cultures of Schooling*. Philadelphia: Falmer Press, 1986.

9. Treatment of gender issues has often been inadequate. See Sikes, P., Measor, L. and Woods, P., *Teachers' Careers*. Philadelphia: Falmer Press, 1985. Recent work is more encouraging. See Nelson, M., 'Using oral histories to reconstruct the experiences of women teachers in Vermont, 1900–1950', in Goodson, I. F. (ed.), *Studying Teachers' Lives*. London: Routledge, forthcoming; and Casey, K., 'Why do progressive women activists leave teaching?: theory, methodology and politics in life history research', in Goodson, I. F. (ed.), *Studying Teachers' Lives*. London: Routledge, forthcoming.

10. Becker, H. S. and Geer, B., 'Latent culture: a note on the theory of latent social roles', in Cosin, B. R., *et al.* (eds), *School and Society: A Sociological Reader*. London: Routledge & Kegan Paul, pp. 56–60, 1971.

11. Goodson and Walker, op. cit., note 1.

12. Sheehy, G., *Passages: Predictable Crises of Adult Life.* New York: Dutton, 1976, and Sheehy, G., *Pathfinders.* London: Sidgwick & Jackson, 1981.

13. Levinson, D. J., *The Seasons of a Man's Life.* New York: Ballantine Books, p. 267, 1979.

14. Ball, S. J. and Goodson, I., *Teachers' Lives and Careers.* Philadelphia: Falmer Press, 1989.

15. Sikes, P., Measor, L. and Woods, P., op. cit., note 9.

16. Lacey, C., *The Socialization of Teachers.* London: Methuen Books, 1977; Woods, P., *Teaching Skills and Strategies.* Philadelphia: Falmer Press, 1990; Hargreaves, A., 'The significance of classroom coping strategies', in Hargreaves, A. and Woods, P. (eds), *Classrooms and Staffrooms.* Milton Keynes: Open University Press, 1984; Pollard, A., *The Social World of the Primary School.* London: Cassell, 1985; and Knowles, J. G., 'Models for Understanding, Preserving and Beginning Teachers' Biographies: Illustrations for Case Studies', in Goodson, I. F. (ed.), *Studying Teachers' Lives.* London: Routledge, forthcoming.

17. Casey, K., 'Teacher as author: life history narratives of contemporary women teachers working for social change', PhD dissertation. Madison: University of Wisconsin, 1988; and Casey, K. and Apple, M. W., 'Gender and the conditions of teachers' work: the development of understanding in America', in Acker, S. (ed.), *Teachers, Gender and Careers.* New York: Falmer Press, 1989.

18. Goodson, I. F., (ed.), *Studying Teachers' Lives.* London: Routledge, forthcoming; and Goodson, I. F., *The Teacher's Life and Work.* Philadelphia: Falmer Press, forthcoming.

Chapter 8

Teacher Development and Instructional Mastery

Michael Huberman

INTRODUCTION

Although life-span or life-cycle research has been progressing for decades, there has been surprisingly little interest until very recently in its applications to teaching. For example, if you scan the index of a recent, and massive, work, the *Handbook of Research on Teaching*,[1] you will find no reference to research on teachers' professional life cycles and only a handful of references to research on teachers' careers.[2] Significantly, those few references relate to research in teacher education with an emphasis on pre-service training, as if the ensuing forty years were less meaningful units of analysis.

To be sure, the tide has turned in the past decade, and I will try to document briefly some of these developments in the first section of this chapter. When examining this literature one can even discern, if dimly, an outline of the modal career trajectories in teaching. In many ways, the Swiss research reported here lends strong support to those trends.

This chapter will begin with a general model of career trajectories in teaching, one which has been designed by interpolating recent research. The model is a useful heuristic for discussing teacher development generally, in response to the following question: *are there discernible 'phases' or 'stages' in the teaching career?* The Swiss data will help to illustrate some plausible responses to that question and, at the same time, will frame some initial answers to the next, more prescriptive question: *what are the characteristics of the more professionally satisfactory or fulfilled careers?* Having argued that perceived instructional effectiveness is one of the core predictors of professional satisfaction, I will then centre more narrowly on *the evolution of instructional skills during the career cycle*. To what extent do teachers become more or less instructionally competent over time, and in which domains? Here again, the Swiss data will form the backbone for this analysis, as well as for the obvious follow-on question: what do teachers actually *do* about areas of classroom instruction in which they feel they are less than fully competent? In studying how teachers go about remedying — or not — their own, self-defined instructional weaknesses, we then cross over to a new terrain: the shape of inservice training and its relationship to the career cycle.

LIFE-CYCLE RESEARCH ON TEACHING: THE STATE OF THE ART

Life-cycle research has certainly been around since philosophers and novelists have been studying lives. The more 'scientific' treatment of lives, however, has followed disciplinary tracks, each with its 'marker' studies or conceptualizations. For example, there is a clear, psychodynamic track running from Freud through Henry Murray and Gordon Allport and culminating in Erikson's eight normative 'life-crises'[3] and Robert White's *Lives in Progress*.[4] There is another, more sociological, track beginning in recent times with the 'Chicago School' and the revival of the oral history tradition, coupled with the development of symbolic interactionism. Along the way, this school has produced some important studies of adult socialization and career patterning, including a seminal study of school-teachers.[5] Still another important influence has been the multi-volume studies of 'life-span developmental psychology'.[6]

Conceptually, there are several ways of analysing the professional life cycle of teachers. In the Swiss research,[7] we have opted for a classic perspective, that of the 'career'. Much of the seminal work on career development has sought, in effect, to identify 'sequences', 'phases' or 'maxicycles' that can describe not only the career paths of individuals within the same profession, but also of individuals across different professions. This does not mean, of course, that these career sequences are invariant, that is, that they always play out in the same progression, nor that they are universal, that is, that all members of a given profession will pass through them.[8] Nor should we have in mind a sequence of temporal segments, but rather a set of spirals that turn back upon themselves, traversing at different 'elevations' many psychological territories we have travelled before.[9]

It would be fair — even charitable — to say that the empirical literature identifying 'phases' or 'stages' in teaching is tentative and uneven.[10] There are, however, some reasonably strong trends which recur across studies, even across studies in different national contexts.

Survival and Discovery

At the phase of career entry, where empirical research is most plentiful, we find the recurrent themes of *survival* and *discovery*. The *survival* theme has to do with reality shock, especially for teachers with no prior teaching experience, in confronting the complexity and simultaneity of instructional management: pre-occupation with self ('Am I up to this challenge?'), the gulf between professional ideals and the daily grind of classroom life, the fragmentation of tasks, the oscillation between intimacy and distance with one's pupils, the apparent inadequacy of instructional materials given the diversity of pupil characteristics — the list goes on.[11]

On the other side of the ledger, the *discovery* theme translates the initial enthusiasm of having one's own pupils, one's own classroom, materials, and yearly programme, and of feeling oneself a colleague among peers. Some of these

123

studies suggest that the survival and discovery dimensions coexist, and that the latter allows the novice teacher to tolerate the former. But there are also one-dimensional profiles, and profiles in which these two themes are absent.

Stabilization

The succeeding phase brings us directly to the classic life-cycle literature and its treatment of commitment, stabilization, and of taking on adult responsibilities. In particular, authors in the psychoanalytic tradition have stressed the significance, in the healthy process of ego development beyond adolescence, of making a commitment to a defined professional role.[12] Making that commitment resolves the danger of ego diffusion through prolonged role dispersion or role uncertainty.

In teaching, the *stabilization* phase corresponds to a subjective choice (a definitive commitment to *this* profession) and to an administrative act (an official appointment or the granting of tenure). As many biographical accounts indicate, such a commitment is not a simple affair, in that it entails ruling out other possibilities (a career in research or in journalism, an artistic career), the double act of choosing and of giving up other choices. This appears to be especially hard for upper secondary teachers, who are often able to keep other options open for several years, and whose initial commitment to teaching is often soft.

Stabilization also means an affiliation to an occupational community, freedom from direct supervision and greater instructional mastery and comfort. One has worked up a rudimentary instructional repertoire that fits most situations encountered in the initial three to four years of teaching, and one is now adding to it, refining it, moulding it to fit one's own, more congenial style of instruction.[13] There is also an attendant sense of 'relief' at having reached this stage, of spontaneity, of pleasure and humour, even a touch of headiness, in the ability to seize the moment, instructionally speaking.[14]

Experimentation/Activism

The *stabilization* phase is probably the most secure in the empirical literature, although it is by no means universal. Beyond this stage, studies diverge. If, however, we take the mainstream — the modal sequence outlined in the literature — we come upon a phase of experimentation or diversification.[15] Here, analysts stress one or more of the following three aspects:

First, the gradual consolidation of an instructional repertoire leads naturally to attempts to increase one's impact. This brings on a small flurry of experiments — with different materials, different pupil groupings, different sequencing. Next, the desire to increase one's impact in the classroom leads to an awareness of the institutional barriers that are constraining such an impact and, from there, to attempts to change the more surreal flaws in the school or school district.

A third line of analysis: having been a few times round the block, teachers may be ready for new challenges, for new stimulation. The implicit theme here is the newly emerging concern with teachers' growing stale in their profession, a malady one sees among older peers.[16]

Taking Stock: Self-Doubts

In most empirical studies, the extent to which *experimentation* gives way to some form of mid-career crisis is not clearly documented. Also, from one study to another the symptoms range from the superficial to the critical — from a gnawing sense of routine to a full-blown, radical reassessment with regard to staying in or leaving the profession. Some analyses insist on the growing sense of monotony somewhere between the 12th and 20th years of teaching; others highlight feelings of disenchantment following attempts to reform practice at the school or district levels. In both cases, there is a moment of *stock-taking*, along with the realization that other careers will have to be ruled out if one does not act quickly. In the larger empirical and epidemiological literature, there is very little evidence for a crisis as typical at mid-life, but there is some stronger support for discernible moments of stock-taking in the course of a relatively calm transition, in the 35 to 45 age range.[17]

Thus to call this an archetypical phase is unwarranted in the face of the data, which may well be lumping together different perceptions occurring at roughly the same time in the teaching career. For example, no study claims that the *majority* of teachers studied reported a mid-career crisis. Some research — ours, for instance — finds up to 40 per cent of the sample saying that, at one or more points in their career, they seriously considered leaving the teaching profession, but many of the reasons given concerned 'moving on' or 'trying out something else' or taking advantage of new career opportunities. Our data also dovetail with others' in showing that men are more subject to 'radical' self-assessments at this point in their career than are women, who appear better able to relate the importance of their career to other commitments in their lives.[18]

Serenity

This is more a leitmotiv than a strong finding in the literature on teacher careers. It is especially present in Peterson's[19] seminal study of teachers in the 45 to 55 age group, most of whom describe a fluid shift from a phase of near-manic activism ('I was young and vigorous . . . I threw myself into a thousand adventures with my pupils') to a phase of more mechanical but also more relaxed, self-accepting activity in class. The gist here is that a gradual loss in energy and enthusiasm is compensated by a greater sense of confidence and self-acceptance. As one of our Swiss respondents put it:

> I don't worry as much about what can go wrong or what went
> wrong during the day. I even forget my work when I come home.
> Mostly, I guess, I don't expect more of myself than I know I can

deliver — no more whipping myself for not being perfect. What I
have to offer is good enough for me and for the pupils, too.

Conservatism

Peterson's and Prick's sub-samples of older teachers (50 to 60) also tend to
complain a lot. They bemoan the new generations of pupils (less disciplined, less
motivated, more decadent), the more negative public image of educators, the
slack or opportunistic nature of school administrators, the lack of commitment
to the profession among younger colleagues. In Peterson's study, there is an
explicit sequence — from *serenity* to *conservatism* — whereas other research is
more equivocal. Here, of course, we intersect with empirical work in the life-cycle
tradition that highlights the link between age and dogmatism, with indications
of increasing prudence, greater resistance to innovations, greater nostalgia for
the past, and more concern with holding on to what one has than with getting
what one wants.[20]

Disengagement

As we shall see in a moment, life-cycle literature emphasizes a trend towards
increasing withdrawal and internalization toward the end of the professional
career. The tone is mostly positive: a gradual disengaging from investment in
one's work to other engagements, and from 'instrumental' concerns to more
reflective pursuits.

More specific work on teachers' professional life cycles provides little more
than anecdotal evidence. Becker[21] found such a trend in his subsample of older
teachers, but attributed it to frustrated ambitions, to an early 'plateauing' in
the profession. Others suggest that the natural consequence of increasing conservatism is that of disengagement from policies and practices of which one
disapproves. Peterson's teachers seem to yearn for calmer years as they
approach retirement. As many sociologists have pointed out, this trend may be
far less psychological in nature than a response to pressures from the environment to cede one's place to younger colleagues and fresher ideas.

A BROAD-BRUSH MODEL OF THE TEACHING CAREER

Having at several points underlined the tentative, often fragmentary nature of
these trends, let me still try to piece them together (see Figure 8.1). As the figure
shows, there is a single stream at career entry, through the stabilization phase.
There are then multiple streams at mid-career, converging again into a single
path at the end. Depending on the previous trajectory, this final phase can be
either serene or acrimonious. The most harmonious trajectory would be this
one:

Experimentation ⟶ Serenity ⟶ (serene) Disengagement

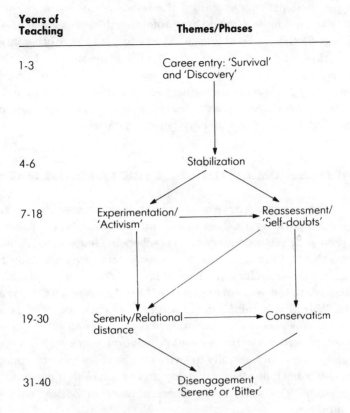

Years of Teaching	Themes/Phases
1-3	Career entry: 'Survival' and 'Discovery'
4-6	Stabilization
7-18	Experimentation/ 'Activism' — Reassessment/ 'Self-doubts'
19-30	Serenity/Relational distance — Conservatism
31-40	Disengagement 'Serene' or 'Bitter'

Figure 8.1. Successive themes of the teacher career cycle: schematic model.

And the most problematic trajectories would be these two:

1. Reassessment ⟶ (bitter) Disengagement

2. Reassessment ⟶ Conservatism ⟶ (bitter) Disengagement

More globally, these trends are consonant with the literature bearing more generally on the professional life cycle. In many ways, Kuhlen's[22] overarching thesis is compelling: a fairly sharp curve of expansion, both in terms of activity and career progression, then a gradual, usually fluid, process of disengagement. But the nature of such a disengagement is controversial. The basic hypothesis is psychological: that of a gradual 'internalization' at 45 to 50 years of age, notably among men.[23] This shift, often associated with metabolic changes, corresponds to Jung's concept of 'individuation', a shift from instrumental activity to introspective reflectiveness, from the narrow self to the archetypal self.[24] Even earlier, Heidegger[25] had worked up an evocative formula for the evolution, with increasing age, from a concern with 'objects of experience' to 'modes of experiencing'.

On the other hand, sociologists have looked elsewhere for determinisms, and other psychologists have shifted the terms of the debate. For example, Maehr and Kleiber[26] have argued that professional 'success' means something different at age 55 than it did at age 25. At 55 one would have other interests and investments that might not be associated with professional advancement in a material sense, but that would be equally 'active'. Reading more, working with two or three colleagues rather than with twenty or thirty, drawing out a modest classroom experiment over several years, are not necessarily signs of a lesser engagement, but simply of another *kind* of engagement.

SOME EVIDENCE FROM THE LIFE-CYCLE STUDY OF SWISS TEACHERS

Since reviews of this study have been published elsewhere,[27] let me summarize some of its main parameters. This was an interview study, conducted between 1982 and 1986 with 160 secondary-level teachers in Geneva and Vaud, of whom roughly two-thirds taught at the lower-secondary level and the remainder taught in the upper-secondary, pre-university division. Four 'experience groups' were chosen: five to ten years of experience, 11 to 19 years, 20 to 29 years and 30 to 39 years. Within this sampling frame (level, sex and years of experience) a random sample was generated. It contained teachers of all subject-matter areas in equivalent proportions to the referent population. Since each interview lasted approximately four hours, usually in two sittings, there was the opportunity to reap the benefits both of a clinical study and of inferential generalization to a larger population. The same study was replicated in Zurich, with strikingly similar results.[28]

In the next few pages, let me try to review the main findings of the segment of the study relating directly to career sequences. Many of these data came from the first question put to respondents, who were asked to review their career trajectory and to see whether they could carve it up into 'phases' or 'stages'. For each phase, they were to provide an overarching name or theme and to note the features constituting that theme. Note that, aside from the constriction of the data into phases, there are no constraints on the informant. She can choose any theme, any sequence, any configuration of features. Also, since this is the opening question, there are no cues inducing a response set. Nor is she probed for explanations, but rather for a descriptive narrative.

Through a series of analytic 'overlays' of individual trajectories, first within subsets of informants (four 'experience groups', both sexes, both levels of schooling — lower secondary and upper secondary), four modal 'sequences' were derived, encompassing 90 per cent of the usable protocols. Let us look at two of these, one in the early years of the career cycle and one near the end:

SEQUENCE 1. 'HARMONY RECOVERED' (5 to 10 and 11 to 19 years of experience).

Painful beginnings ⟶ **Stabilization** ⟶ **Experimentation**

Must one begin painfully? Not necessarily, but one third of the sample lived their initial experience that way, defining the first phase exclusively in these terms. Elsewhere in the study our respondents were asked to go over their initial year of teaching in some detail. Close to a half recited a familiar litany: a sense of being overwhelmed, continual trial-and-error, vacillation between excessive strictness and permissiveness, exhaustion, difficulties with pupil discipline, fear of judgements on the part of other teachers or administrators, intimidation by some pupils. Also, these descriptions came *after*, not before, the formal programme of teacher preparation — a finding not restricted to Switzerland nor even to studies of European teachers.

The stabilization phase is, as we saw, a staple of the life-cycle literature, and the Swiss data reflect closely the trends of other empirical work. This is a mostly positive phase, with its multiple components of commitment to the profession, acquisition of tenure, consolidation of a basic pedagogical repertoire and integration in a group of professional peers. And this phase gives way to another, archetypal theme: experimentation within and outside the classroom, in order to get a better shot at the instructional outcomes one is after, and which are being depressed by curricular or institutional constraints.

Now for a look at the last modal career sequence:

SEQUENCE 4. 'RENEWAL' with a positive or negative issue
(11 to 19, 20 to 29, 30 to 39 years of experience)

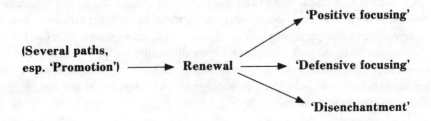

This is the most representative trajectory in the sample, comprising some 40 per cent of the teachers of the three age groups. The term 'renewal' (other informants speak of 'reform' or 'major change') implies structural reform here, and is primarily linked to structural changes enacted in Geneva between 1962 and 1972. There was, in addition, the influence of the so-called 'events of May 1968' in Paris, the students' revolution. All secondary schools were affected, as were many primary-school teachers who taught in the upper grades and were assimilated into the 'orientation' schools. This constituted a promotion in terms of status, working hours and salary, hence the 'promotion' theme mentioned on the chart.

As the chart shows, 'renewal' is the determinant of successive phases, in this case of the ultimate one. *Positive focusing* is our term for this; respondents spoke of 'cultivating my garden' or of 'doing my thing' or of 'specializing', although the term 'focusing' was also explicitly present. We chose to call this scenario 'positive' for two reasons: our informants construed it this way, and it contrasts thematically with the next scenario.

The gist of informants' accounts was that the 'renewal' phase had been expansive; teachers now want to contract. This meant focusing on a preferred grade level, subject matter or type of pupil; disinvesting in school work and increasing outside interests; reducing contacts with peers other than those of one's most convivial group; avoiding additional administrative tasks or out-of-hours commitments; and not getting involved in future school-wide innovations. As noted, the tone is resolutely positive, but there is a clear sense of pulling back; something, even, of a narcissist entitlement: 'I've done my share; now leave me alone to do what I want'.

Defensive focusing has many of the same features: specializing, reducing commitments, using seniority to carve out a comfortable schedule, relating only to a small circle of peers. The tone, however, is different. These are essentially people who were brought kicking and screaming through the 'renewal phase'. They are traditionalists who disapproved of the majority of changes enacted and who disapprove of the outcomes. In some ways, the first portrait painted by Ivor Goodson in the previous chapter, that of an unrepentent elitist pulled unwillingly through comprehensive school reform in the UK and who then shifts his professional energies outside the school, is an apt illustration.

Disenchantment is a respondent's term, and it carries a sense of bitterness. Most informants approved of the 'renewals' but judge the sequel much like the defensive focusers: amorphous pupils, Babbitt-like administrators, ill-advised policies, mindless paperwork. There are, however, two new chords. First, the themes of 'fatigue' and 'lassitude' come through clearly. Next, there is bitterness over the failure of the reforms, much of it directed at 'turncoat' administrators who failed to follow through when the going got rough. Most of these informants are men.

PREDICTING THE POSITIVE FOCUSERS AND THE OTHERS

Trends in the Swiss data, then, seem to mirror fairly well both some of the more fragmentary findings of research on the teaching career and the overarching patterns found in the life-cycle literature more generally. More intriguingly, these findings beg some obvious, important questions. For example, what distinguishes teachers who end their careers in a phase of positive focusing from those who focus negatively or who disengage bitterly? And what does that tell us about the royal roads to career satisfaction or dissatisfaction? To what extent can these career paths be managed or even influenced by others?

In effect, we spent a lot of time on attempts to predict the later phases of teaching from earlier ones. Essentially, we boiled down data from the leitmotivs and features mentioned by informants for each career phase. By generating factor scores for each informant, we were then able to see which features within which leitmotivs discriminated between older teachers reporting an ultimate phase of 'satisfaction' and those describing that phase in terms of 'disenchantment'.

It turned out that, statistically at least, the ultimate discriminant analysis was powerful (canonical r = 0.84, p < 0.001), predicting correctly 89 per cent of the cases of 'disenchantment' and 97 per cent of the cases of 'satisfaction'. But it did not predict them early; that is, before teachers were about 12 or 15 years into their career. Still, the few early predictors that emerged are suggestive. Put briefly: teachers who steered clear of reforms or other multiple-classroom innovations, but who invested consistently in classroom-level experiments — what they called 'tinkering' with new materials, different pupil grouping, small changes in grading systems — were more likely to be satisfied later on in their career than most others, and far more likely to be satisfied than their peers who had been heavily involved in school-wide or district-wide projects.

So 'tinkering', together with an early concern for instructional efficiency ('getting it down to a routine, getting the materials right for most situations I run into') was one of the strongest predictors of ultimate satisfaction. Inversely, heavy involvement in school-wide innovation was a fairly strong predictor of 'disenchantment' after 20 or 25 years of teaching. Tending one's private garden, pedagogically speaking, seems to have more pay-off in the long term than land reform, although the latter is perceived as stimulating and enriching while it is happening.

Two other factors were predictive of professional satisfaction later in the career cycle. The first was a *slight, spontaneous role shift when one began to feel stale*. In this subset of teachers, every fourth or fifth year brought with it a change in grade level, subject matter, school building or academic stream; one might move, say, to slightly older pupils in a less academic stream and teach more history and less Latin in one's subject-matter mix. 'Keeps the brain cells from dying off', said one informant, 'and gives me a bigger bag of tricks in the classroom'. Note that these people are not warding off stagnation by leaving the classroom but by drawing on what diversity there is — and there is plenty — within the bounds of classroom instruction.

The second factor was, strictly speaking, more associated with long periods of professional satisfaction than with a career that ended on that note. It had to do, simply, with *the experience of achieving significant results in the classroom* — with a long, almost magical string of years in which apathetic pupils came alive, classrooms buzzed with purposeful activity, relationships with pupils were intense, and performance levels were well above the average. In many instances this corresponded to a major instructional shift on the teachers' part — to a new set of didactic materials, to a more diagnostic approach, to an interest-centred curriculum — which brought in its wake some exceptional results,[29] but there

131

were other influences at work as well. For example, a diabolical string of unmanageable classes could put an end to these 'magical years'. This suggests — and is worth attending to — that many sources of career satisfaction and dissatisfaction in teaching are beyond any one teacher's volitional control; they depend mostly on the lottery of the year's assignment of pupils, but also on the enlightenment or obtuseness of the newly assigned department head or school principal, on the wisdom or folly of the district's choice of reading, language or science programme, and so on.

MASTERING THE COMPONENTS OF TEACHING

As one reviews the trends outlined above, there emerges an image of the harmonious teaching career that is perhaps surprising in its simplicity. It would seem that the secondary-school teachers in our sample thrive when they are able to tinker productively inside classrooms in order to obtain the instructional and relational effects they are after. To do this, they appear to need manageable working conditions, opportunities to experiment modestly without strong sanctions if things go awry, periodic shifts in role assignments, access to collegial expertise and external stimulation, and a good shot at significant learning outcomes for their pupils. In the best cases, our informants sought out these conditions themselves. More prescriptively, one can imagine that people may often have to be nudged; for example, they might be nudged to try out *all* the parts of a new science module, nudged to take on, periodically, a higher or lower grade level or pupils in another academic track, or nudged to check out more closely what their more dynamic peers are doing. In other words, the strongest sources of career satisfaction may lie potentially under our noses, in the classroom, provided that some minimal conditions — some slack, variety, challenge and tolerable work assignment — are met.

If these conditions are not met, there is some cause for alarm. For example, levels of career satisfaction in our sample were distinctly higher for women than for men, and for part-time teachers than for full-time people.[30] Essentially, this meant that people with a heavy investment outside their work, be it childcare or an avocation, were happier with their teaching careers than their full-time and — the case for many men — heavily engaged colleagues. If strong engagement in your work buys you misery and part-time employment buys you happiness, there must be something wrong with the work conditions, not necessarily day-to-day but over the long term.

This being the case, one could claim that a number of malcontented men might be those having sought, but not obtained, administrative posts at an earlier point in their career. In the Geneva context this is unlikely (fewer administrative posts, relatively small salary differential, marginal status enhancement, 'rotation' system among department staff for the role of department head). On the other hand, there may well have been resentment among lower-secondary teachers who did not make it into the more elitist streams of the upper-secondary schools.

But we have strayed a bit from the line of reasoning on which we have just embarked. If career satisfaction is tied up with the tasks and conditions of class-room instruction, we need to ask three questions. First, which facets of one's work matter the most? Next, how well are these facets mastered at different points in the career cycle? Last, how do teachers go about mastering those facets with which they are having trouble?

There are some data elsewhere in our life-cycle study that can help to answer some of these questions. Working from what is best known as the 'perceived problems' approach[31] we developed a checklist designed to measure the skills which secondary-school teachers would deem the most important. This was a long, perilous enterprise, involving multiple respondent panels and several interactions. We were not after a prescriptive list, nor were we interested in the factors derived from correlational studies of teacher effectiveness. Rather, we were after core features of professional activity that teachers would acknowl-edge as such, on their own terms and with their own weightings.[32]

Once derived, piloted and correlated with segments of comparable instru-ments, we took the 18-item checklist to our 160 informants and asked them to estimate their current levels of mastery; and, for those fully or mostly mastered, to estimate how many years it took them to get on top of each facet. For example, Table 8.1 shows a distribution of the facets which appear to have been mostly or fully mastered by at least 65 per cent of our informants. It is possible — even likely — that some of these estimates are inflated, and that a response of 'mostly' mastered is more accurately one of 'more or less' mastered. All the same, note that, for 8–17 per cent of the sample, including at least 40 per cent with more than 20 years of teaching experience, these facets are not mastered.

Continuing in this vein, Table 8.2 shows the most problematic facets — the ones mastered by no more than 60 per cent of the sample. Four of these five aspects are resolutely instructional, and at least two pose problems for at least a third of the sample. Since all respondents have at least five years' experience under their belts and the majority have at least fifteen, we can assume that a large number of experienced teachers are having trouble with aspects of their work which they themselves acknowledge to be central ones.

For roughly half of the 18 facets, 67 per cent of those respondents who claimed to be fully or mostly in a situation of mastery said that it had taken them at least five years to get there. For three of those facets (pupils below grade level, various modes of work in the classroom, a sense of being as competent as one's experienced peers), 67 per cent of the respondents claimed that they had needed six to ten years.

How did they get there? How did the others try to get there? These are, of course, critical questions in that we are addressing what teachers claim to be core components of their work, and for which mastery did not come easily — if, in fact, it came at all. The answers are instructive, and they lead us to the

Table 8.1. Facets of teaching mastered by 65 per cent of the sample (n = 160)

Facet	Mastered?							
	yes		mostly		no		n/a*	
	n	*%*	*n*	*%*	*n*	*%*	*n*	*%*
Having a variety of lessons and materials that address most situations	127	79	17	11	12	8	4	2
Feeling as professionally competent as the experienced peers in my reference group	125	78	7	4	15	9	13	8
Finding the right standards — not too demanding nor too lax	125	78	16	10	18	11	1	0.6
Accepting unsuccessful days or weeks philosophically	116	73	10	6	34	21	—	—
Feeling generally competent as a pedagogue	109	68	26	16	18	11	7	4
Getting back on top of a class with which the year began dismally	64	67	13	14	12	13	7	6
Covering the prescribed curriculum without overloading lessons and exercises	104	65	20	13	27	17	9	5

*n/a = judged not applicable

Table 8.2. Poorly mastered facets of teaching: marginal data (n = 160)

Facet	Mastered?							
	yes		mostly		no		n/a*	
	n	*%*	*n*	*%*	*n*	*%*	*n*	*%*
Acknowledge, without over-reacting, criticism from others	95	59	16	10	34	21	15	10
Work in different modes: collectively, in groups, individually	91	57	13	8	42	26	14	9
Be instructionally effective for both rapid *and* slow pupils	65	41	24	15	59	37	12	7
Generate, sustain interest on the part of poorly motivated pupils	64	40	49	31	44	28	3	1
Bring up to speed the pupils starting the year below grade level	54	34	33	21	52	33	21	13

*n/a = judged not applicable

intersection between inservice training and professional development more generally (see Table 8.3). In 90 per cent of the cases, which covers the full set of facets, our respondents say they act alone 'in my corner', on their subject matter or on small experiments in which materials or instructional modes are varied incrementally until a promising mix is found, then consolidated. Next in importance, but well behind, comes work with a small group of colleagues. Note that we are still in a small, bounded, informal universe, and we have used up 74 per cent of the responses. Inservice offerings come next, but they seem to be relatively underutilized for strictly instructional purposes — despite the fact that offerings in Geneva and Vaud are munificent. They may well serve other, useful purposes, such as keeping up to date in one's field, having some interesting exchanges, making new contacts and so on, but they are distal to the core components of classroom mastery.

Table 8.3. Attempts to achieve mastery of core facets of teaching (n = 93)*

Type of attempt	Number of responses	Percentage of responses	Percentage of cases
Little experiments — trial and error	56	39	58
Personal research on one's subject matter	31	22	32
Work with a small group of colleagues	19	13	20
Inservice training	18	13	19
Work on one's own personality or work habits	11	8	11
Recourse to specialists	2	1	2
Other attempts (miscellaneous)	6	4	6

*Multiple responses (n = 143)

ARTISANRY, TRAINING AND CAREER DEVELOPMENT

These analyses are beginning to funnel into some strong assumptions. The strongest, perhaps, is that *the best scenario for satisfactory career development is through a 'craft' model.* Essentially, teachers are artisans working primarily alone, with a variety of new and cobbled-together materials, in a personally designed work environment. They gradually develop a repertoire of instructional skills and strategies, corresponding to a progressively denser, more differentiated and well-integrated set of mental schemata; they come to read the instructional situation better and faster, and to respond to it with a greater variety of tools. They develop this repertoire through a somewhat haphazard process of trial and error, usually when one or another segment of the repertoire does not work repeatedly. Somewhere in that cycle they may reach out to peers or even to professional trainers, but they will typically transform those inputs into a more private, personally congenial form. When things go well, when the routines work smoothly and pupils are attentive and productive, there is a rush of craft pride that translates into what has come to be called 'self-efficacy'[33] or, for our purposes here, 'personal teaching efficacy'.[34] That sense of efficacy then drives the quest for further experimentation and, within that cycle, leads to a more active scanning of the environment for new skills or materials. When things do not go well, cycles of experimentation and scanning are intensified. I have tried, elsewhere, to spell out these points a bit more.[35]

A second assumption is that *the shape of inservice training most likely to further such a model will need to be grafted on to the ways in which teachers spontaneously go about tinkering with their classrooms* — alone, with a small group of colleagues, in informal and idiosyncratic ways, much as we say in Table 8.3. This, in turn, will call for a radical shift in the ways in which most inservice offerings are provided. Whereas we have spent many years developing fully equipped district or regional centres, we should probably have invested in a thousand makeshift bungalows set near a small cluster of schools.[36]

The problem with both these assumptions is that they derive from best-case scenarios: from teachers who continue to tinker actively within their instructional setting, to generate variety when classroom routines are fully consolidated, to reach out spontaneously for new inputs. Yet our life-cycle research, along with others', turned up large cohorts of teachers who disengaged after only 10 or 15 years of experience, or who made no attempts to change instructional practices which they themselves judged to be problematic. It is noteworthy, of course, that these people tended to feel professionally dissatisfied. But that does not tell us how to intervene. Clearly, the 'spontaneous experimentation' model outlined above does not fit them, at least at later stages in their careers. Nor does the regnant model of staff training seem to apply,[37] in that it assumes a pliant, slightly compulsive public of teachers willing to assimilate conceptual inputs, attend closely to models, submit to critical feedback in their attempts to change ongoing instructional practice, and be coached via hands-on assistance from consultants and peers. The evidence is strong that this model works better than conventional, looser modes of staff development, most of which lack the key components of structured practice, feedback and coaching. But it is uncertain that this approach works especially well for more passive, more disengaged teachers, or even that more active, experienced, individualistic teachers will go with these kinds of highly scripted and codified procedures, and ones that do not necessarily address the peculiar mix of problems and opportunities that they are contending with at the moment.

On the basis of what we have seen earlier in this chapter, and with the objective of reaching all species of experienced teachers, I propose to work in four directions. Spelling out each one calls for far more detail than the length that this chapter allows, but let me touch briefly on all four.

First would come the attempt to increase the number and quality of colleagues or experts to whom teachers turn spontaneously in the course of their private tinkerings and experimentation in their classrooms. When I am in trouble, or when I am looking for new geography materials, I am likely to turn to another geography teacher in my building, or to one I met at an inservice course, or to one I know from student teaching days. All are relatively close by, trust-worthy and of potential help. They may not, however, have anything to offer me that I do not already have; they are not necessarily the highest-quality sources in my environment, but they *are* in my network. The trick, then, is to expand the network — to include a greater number of people, including some craftspeople likely to have some new tricks to teach me. This is the kind of endeavour that many teachers' centres are skilled at, but there are other models of networking that are equally effective.

In line with this strategy, we would probably need to decentralize the resources to generate and sustain such networks; that is, to move the budgets for released time, materials and consultants closer to the people using them than to the administrators and centres providing the services. This is no small task; it entails the creation of a private-sector mentality within a public-centre manage-ment, and it strips the number of administrative jobs in the district. Unfortu-nately, both of each measures violate the laws of bureaucratic physics. Note that here we enter into the logic of a supply-side economy of staff development: groups of teachers across schools or subgroups of teachers within schools applying for and 'spending' resources for collaborative work which typically includes a con-ceptual, observational and experimental phase. Our experience in Geneva, for example, has been that the shifting of these resources out of the central office has done wonders for the responsiveness of staff development centres, which are redundant if they are not called upon. There is a world of difference between a centre which devises and offers courses and one which provides backing for tem-porary groups of teachers working in a problem space that is collectively mean-ingful and is usually of some urgency.

Next, we would have to deal with (a) the more passive, disengaged, morbidly suspicious colleagues in the profession, and (b) with the tendency of spontaneous working groups of teachers to fly off in several directions for several weeks at a time. This entails some deliberate recruitment into a network of people who would otherwise have worked alone. It also entails, for some of the activities, some structuring or technical assistance on the part of peers, experts or consultants. But the key lies in the ways by which the group works through its tasks and, in particular, *the necessity of each member actually to experiment in the classroom with the skills or strategies that emerge from discussions and observations.* As the French say, 'il faut passer à l'acte'. Staff development activities that include actual experimentation over time, along with some collection of data before, dur-ing and after these attempts, are far more likely to produce durable instructional change.[38] I have tried to argue above that the chief *reason* why this mode is effective is that it involves the kind of tinkering which teachers use spontaneously to test, improve and derive pleasure from their work. Loosely structuring this pro-cess should raise it to a much higher power when one brings into it peers trying out similar approaches, opportunities for ongoing exchange, access to consultants or to fellow craftspeople slightly more skilled in this area than oneself and, probably, more intensity and care than one would spontaneously put into it if one were alone.

Finally, we might bring in a component I have deliberately avoided until now: the 'work place' conditions within the school itself. There has been pioneering and exciting work[39] on the institutional conditions which foster collaboration and experimentation among school staff. Unfortunately, much of it has to do with conditions of leadership that appear to be exceptional and unstable; they are not easily built into the warp of conventional schools nor even sustained when exceptional principals leave the building. School buildings, like schoolteachers, have life cycles of their own, with phases never to be recaptured. Nor has it been shown conclusively that higher levels of interaction and co-ordination among groups of teachers translate into measurable changes at the classroom level. In effect, the artisan model — working alone, in unique conditions, with unique tools and in a personally congenial mode developed over a long period of isolation — is a difficult one to change. There is some good evidence, however, that collective attempts to revise practices within individual schools can be successful.[40]

Qualitative improvements in the school as a work place might make a demonstrable, long-term difference — provided that they translate into the kinds of instructional mastery that seems to enhance satisfaction with one's work as an artisan of learning. We might even find that the professional life cycle of teachers within these places plays out differently as compared with the trajectories shown earlier — that there are schools in which staff members do not disengage later in their careers, do not end up uniquely tending their own gardens, do not feel the stale breath of routine after only eight to ten years into the profession, and in which one only hears stories about mid-career crises in buildings other than in one's own.

NOTES

1. Wittrock, M. (ed.), *Handbook of Research on Teaching* (3rd edn). New York: Macmillan, 1986.

2. Floden, R. and Huberman, M., 'The state of the art of research on teachers' professional lives'. *International Journal of Educational Research*, 13 (4), pp. 455–66. Special issue of IJER, *Research on Teachers' Professional Lives*, 1989.

3. Erikson, E., *Childhood and Society*. New York: Norton, 1950.

4. White, R., *Lives in Progress*. New York: Dryden, 1952.

5. Becker, H., 'The career of the Chicago schoolmaster'. In Becker, H. (ed.), *Sociological Work: Method and Substance*. Chicago: Aldine, 1970.

6. Baltes, P. and Brim, O., *Life-Span Development and Behavior*, Vol. 6. New York: Academic Press, 1984.

7. Huberman, M., Grounauer, M. -M. and Marti, J., *La vie des enseignants.* Paris and Lausanne: Delachaux & Niestlé, 1989; and Huberman, M., 'The professional life cycle of teachers'. *Teachers College Record*, 91 (3), pp. 31–57, 1989.

8. Super, D., 'Coming of age in Middletown'. *American Psychologist*, 40 (4), pp. 405–14, 1980.

9. Shneidman, E., 'The Indian summer of life: a preliminary study of septuagenarians'. *American Psychologist*, 44 (4), pp. 684–94, 1989.

10. For a more complete treatment of this and the following points, see Huberman, 'The professional life cycle of teachers', op. cit., note 7; and Huberman, M., 'On teachers' careers: once over lightly, with a broad brush'. *International Journal of Educational Research*, 13 (4), pp. 347–62. Special issue of IJER, *Research on Teachers' Professional Lives*, 1989.

11. See, for example, Veenman, S., 'Perceived problems of beginning teachers'. *Review of Educational Research*, 54 (2), pp. 143–78, 1984.

12. White, op. cit., note 4.

13. Watts, H., *Starting Out, Moving On, Running Ahead.* San Francisco: Teachers' Centers Exchange, 1979.

14. Peterson, W., 'Age, teacher's role and the institutional setting'. In Biddle, B. and Elena, W. (eds), *Contemporary Research on Teacher Effectiveness.* New York; Holt, Rinehart, 1964; and Lightfoot, S., 'The lives of teachers'. In Shulman, L. and Sykes, G. (eds), *Handbook of Teaching and Policy.* New York: Longman, 1985.

15. Sikes, P., 'The life cycle of the teacher'. In Ball, S. and Goodson, I. (eds), *Teachers' Lives and Careers.* Lewes: Falmer Press, pp. 27–60, 1986.

16. Cooper, M., *The Study of Professionalism in Teaching.* Paper presented at American Educational Research Association, New York, 1982; and Prick, L., 'Satisfaction and stress among teachers'. *International Journal of Educational Research*, 13 (4), pp. 363–77. Special issue of IJER, *Research on Teachers' Professional Lives*, 1989.

17. Hunter, S. and Sundel, M., 'An examination of key issues concerning mid-life'. In Hunter, S. and Sundel, M. (eds), *Midlife Myths.* Newburg Park, CA: Sage, pp. 8–28, 1988.

18. See, for example, Prick, L., *Career Development and Satisfaction among Secondary School Teachers.* Amsterdam: Vrije Universiteit Amsterdam, 1986.

19. Peterson, op. cit., note 14.

20. See, for example, Riley, M. W., Hess, B. B. and Bond, K. *Aging and Society*, Vol. 1. New York: Russell Sage, 1968.

21. Becker, op. cit., note 5.

22. Kuhlen, R., 'Developmental changes in motivation during the adult years'. In Birren, J. (ed.), *Relationships of Development and Aging.* Springfield, IL: Thomas, 1964.

23. Neugarten, B. and Datan, N., 'The middle years'. In Arieti, S. (ed.), *American Handbook of Psychiatry*, Vol. 1. New York: Basic Books, pp. 492–608, 1974.

24. Jung, C., 'The stages of life'. In *Collected Works*, Vol. 8. Princeton, NJ: Princeton University Press, Bollingen Series XX, pp. 749–95, 1930.

25. Heidegger, M., *Being and Time.* New York: Harper & Row, 1926.

26. Maehr, M. and Kleiber, D., 'The graying of achievement motivation'. *American Psychologist*, 37 (4), pp. 787–93, 1981.

27. Huberman *et al.*, *La vie des enseignants*, op. cit., note 7; Huberman, 'The professional life cycle of teachers', op. cit., note 7; and Huberman, M., *Teacher Professionalism and Workplace Conditions.* Paper presented at Holmes Group seminar on 'Conceptions of teachers' work and the organization of schools'. East Lansing, MI: Michigan State University, 1988.

28. Hirsch, G. and Ganguillet, G., *Einstellungen, Engagement und Belastung des Lehrens: Ein lebernsgeschichtlicher Ansatz.* Zurich: Päd. Abteilung der Erziehungsdirektion des Kantons Zürich, 1988.

29. See for similar evidence: Guskey, T., 'Attitude and perceptual change in teachers'. *International Journal of Educational Research*, 13 (4), pp. 439–53. Special issue of IJER, *Research on Teachers' Professional Lives*, 1989.

30. See for similar trends: Prick, op. cit., note 18; and Prick, 'Satisfaction and stress among teachers', op. cit., note 16.

31. See, for example, Cruickshank, D., Kennedy, J. and Myers, B., 'Perceived problems of secondary school teachers'. *Journal of Educational Research*, 68 (2), pp. 155–9, 1974.

32. For more details, see Huberman, M., 'What knowledge is most worth to teachers?: a knowledge-use perspective'. *Teaching and Teacher Education*, 1 (3), pp. 251–63, 1985.

33. Bandura, A., 'Self-efficacy: toward a unifying theory of behavioral change'. *Psychological Review*, 84, pp. 191–215, 1977.

34. Smylie, M., 'The enhancement function of staff development: organizational and psychological antecedents to individual teacher change'. *American Educational Research Journal*, 25 (1), pp. 1–30, 1988.

35. Huberman, M., 'Teacher careers and school improvement'. *Journal of Curriculum Studies*, 20 (2), pp. 119–32, 1988.

36. Huberman, op. cit., note 32; and Howey, K. and Vaughan, J., 'Current patterns of staff development'. In Griffin, G. (ed.), *Staff Development*, 82nd Yearbook of NSSE, Chicago: University of Chicago Press, pp. 92–117, 1983.

37. See Joyce, B. and Showers, B., 'Improving in-service training: the messages of research'. *Educational Leadership*, 37, pp. 379–85, February 1980; Wade, R., 'What makes a difference in in-service teacher education?: a meta-analysis of research'. *Educational Leadership*, 42, pp. 48–54, 1985; and Daresh, J., 'Research trends in staff development and in-service education'. *Journal of Education for Teaching*, 13 (1), pp. 3–11, 1987.

38. See, for example, Hoover, N. and Carroll, R., 'Self-assessment of classroom instruction: an effective approach to in-service education'. *Teaching and Teacher Education*, 3 (3), pp. 179–91, 1987; and Loucks, S. and Melle, M., 'Evaluation of staff development. How do you know it took?'. *Journal of Staff Development*, 3, pp. 102–17, 1982.

39. See, for example, Little, J., 'Norms of collegiality and experimentation: workplace conditions of school success'. *American Educational Research Journal*, 19 (3), pp. 325–40, 1982; Little, J., 'Teachers as Colleagues'. In Richardson-Koehler, V. (ed.), *Educators' Handbook*. New York; Longman, pp. 491–519, 1987; Rosenholtz, S., 'Effective schools: interpreting the evidence'. *American Journal of Education*, pp. 352–87, May 1985; and Rosenholtz, S., Bassler, O. and Hoover-Dempsey, N., 'Organizational conditions of teacher learning', *Teaching and Teacher Education*, 2 (2), pp. 91–104, 1986.

40. See, for example, Leithwood, K. and Montgomery, D., 'The role of the elementary school principal in program improvement'. *Review of Educational Research*, 52 (3), pp. 309–39, 1982; Stevenson, R., 'Staff development for effective secondary schools: a synthesis of research'. *Teaching and Teacher Education*, 3 (3), 1987, pp. 233–48; and Rosenholtz, S., 'Education reform strategies: will they increase teacher commitment?'. *American Journal of Education*, pp. 534–62, August 1987.

Chapter 9

Contexts for Teacher Development: Insights from Teachers' Stories

Danielle Raymond, Richard Butt and David Townsend

INTRODUCTION

This chapter draws on a long-term research project which uses teachers' autobiographies to understand the nature of teachers' knowledge and development. The project forms part of an increasing body of research which uses biographical methods to understand teachers' lives, careers, cultures and life-worlds.[1] In this chapter we suggest ways to support and facilitate teacher development. In order to do this, we first present condensed accounts of three teachers' autobiographies. Through an analysis of these three cases, and from a preliminary examination of over 80 teacher autobiographies, we then discuss some general characteristics of, and conditions for, teacher development. Finally, we evaluate collaborative autobiography as a process for gathering teachers' stories not just for the purpose of research, but also for facilitating teacher development.

In this chapter, the *descriptive* sense of teacher development refers to how teachers actually develop and have developed through the current social conditions of their lives, careers, and experiences of existing educational cultures and contexts. The *intentional* sense of teacher development refers to it as something which can and should be promoted and enhanced. This has more usually been called professional development. Our purpose, in this chapter, is to describe how teacher development appears to occur in the descriptive sense and then transpose descriptive understanding into an intentional sense of teacher development in the latter part of the paper. This shift is also, in a sense, a shift from *event theory* (speculation as to how teacher development occurs) to *praxiological theory* (speculation as to the best means to reach agreed ends).[2] Our aim in this is not to be prescriptive about teacher development, but to identify generic conditions, actions, and contexts which can be created and adapted by teachers and others to assist specific professional development projects.

Danielle Raymond, Richard Butt and David Townsend

THE NATURE OF TEACHER DEVELOPMENT

Three Stories of Teacher Development

Lloyd Lloyd is the third youngest in a family of ten children born to Japanese-Canadian parents. Lloyd, a 38-year-old teacher with 12 years of experience, teaches grade six children of average and below average ability. At the time of the study, he had been at the same school for the previous 11 years and had also been an administrative assistant for four years.

Lloyd's present pedagogy, along with his personal and professional development history, embody three basis aims: *survival*, *safety* and *success*. These aims articulate his relationships to himself, to his personal and cultural history, to his career progression and to his socio-economically disadvantaged pupils. For Lloyd, these aims express strong mutual interests which he translates into a common goal: to move up. This goal is mediated by an image of *family* that gives a strong human quality to his teaching. Through his past sufferings of cultural deprivation this image of family allows him to empathize with his students and provide them with a nurturing environment, structure and direction.

Lloyd's three basic aims are embodied in the social development curriculum he has created for his students. This curriculum derives directly from his personal background and family life, although he also relates it to the needs of his lower socio-economic pupils for upward mobility within the school system. These values were emphasized by his parents and were successful in helping the family to be upwardly mobile. His basic aims are also contained within his academic curriculum, where he takes care to cover institutionalized requirements, including what he thinks are the basics, in a logical, well-planned, sequential, structured and organized fashion. From his experience, these students need to know this material to make sure they move up. His parents' moral sense contributes to his commitment to 'covering' the curriculum. Their work ethic, combined with the need for safety, survival and successful upward mobility, is translated into finding what is acceptable from external guidelines, policies and other resources.

When describing his professional development, Lloyd claims that since the beginning of his career when he learned the basics of teaching, he has changed very little. He locates the main sources of his present pedagogy in his family's basic values, in his experience of cultural deprivation and in his own experience as a pupil. These latter experiences, encapsulated in the influence of his grade five teacher, whom he calls his 'white mother', laid the grounds for the hard work in his first years when he developed materials and worksheets that would teach the basics in a very structured manner.

> Since I learned most of my skills, it seems, from Mrs Hunt, I still
> can remember some of her strategies, many of which were of the
> rote memory type of activities. This had led me to believe that
> with students who are unable to conceptualize data (such as I was

in those days) the use of a similar approach is effective. I try to
use it with my modified students and it seems to be working.

On such firm personal grounds, professional development experiences and
activities are used to strengthen and reinforce deeply ingrained orientations. In
the first years of his career, after a disappointing team-work experience, Lloyd
withdraws to become what he calls 'a closet teacher'. He pulls himself through
with hard work, mainly doing his own thing and making sure his underprivileged
pupils are successful. Later, he becomes more outwardly directed, encouraged
by his involvement with colleagues in an objectives-based education project
that serves to reinforce his disposition for fundamentals, structure, sequence
and organization. Other sources of professional development have served more
immediate, instrumental, technical and acceptance needs. Lloyd evolved, then,
in a professional sense, very early in his career, through his hard work at becoming *his* interpretation of what external sources and internalized cultural and
familial values might see as 'the best possible teacher'. Following this early
development of his teaching competence, he has changed very little. If he has
done so at all, it is in response to mandated policies, changes in roles, or through
technical elaboration of existing skills. Professional development experiences
have allowed him to become more explicitly what he already is.

Glenda At the time of our study Glenda was a 44-year-old teacher with nine
years of experience, two of them in Pakistan. She teaches English as a second
language (ESL) to refugee and immigrant children of low socio-economic status.
She also works as a resource person with regular teachers who have children
with different linguistic and cultural backgrounds in their classrooms.

Within a language development approach, Glenda's pedagogy uses themes
that capture pupils' interests around which she organizes activities that encourage communication. Errors are considered developmental in nature, and students correct themselves as their proficiency increases. They learn and develop
at their own pace as they become ready for the next steps. Glenda does not use
behavioural objectives. She builds her curriculum out of her students' cultural
heritages and communication needs. Two core ideas in Glenda's pedagogy are
self-directedness and self-determination. In her self-directedness Glenda lives
the notion of teacher-as-learner in the classroom where everyone participates in
deciding where to go and what to do next.

Glenda describes her development in terms of a 'slow motion film of a seed
developing and growing into a blossom'. She describes this slow blossoming
process in terms of five phases: 'planting the seed', 'nurturing', 'the bud begins
to open', 'full bloom', and 'planting again'.

Planting the Seed. Glenda's parents, particularly her father, planted the
seed for respect for others as early as the night before she entered grade one,
when he told her that children of different skin colour, eye shape or hair type
would nevertheless be like her because they all had feelings and would all want to
be happy.

Nurturing. Her schooling years provided for the 'development of a strong root system and a stem' in nurturing the seed of interest for other cultures. In grade school, she sought out as much information as she could on other cultures. In high school, Ted Aoki, her social studies teacher (and since then a leading writer on the humanistic character of teaching), made her realize that all this 'information' was personal and humane, and had meaning that affected her as a member of humanity. Ted Aoki was not only a model of what a teacher should be, he also became her mental mentor — a sort of conscience.

The Bud Begins to Open. The bud that appeared at the end of the stem in high school remained closed for several years of teaching home economics, followed by marriage, children and suburbia. Only when her husband joined the Canadian diplomatic corps and was posted to Pakistan did Glenda resume her interests in other cultures. A number of traumatic and paradoxical experiences she identifies as 'culture shock' moved her through euphoria, frustration and irritation, and rejection of the Pakistani culture. This, combined with the oppressive climate of a traditional marriage, and the hierarchical nature of the diplomatic corps (which even denied them something as trivial as a hall table lamp because of their junior status), led to a cathartic outburst and drastic change. In the midst of this personal turmoil, Glenda turned to Ted Aoki, her mentor, and realized that she had to find the personal and humane element in Pakistan. She took an interest in Pakistani people's lives, families, beliefs and dreams. Slowly, while teaching at the International School of Islamabad, the bud began to open. Discussions with her grade ten class of students from 14 different countries brought her to close the teacher's guide and return students' workbooks to the store room. The knowledge about cultural differences was right there in front of her — specifically as it related to the role of women in different cultures.

Full Bloom. Back in Canada, Glenda started teaching ESL at the elementary level, a context that suited both her old and new dispositions. She soon realized that her linguistic-orientated background was getting her into deep trouble and she felt incompetent when questioned by teachers on what to do to help minority children. She put together a professional development plan for herself that involved classroom observation, learning from peers about language-orientated programmes, enrolment in a reading course, and selected courses and workshops on practical applications, classroom strategies and resources. A *personal pedagogy* emphasizing a *developmental approach* slowly emerged over the next four years.

Planting Again. Grounded in a pedagogy that feels enjoyable and comfortable for both her and her students, Glenda now shifts the focus of her efforts beyond the classroom into the development of quality intercultural education throughout the school system.

Glenda's development as a teacher, deeply rooted as it is in early family and schooling influences, has also involved watershed personal experiences in her adult years, experiences that brought her to shun direction by others, to become the author of her own actions, and to begin to understand others on their own terms. Her more recent professional development activities in terms of courses, workshops and so on, and her practical elaboration of her teaching skills and competencies, have therefore taken place through a long process of personal liberation from mandated societal roles, a process that took many years of her adult life. This committed teacher, in full bloom, plants again from a ground that she now knows as her own.

Stephanie Stephanie is 40 years old and teaches grade four in the suburbs of a medium-sized city. Stephanie acquired her 20 years of teaching experience in six different schools. She has taught all grade levels, both as a regular teacher and as a specialist in music and physical education.

A chronicle of Stephanie's professional development activities reveals that she did not attend any particular courses or sessions during the first seven years of her career. During the following 10–11 years she acquired a BEd, a certificate in Educational Technology and a master's degree. She also attended numerous workshops and conferences, especially activities sponsored by the professional association of language arts teachers. Then she took a one-year sabbatical, during which she took some ESL classes. A year ago she got involved in this biographical study that she saw as 'an occasion to reflect on what I was doing'. This sketchy summary, however, does not begin to get at some substantial aspects of Stephanie's development that we need to consider in order to understand what kind of teacher she is in general and why, in particular, she suddenly switched to taking more organized professional programmes.

First, there is the question of Stephanie's commitment to teaching. It has not always been of the same scope or intensity. For the first seven years she was rather unsure about her commitment. She hinted that she might not have freely chosen her own career orientation. Her mother, sisters and brothers are all teachers and she did not want to disappoint them. People investing themselves in you, she said, create obligations that can transform a career, even a life, because it causes you to make choices that are not always according to your own tastes.

After pre-service education Stephanie completed one year at pre-med school and considered, during her first seven years as a teacher, whether to ultimately pursue a medical career instead. By that point, however, she reached a stage where she 'dropped that idea and committed herself to teaching'.

The next ten years of intensive and ongoing formal and informal professional development activities are a clear expression of her commitment. Professional development absorbed most of her time. In her eighth to twelfth years she was involved in a new art school where parents, teachers and the principal worked together for the success of the project. Over the following five years, she seems to have been trying to achieve some balance between her personal and her professional lives, not unlike the mid-career teachers described by Huberman in Chapter 8. She takes care of herself and gets involved in activities where she looks for a greater self-understanding, including her participation in this study. During the past two years, her commitment to teaching has not been so engulfing. She also now seems to be trying to colour her teaching with insights gleaned from personal sources. Thus, while on the surface there seems to be a withdrawal from *institutionalized* professional development activities, her professional development has simply taken a different tack. Stephanie now seeks a more *personal* anchorage for her professional growth.

What was Stephanie exploring through her professional development in the sense of her immediate understanding of, and approach to, teaching? Biographical materials reveal that some of the most important changes with which she had to struggle during her twenty years of teaching were changes in 'a central idea in her philosophy of teaching', 'the idea of responsibility in the learning process'. This 'idea' concerning specific teaching practices has undergone several transformations over the years.

When she started teaching, Stephanie felt that a teacher was totally responsible for the learning in the classroom. This view was embodied in practices emphasizing total classroom control such as 'not doing her own thing while children work'. This initial configuration of the idea of responsibility has several roots in her biography. In her images of the good teacher from her own schooling are imperatives derived from her family of teachers who 'were also "big workers" and put teaching at the centre of their lives', and from her upbringing, where she got the sense that in life *one fulfils obligations to others* and does not go around exploring *one's own choices*. This initial personal grounding of the idea of responsibility was further drilled into her in a pre-service programme emphasizing classroom control and teacher dedication. Moreover, as the youngest in the family she had lacked contact and experience with children, and therefore lacked opportunities to see what they could bring of their own to the learning process.

A first dent in this idea of teaching as control occurred in her sixth year of teaching, when she changed her status to a music and physical education specialist. No longer responsible for teaching the 'most important' subjects such as languges, arts and maths, and feeling less weight on her shoulders, she started to 'relax and to have more interesting contacts with children'. Also, in a different teaching environment where furniture could be moved around, she started experimenting with different teaching practices where children became progressively involved in the choice of activities and lesson content. She was also less insecure now about classroom discipline. She expected that there would be noise and that 'children would not be aligned like onions in a garden'. But, if this seemed to be possible in music and physical education, what about other subject matter areas?

A second series of changes was initiated by another modification of Stephanie's teaching assignment to a grade three regular teaching position in a new art school. In this school, everyone was involved in planning and decision-making and worked as a team. She felt support from colleagues and from the principal to explore practices where she 'would not teach with chalk in her hands with the kids sitting there listening'. This, she said, was a significant moment in the development of her idea of responsibility:

> It is at that moment when I started at Sacred Heart [school] that
> I really started to centre my teaching around the child and not
> around my own role.

Her teaching practices in all basic areas gradually moved towards more involvement of the children in activities, lesson content, and evaluation processes. This was the time when her involvement in formal professional development activities peaked and also when the children provided inspiration for her:

> It is through contact with the children that I gradually realized
> that things could be different, that the child could take more
> room and that it would be positive.

Stephanie went on to explore more 'of the idea of open education', particularly the 'learning centre' and various practices pertaining to what she now calls 'child-centred' teaching. But several factors seem to have set limits on how far she will go in sharing the responsibility for learning with pupils. First, she realized that she 'bumps against' what she refers to as 'her own nature'. She still wants to control the organization of the classroom environment and she realizes that, while it appears that she consults with the children on the learning centres, she none the less tells them how to set them up. Second, after five years, following a disagreement with her colleagues at the art school, she asked for a new assignment and started teaching in another school where she changed grade levels each year, unable to find another teacher also willing to set up her classroom in learning centres. Feeling overworked, exhausted and isolated, Stephanie eventually dropped the learning centre idea and worked from a view of responsibility where children were not involved in decisions pertaining to the general organization of the classroom, but could still pick up themes and at their own pace during particular learning activities. She summarizes her present position as follows:

> My objective is not to have children make all the decisions, so
> they'll be sitting on my head in the classroom. But I want them
> to feel that I am close to them.

Again, in Stephanie's case, we can see that the process of teacher development has to be understood in relation to personal sources, influences, issues and contexts. While changes in status and institutional mandates provide both possibilities for, and limitations to, her development, there is also a deeper, more personal struggle to carve *her self* out of several conflicting influences, some of them deeply ingrained ones that she refers to as 'her own nature'. Paradoxically, however, this 'nature' is as much imposed by others as it is her own. Her professional development is, in this sense, an enactment of a long process of creating *her self*, of making and living out the consequences of a biography.

GENERAL CHARACTERISTICS OF TEACHER DEVELOPMENT

What insights and conclusions can we draw from these three teachers' accounts of their personal and professional development? What do their biographies tell us? In the most general sense, they draw our attention to the fact that in order to begin to facilitate teacher development we first need to understand how it already occurs. This involves a number of further questions that need to be addressed. What are the major substantive sources of teacher development? What helps or hinders changes and growth in teachers? What events, contexts, conditions and relationships have a telling impact on teachers' professional knowledge and practice? And how can we foster teacher development in a way that allows for healthy individuality as well as collegiality? Understanding teacher development in these descriptive senses should enable us to enhance that process further through explicit and intentional attempts at professional development.

The Primacy and Persistence of Early Personal Experience

The foregoing accounts of three teachers' development emphasize the importance of pre-teaching influences and processes for their professional identity as well as for framing the way they change during their careers. As Goodson argues in Chapter 7, pre-training experiences provide the foundations which not only influence the way a teacher begins to teach, but also act as lifelong references for teacher identity even when these grounds are shaken by later classroom experiences.

The power of pre-training personal influences is evident even at later stages of teacher development, in the ways and the very terms by which teachers describe these influences. For instance, Lloyd calls his 'three basic aims' the values of survival, safety and success that were emphasized by his parents, and that he has carried into his pedagogy and his own professional development. 'Survival, safety and success' are basic to his own fabric as a person and as a teacher. Glenda encapsulates in the word 'conscience' her high-school social studies teacher's contribution as a model of what a teacher should be. Stephanie summarizes in the phrase 'her own nature' a fundamental aspect of her teaching self. This aspect concerns the issue of responsibility, and is derived from images of 'the good teacher' present in her own schooling and enacted by family members who put teaching at the centre of their lives. The terms chosen to describe the impact of family and schooling experiences point to long-lasting and deeply set dispositions that remain at the core of the teacher's developmental process throughout a career. Moreover, 'my three basic aims', 'my conscience' and 'my own nature' reformulate teacher development in existential terms as a process that is inseparable from the construction and expression of the teacher's personal identity. Whether influences from later experiences confirm, challenge or even invalidate these initial dispositions, these later influences inevitably brush against this fundamental personal ground. As Louden (Chapter 11) and Oberg and Underwood (Chapter 10) also show, it is against this personal ground that teachers appear to assess their opportunities for professional development.

The depth of pre-teaching influences is also underlined by the language which teachers use to describe how these initial dispositions were acquired. Lloyd tells how his parents 'had an uncanny ability to *engrain* these values of theirs into their children without the use of physical force or verbal abuse'. Glenda depicts her father's influence on her identity as a teacher of ESL in terms of his 'planting the seed' of respect for others. Stephanie's preoccupation with the teacher's responsibility in the learning process was 'drilled' into her by teachers in her family and in her own schooling.

Teachers' words for the kind of impact on their teaching and for the processes by which this impact is felt to have been achieved point to the strength, depth and persistence of personal pre-professional history in shaping their development as teachers. This also seems to be the case for many other teachers. From a preliminary analysis of our collection of over eighty teacher autobiographies, regardless of subject, grade level and other contextual teaching factors, we can discern that various sources and influences (parents, relatives, schoolteachers, the nature of the family, home, ethnicity, religion and location) from the teachers' pre-professional life history are continually evoked and reconstructed to establish a firm emotional and moral ground that helps form teachers' professional commitment and identity. Informal and formal professional activities, challenging innovations or teaching experiences all seem to be assessed against this personal ground, even at later stages in these teachers' careers.

Through Lloyd, Glenda and Stephanie we can understand Nias's notion of the 'substantial self': the person we bring into the classroom context and its impact on teaching. 'If we wish to understand teachers we must attempt to learn more about these personal dispositions . . . the deeply held substantial view of selfs.'[3] Many teachers within contemporary classroom contexts feel a need to defend and affirm the substantial self. Nias speculates that these needs lead to a self-reinforcement of isolation and privacy to avoid differences and lack of agreement with colleagues.[4]

This should not be understood as implying that teachers' orientations are so deeply set when entering pre-service education that no significant further professional development is possible. Rather, the 'apprenticeship of teaching'[5] that occurs before pre-service education seems to delineate broad areas for future development. These early grounds for teacher development can subsequently be reshaped in various conscious and unconscious ways and, in turn, can influence classroom practice in many different ways. Yet, regardless of all these transformations, teachers do not appear to lose track of where they come from. Significant people, events or relationships that occurred prior to teacher education are repeatedly invoked to infuse meaning and purpose to these transformations. Conversely, if classroom realities or imposed institutional changes challenge the teacher at the very core of these developmental areas, these might precipitate inner struggles and deeply felt contradictions leading to slow transformations, disaffirmation or possibly withdrawal.

Professional Development as Personal Development

Already made uniquely idiosyncratic by pre-training experiences, teacher development seems to become even more personal during the teacher's career. First of all, while varieties in teaching contexts have to be dealt with on a situation-by-situation basis, they are also interpreted by each teacher according to his or her particular configuration of basic teaching dispositions. This configuration frames teachers' understanding of classroom reality and their development of pedagogy. Teachers do not just encounter experiences and resources in their schools and classrooms. They seek them out and judge their relevance for their own development. The type, number, and timing of these experiences form a unique amalgam for each teacher — the result of a dynamic interaction between context and personal biography. Thus biography does not only influence the teacher's response to context and opportunities, it can also help select and guide the search for particular professional development opportunities. Glenda aptly describes this personal process:

> Professional development is an all-encompassing term to me
> which might include the discussion of students' progress with the
> classroom teacher, acting as an adviser on a school newspaper,
> serving on a district committee, presenting a workshop, reading a
> professional journal, attending a conference, taking a university
> course or reflecting on a particular student. All of these and
> hundreds of other activities that cause me to think and talk about
> education and kids, I consider to be professional development. I
> see professional development as a very personal process where *I*
> determine areas where I want to increase my understanding and
> abilities.

CONTEXTS AND CONDITIONS

Commitment and Person–Context Interactions

From our case studies, it is clear that our teachers had evolved a strong commitment to children which came out of deeply personal roots: survival, safety and success for Lloyd, self-determination for Glenda and responsibility for Stephanie. These personal roots appear to provide both the seeds and the drive for self-improvement. Lloyd's early preoccupation with becoming the *best possible* teacher and Glenda and Stephanie's later decisions to pursue *self-initiated* professional development are examples of this. At one point or another, Lloyd, Glenda and Stephanie all integrated their commitment, their professional development and their pupils' needs through working in contexts that matched their predispositions. How many teachers, it is worth asking, are able to achieve this and how?

We have seen that in teachers' life-stories the person the teacher is and the context in which the teacher works can be *congruent*. Here, the teachers' intentions and the contingencies of the context more or less match each other, as in the case of Lloyd and Glenda. However, there may also be dilemmas, paradoxes and contradictions between the person and the context which the teacher has to negotiate. Here the person and the context are in a *dialectical* or *dialogical* relationship. A third possibility is that the interactions between person and context may be *problematic* owing to mismatches between personal professional dispositions and rather extreme constraints of the context. As Hargreaves notes, 'all teaching takes place with contexts of opportunity and constraint'. Unfortunately, many contexts within the working lives of teachers are characterized by constraints leading to survival-based patterns of teaching and an emphasis on coping, pupil control, routinization and habit.[6] Denscombe[7] suggests that we can understand this routinization as the teachers' response to a structure not of their own making, and a work context which is so constrained that the opportunities for teachers to create personal meaning is minimized. He makes the additional point that these individual responses have evolved into a powerful work culture of collective patterns and practice.

Teacher commitment within such contexts is obviously problematic. Woods sheds light on this issue in an ethnography which focuses on students' responses to schoolwork. He comes to the conclusion that open negotiation with pupils regarding the nature of classroom work is at the heart of being a good teacher, since the 'most meaningful activities to many of the pupils were those which made sense within their own culture pertained to the private sphere'.[8] He goes on to say that this is also true for teachers. We have noticed too, in our collection of life-histories, that where teachers have been able to build a personal bridge to the context of teaching — for themselves and their students — a strong sense of both teacher and pupil commitment evolves. This is clearly the case with Lloyd, Glenda and, in certain contexts, with Stephanie. In these circumstances teachers move from teaching as 'a kind of secondary going through the motions'[9] where their substantial self is *separate* from work, where they are not committed and where they feel a need to maintain and *defend* the substantial self, to a situation where they can include, affirm and evolve their self through their teaching.[10] In these latter circumstances, teachers might evolve a powerful combination of all four types of commitment which Nias[11] discovered: commitments to caring, to the pursuit of competence, to developing and maintaining a personal identity as teacher, and to career continuance.

Individualism and Collegiality

For Stephanie, Lloyd and Glenda, long periods of individual and somewhat isolated development that seem to take place in phases are sometimes punctuated by contexts where they work successfully with others. These appear to be seen as significant if only because of the breakdown of isolation and the provision of mutual support and interest that come with it. Lloyd and Stephanie, in particular, talk of contexts where groups of teachers work together, bonded by similar compelling visions and commitments. The issues, concerns and problems that arise are dealt with co-operatively and collegially. There is mutual support and encouragement to deal with the challenges set and an environment for and willingness to take the associated risks. These positive collegial contexts are mirrored by ones where interactions with colleagues are more negative. Some hinder teacher development and even cause regression, as we see with Lloyd's withdrawal and Stephanie's transfer from the child-centred school. Stephanie's new school with its different pedagogical tone and less collaborative climate also forces her to moderate her image of teaching.

It is not surprising, given the conditions of constraint under which many teachers work and given the culture of isolation, conservatism and privatism which surrounds their practice,[12] that 'teaching is a lonely profession'.[13] The *usual state* of professional development, then, inevitably becomes one of long periods during which individuals work alone. It is not just a matter of teachers being prevented by timetables and lack of time from working together. There is also evidence of some resistance to participatory activity, and of conflicts even when teachers do attempt to collaborate.[14]

Within our collection of teachers' life-stories which did not specifically *solicit* any particular comment related to relationships with colleagues, 98 per cent of teachers wrote about intercollegial relations, 80 per cent mentioned negative interactions with colleagues as significant, and 60 per cent perceived positive interaction with peers as telling aspects of their working life. Forty-five per cent of teachers wrote of incidents and relationships involving administrators that were positive and 75 per cent wrote of such incidents that were negative aspects of their working contexts over time.[15] Intercollegial relations, then, are a significant aspect of work life which have telling impacts on teachers' work. Even though there are positive aspects to intercollegial relations, they are often outweighed by negative interpersonal contacts. It is not surprising then, given the other constraints under which teachers work, that many teachers choose social isolation to maintain and defend their sense of self. To venture forth and interact can open the door to accountability, value difference, criticism and lack of agreement. Thus the general conditions of poor social relations, lack of a common language and poor communications often prevail.[16] While collegiality and collaboration are clearly problematic, there is evidence to suggest that, given the right conditions, context and processes, they can be very powerful supports for teacher development.

As teachers engage in these individual and group activities in their specific contexts of work, they do not and cannot ignore broader responsibilities related to the mandated curriculum and other external constraints. Lloyd, Glenda and Stephanie take these mandates seriously but they also *reinterpret* them to reflect their own values, personal predispositions and contextual needs. This capacity and willingness to reinterpret external mandates protects these teachers from the alienation and denial of self that would otherwise come with compliance. By taking responsibility for reinterpretation, Lloyd, Glenda and Stephanie take ownership of their educational projects. This is not to say that all teachers do this or can do this, or that all contexts and external agendas are open or appropriate to reinterpretation. It does, however, raise the question as to how teachers develop the capacity and the confidence to reinterpret external mandates in a way that is compatible with their own grounded dispositions and their pupils' needs as they see them. Our data suggest that consciousness of their own values, predispositions, evolving styles and their own biographical development as a person and a teacher provides a fundamental base for the reinterpretation of external prescriptions.

DISCUSSION AND IMPLICATIONS

From reflecting on three teachers' stories, and on our experience of working with over 80 teachers' autobiographies, several possibilities emerge for creating contexts which might facilitate teachers' development.

The link between personal and professional dispositions makes it important for teachers to have opportunities to examine their own personal commitments, histories, and teaching styles. Discovering and making explicit the roots of their commitment, understanding the personal grounds that underlie their professional work, being clearer about the types of educational contexts that best suit their biographical dispositions — all these kinds of reflection might assist the process of teacher development.

Contexts which enable teachers to collaborate in solving common problems in a focused way also appear to enhance teachers' own individual efforts at development. This seems to support the idea of school-initiated and school-based projects, although cross-school groups of teachers with similar interests might also provide helpful contexts for collaboration where there are common interests to be shared. By their voluntary, self-initiated nature, these activities encourage individual and collective teacher ownership. The mutual interests, trust and support that develop within groups appear to provide the encouraging environment necessary for taking individual and collective risks. A collective commitment and challenge provokes and requires action and the collective climate that develops also supports and promotes that action.

However, collaborative efforts often get squeezed out by the press of daily classroom reality, lack of time and the culture of the school.[17] 'There are few vehicles in school for collegiality'[18] and 'few schools sustain strong norms of collegiality and experimentation'.[19] Where such efforts are supported by external agencies, structures and resources, *and* internal norms, they stand a better chance of continuing. Lloyd's collaborative project survived for a number of years, partly because the school district was committed to it and provided time, resources and support. Stephanie's most productive context was within the arts school aided by support from the whole school staff, the principal and the parents. Since collegiality and collaboration are apparently related to more successful teacher development, it is important to identify the organizational character-istics germane to collaborative projects so that we may improve schools as a context for teachers' co-operative learning. The literature on collegiality is beginning to reveal conditions and generic practices that corroborate our life-history research and appear to foster collegiality and teacher development. Studies of schools and of school-based projects, particularly of those rare exam-ples of collegiality that already exist, have yielded some useful hints.

In terms of maintaining room for the personal meaning essential for com-mitment and individuality within collective efforts, the work of Lieberman and Miller[20] has revealed that teachers must be regarded as experts with respect to their own classroom reality. Their personal styles must be seen to have value. They need help in articulating their styles. And they need a dialogue to evolve collective projects out of individual concerns. The personal meaning of work can also be enhanced when it provides a mutually agreed organizing principle, serves sociability needs, sustains status and self-respect, establishes personal identity, provides a routine, distracts from worry, offers achievement and contributes to a cause.[21] In terms of involving teachers in collaborative projects, both our work[22] and others'[23] speaks of staged voluntarism whereby teachers are given the choice of participation, with whom they participate, how and for what pur-poses. Despite their privatism, teachers commonly express a need for a shared set of goals.[24] This aids collegiality as does shared understanding, shared investment and risk, collective participation in project implementation, a focus on specific problems, frequent meetings and continuing projects that are congruent with professional norms.[25] Bird and Little[26] also found that collegiality was supported when agreements about desired practice were promoted and a common language developed to describe and analyse it. In addition they found that, within the few schools that sustained strong norms of collegiality and experimentation, there were specific staff discussions of teaching practices, teachers observed each other at work, they worked together on plans and materials, and they learned from and with each other. They found that collegiality and experimentation will occur when teachers and principals describe and call for it, model it, provide support, reward it and defend it. Lieberman[27] in her description of collaborative research claimed that, regardless of the context, team deliberation has been shown to produce knowledge and self-learning for teachers, provide powerful professional development and encourage greater collegial interaction.

We have attempted to create these sorts of conditions for collaboration during the last seven or more years in projects of our own. Glenda and Lloyd and other teachers who have engaged in the process we call *collaborative autobio-graphy* claim it has helped them understand both their own and others' teaching in a deeply personal and professional way. Our enquiries into teacher development through the examination of teachers' autobiographies have encouraged us to look at collaborative autobiography as one kind of context which can provoke and promote better teacher development. We have found that the context necessary for the process of collaborative autobiography satisfies most of the conditions that facilitate teacher development, especially if conducted with school-based groups that include at least one administrator.

Preferably, professional development should be self-initiated. In order to know what we wish to do next, however, we need to know ourselves, who we are, and how we came to be that way. Most of us are not as aware of this as we might be. For this reason alone, we would argue that for teachers and, indeed, other professionals, developing an autobiography, perhaps in collaboration with others, is a fundamental form of personal and professional enquiry — *basi research* that is needed to know what to focus on and how, in each teacher's development.

We have been enabling groups of teachers and administrators to construct personal and professional autobiographies as a platform from which to launch into school-based projects. We work through four phases of activity in cooperative groups — a depiction of the context of each teacher's current working reality, a description of their current pedagogy and curriculum-in-use, reflections on their past personal and professional lives to assist their understanding of present professional thoughts and actions, and, finally, a projection into their preferred professional futures arising from a personal critical appraisal of the previous three accounts.

The method of collaborative autobiography is described in detail elsewhere,[28] but the following brief synopsis will characterize its main elements. Each member of each group, including the facilitator, presents oral excerpts from a self-instructional guide related to teachers' life-stories which they have completed independently. The rest of the group ask questions and share points of similarity and difference in experience to gain deeper understanding of each presenter and to assist each presenter to clarify his or her own understandings. To facilitate a high quality of personal reflection, sharing and collaboration, a number of conditions are essential to the process. They include making 'I' statements, accurately identifying and describing feelings, being frank and honest, engaging in non-critical acceptance of others, and providing confidentiality. Participants are reminded that they have complete control over the level of disclosure they decide to make about personal and professional aspects of their lives. Levels of disclosure may vary from one context to another. These contexts include group discussion, private conversations with someone in the group, discussion with the facilitator, and the self-instructional booklet which is confidential to the teacher. The experience of the process, then, can manifest itself at multiple levels. The autobiographies are individual and personal, yet they evolve through a process which is also collective and collaborative while being reflective. In addition, the process is also action- and practice-orientated.

Autobiography is experiential in itself, encouraging reflection-on-experience and a responsibility for one's own story. But being self-initiated requires support. Writing one's autobiography is easier when supported and catalysed by colleagues who live in the same place. The seminar in collaborative autobiography provides just such a context — where all are teachers and learners, where all risk together, where the group builds mutual trust, and where an accepting and affirming environment is created. Since the context is created by participants there is usually a healthy match between person and context. Similarities affirm, and differences offer a dialectic. Through this process teachers work on their concerns. Within the life-history seminar teachers can be mentors for each other in turn, as excerpts from their stories are shared and discussed.

By the end of the two-day seminar in collaborative autobiography, teachers have a deeper understanding of their own and their colleagues' teaching and how it came to be that way. In addition, each teacher has an individual professional development agenda for the future. We then engage in an exercise which asks each group to identify its collective concerns in order to plan its agenda for the future. Lastly, each group of teachers and one administrator is asked to identify a common project which it can pursue that addresses, as far as is possible, both individual and collective agendas. Groups then engage in school-based projects which include agreed foci, regular meetings, interclass visitation, problem-solving and forms of action research.[29] If we compare this process of collaborative autobiography and school-based projects with the common conditions for productive teacher development noted from teachers' stories and the literature, they are very well-matched. We conclude, then, that *collaborative autobiography*, besides being a useful means for research into teacher development, is also a potentially powerful means for assisting that development. It provides an interpersonal challenge within an interpersonal context that in turn offers support and a sheltered environment for taking risks.

What we think this process offers, more than other attempts to provide for collegiality and collaborative teacher development, is the simultaneous focus on individuality[30] as well as the collective project. While individual teachers, through autobiography, are able to identify deeply felt dispositions and concerns, they are also learning and understanding from other teachers' stories and, since the possibility of sanction and judgemental behaviour is diminished, the possibility of appreciation is enhanced. This is particularly important if we are to foster inter-class visitation. It is made easier if you know your visiting peer understands why you teach the way you do. Finally, the problems and concerns that are addressed by the projects arise from deeply personal, classroom and school sources through which teachers can reinterpret external initiatives, as opposed to many so-called school-based projects which are little more than teacher reactions to external reforms or mandates.

CONCLUSION

Drawing on data from detailed case studies of three teachers' life-stories and from a collection of over 80 others, this chapter has attempted to illustrate the nature of teacher development from the teacher's perspective. Teachers' stories clearly illuminate the way in which teachers' early personal experiences and personal development have a profound influence on who they are and who they become as teachers. Since these personal dispositions shape teachers' encounters with career situations and contexts, the inevitable individuality of professional development is underlined. Simultaneously, however, teachers' stories show the powerful effects that collegiality and teachers working on common projects have on teacher development. Even though these effects are corroborated to some extent by the literature, teachers' experiences of norms of experimentation and collegiality remain rare, given the cultural conditions and constraints under which teachers work. Activities and outcomes described in this chapter add to the existing knowledge about contexts and conditions which have been shown to promote collegiality, school-based projects and professional development.

Collaborative autobiography, the method used to gather teachers' stories for this project, provides one such context which has the potential to create a healthier inter-collegial culture in schools so that both individual and collective professional development needs might be met in school-based projects.

NOTES

1. Butt, R. L. and Raymond, D., 'Studying the nature and development of teachers' knowledge using collaborative autobiography'. *International Journal of Educational Research*, 13 (4), pp. 403–419, 1989; Ball, S. J. and Goodson, I. F. (eds), *Teachers' Lives and Careers*. Lewes: Falmer Press, 1985; Hargreaves, A., *Two Cultures of Schooling: The Case of Middle Schools*, Lewes: Falmer Press, 1986; Huberman, M., 'Teacher careers and school improvement'. *Journal of Curriculum Studies*, 20 (2), pp. 119–32 1988; Krall, F. R., 'From the inside-out: personal history as education research'. Occasional Paper Series, Edmonton: University of Alberta, Department of Secondary Education, 1988; Pinar, W., 'Autobiography and the architecture of self'. *Journal of Curriculum Theorizing*, 8 (1), pp. 7–36, 1988; Sikes, P. J., 'The Life Cycle of the Teacher'. In Ball, S. J. and Goodson, I. F. (eds), *Teachers' Lives and Careers*. Lewes: Falmer Press, pp. 27–60, 1985; and Woods, P., 'Conversations with teachers: some aspects of the life history method'. *British Educational Research Journal*, 2 (1), 1985, pp. 13–26, 1985.

2. Maccia, E. S., 'Curriculum theory and policy'. Paper presented at AERA, Chicago, 1965.

3. Nias, J., 'The definition and maintenance of self in primary schools'. *British Journal of Sociology of Education*, 5 (3), p. 268, 1984.

4. Ibid., p. 275.

5. Lortie, D. C., *School Teacher: A Sociological Study*. Chicago: University of Chicago Press, 1975.

6. Hargreaves, A., 'Teaching Quality: A Sociological Analysis'. *Journal of Curriculum Studies*, 20 (3), p. 219, 1988.

7. Denscombe, M., 'The work context of teaching. An analytic framework for the study of teachers in classrooms'. *British Journal of Sociology of Education*, 1 (3), pp. 279–92, 1980.

8. Woods, P., 'Negotiating the demands of schoolwork'. In Hammersley, M. and Woods, P. (eds), *Life in School: The Sociology of Pupil Culture*. Milton Keynes: Open University Press, p. 225, 1984.

9. Ibid., p. 233.

10. Nias, op. cit., note 3, p. 275.

11. Nias, J., 'Commitment and motivation in primary school teachers'. *Educational Review*, 33 (3), pp. 181–90, 1981.

12. Lortie, op. cit., note 5.

13. Sarason, S. B., Levine, M., Goldenberg, I., Cherlin, D. L. and Bennett, E. M., 'Teaching is a lonely profession'. In *Psychology in Community Settings: Clinical, Educational, Vocational, Social Aspects*. New York: John Wiley, 1966.

14. Hargreaves, A., 'The rhetoric of school-centred innovation'. *Journal of Curriculum Studies*, 14 (3), pp. 251–6, 1982.

15. Butt, R. L., Paul, J. and Smith, J., 'Collegial relationships and professional development: the interpersonal context of teachers' work'. Invitational conference on Ethnography and Teachers' Worklives, St Hilda's College, Oxford, September 1988.

16. Lieberman, A. and Miller, L., 'Synthesis of research on improving schools'. *Educational Leadership*, 38 (7), pp. 583–6, 1981; Lieberman, A. and Miller, L., 'School improvement: themes and variation'. *Teachers College Record*, 86 (1), 1984, pp. 4–19; Lieberman, A. and Miller, L., *Teachers, Their World and Their Work: Implications for School Improvement*. Alexandria, VA: Association for Supervision and Curriculum Development, 1984; Lieberman, A., 'Collaborative research: working with, not working on'. *Educational Leadership*, 43 (5), pp. 28–32, 1986; and Lieberman, A., 'Collaborative work'. *Educational Leadership*, 43 (5), pp. 4–8, 1986.

17. Hargreaves, A., 'Cultures of teaching'. In Goodson, I. F. (ed.), *Studying Teachers' Lives*. London: Routledge, 1990.

18. Sarason, S., *The Culture of the School and the Problem of Change*. Boston: Allyn & Bacon, p. 109, 1982.

19. Bird, T. and Little, J. W., 'How schools organize the teaching occupation'. *Elementary School Journal*, 86 (4), p. 498, 1986.

20. Lieberman and Miller, 'Synthesis of research on improving schools', op. cit., note 16.

21. Woods, op. cit., note 8, p. 233.

22. Townsend, D. and Butt, R. L., 'Collaborative autobiography, action research, and professional development'. Paper presented at AERA, Boston, April, 1990.

23. Lieberman and Miller, 'School improvement: themes and variation', op. cit., note 16; and Little, S. W., 'Seductive images and organizational realities in professional development'. *Teachers College Record*, 86 (1), pp. 84–102, 1984.

24. Nias, op. cit., note 3, p. 277.

25. Little, 'Seductive images and organizational realities in professional development', op. cit., note 23.

26. Bird and Little, op. cit., note 19.

27. Lieberman, 'Collaborative research: working with, not working on', op. cit., note 16.

28. Butt, R. L., 'An integrative function for teachers' biographies'. In Milburn, G., Goodson, I. F. and Clark, R. J. (eds), *Reinterpreting Curriculum and Research: Images and Arguments*. London, Ontario: Falmer Press, 1989.

29. Townsend and Butt, op. cit., note 22.

30. Hargreaves, A., 'Individualism and individuality'. *International Journal of Educational Research*, forthcoming.

Chapter 10

Facilitating Teacher Self-development: Reflections on Experience*

Antoinette Oberg and Susan Underwood

INTRODUCTION

This chapter explores what can happen when a teacher begins to trace her way of being in the actions and interactions of the classroom. The exploration is rooted in congruent experiences of a 36-hour graduate-level university course.

In contrast to many professional development situations, the one described in this chapter had all the advantages (and disadvantages) of a university credit course. That is, there were 36 hours of regularly scheduled meetings, norms that supported the investment of 72 to 100 hours of time outside class by students, and a comprehensive plan worked through by one or two instructors for the whole period. There was also the spectre of grades to be assigned at the end of the course, in which one of us was teacher and one of us was student. It begins, as all explorations do, from a point of departure — a departure from the known and the mapped.

As teacher and student embarking on this journey, both of us are aware of the well-travelled paths of teacher development. These routes are set with goals and objectives to mark the way and evaluation criteria to ensure the destination is reached. But what we question belongs to 'the road less travelled'. Our question is, 'What happens to the quality of a teacher's experience when a teacher turns to that experience as a source of reflection?'. The process of reflection is the one we have followed as teacher and student within a graduate course and as co-authors of this chapter.

In undertaking a journey, a traveller bespeaks a purpose. She leaves her home and ventures forth not merely because of the pleasures of the trip but because of a desire to understand or experience those marvels of which she has heard rumours. What she knows is that something may exist which can enrich her present situation; what she does not know is how or where, or indeed whether, she will discover its presence. The teacher development with which we are concerned involves a search for an unknown quality. It is not the product of an applied theory, nor will it follow the same path given different participants in

---

* Paper presented at the invitational conference on Teacher Development: Policies, Practices and Research, Ontario Institute for Studies in Education, Toronto, February 1989.

the search. This quality of unpredictability is the very dimension of teacher development that we find intriguing.

Each teacher's development is unique, affected by his or her history, insights, talents, and desires. To move consciously towards a fuller sense of what it means to be a teacher, this unique human story must be told. In this way, the teacher can voice his or her experience and, through recognition of the place upon which he or she stands, move beyond what is presently known.

We begin our story during a curriculum foundation course in which teachers and other professionals were asked to reflect upon their practice in the hopes that they would come to an awareness of their actions and convictions within their professional lives. As a class, we shared our stories and interpretations, and in doing so we wove into the fabric of our lived experience yet another thread, the thread of ongoing critical reflection. It strengthens the quality of the overall design and is likewise enhanced by other strands of various hues. The theory which we thus create is not separate from our practice, either as source or product. It is simply how we speak of what we do in those moments when our actions are in tune with our intentions. Theory, spoken of as an integral aspect of experience, is not static but ever shifting — like Heidegger's 'groundless ground'. We theorize in response to our experience and our experience is informed and shifted by our theory, a dialogical relationship which composes understanding.

In writing this chapter, we have allowed its dialogical nature to suggest both form and content. The structure of conversation reflects the manner in which we have arrived at insight into the development of teacher awareness. Though responses will vary whenever conversation is initiated, its attraction is universal: a gradual disclosure of self and other that becomes its own experience. Although written in two voices, this chapter is the journal of such a shared discovery.

In venturing beyond what we have previously understood we have turned to experience as a guide, observing the natural landmarks of the terrain and progressing tentatively. We do not seek to define routes or to stake claims. Rather we seek to enter our experience ecologically and thereby to create for ourselves and others an integrated understanding of teacher development, how it may be fostered and its meaningfulness to practice.

ACT 1: A COURSE OF SELF-DEVELOPMENT

Each September is a new beginning. For the teachers who come to my curriculum foundation course, it is the beginning of a graduate programme which they have selected and have been selected for. For me, it is a venturing forth into an area which I cannot map beforehand: teacher professional development. We come to the course, students and I, with mixed emotions: eagerness, apprehension, scepticism, curiosity. Students expect their uncertainties to be quelled on the first day by a clear statement of course content and requirements. I know these cannot be clearly understood until after the course is over.

To me, the course is like a stage. It is a space that I construct and fill with props. Everyone who comes is invited to create a play based on his or her own past professional experience. The props are readings, assignments, frameworks, and questions. These elements are selected, arranged and presented in such a way as to encourage thoughtful reflection on what is taken for granted in professional practice. Each person is invited to seek out the commitments and convictions embedded in his or her daily practice. I call this a search for ground, using 'ground' metaphorically as the place where one stands (in the present), as the locus of one's roots (in the past), and as the source of nourishment for growth (into the future). The ground on which one stands shows who one is at that time; that is, it composes one's judgements, purposes and direction. The story of how this ground changes over time is the story of one's life.

The aim of this ground probing is to engage in an intensely personal and yet objectively critical examination of oneself as a professional educator. Achieving the latter is achieving perspective on oneself and one's situation, and with perspective comes the possibility of liberation from the confinements of limited understandings and limiting situations.

When I set the stage in the foundation course, the props I bring along are a collection of readings which invite fresh looks at ordinary curriculum practices, a short speech on the nature and promises of reflection on practice (which I know will not be intelligible until the course is finished), and a brief outline of the sequence and sort of writing that is likely to facilitate the reflection called for. I suggest that the writing proceed in three stages: first, detailed, literal descriptions of actual events from daily practice from an insider's point of view; second, review of those descriptions seeking a deeper understanding of what is there and what it means, that is, seeking their ground; and third, another reconsideration, this time expanding the horizon of both the enquiry and the enquirer, pushing the enquiry into the future tense and the enquirer into the nexus of social and political interests in which his or her classroom, office, school are embedded. To lay the groundwork for this developmental writing, students are asked to keep a journal of their experiences during the course.

Beyond these meagre preliminaries, what happens is up to the 'actors' who join the class. With their particular backgrounds, talents and interests, they create their own 'plays'. To begin with, they write stories of their own professional lives. I listen and respond with comments, questions and suggestions that encourage them to look more deeply into their stories. As they revisit their early writings, students create new stories that they did not know before, revealing to themselves as well as to me where they stand on the stage of life. Then, in their final revisitation of their term's work, they place their stories in a larger social and political context and envisage a new performance, as they imagine it will be tomorrow in their classrooms and offices.

SU: A scriptless actor, upon entering a stage bereft of the standard set, soon begins to intuit the nature of the drama in store. Just so, as a student entering a course in which assignments were invitations to pause, to reflect, to question, I sensed at once that this course would be a place where the challenges were unlike others. There would be no lines to memorize or roles to learn, no omnipotent director. What there would be, however, was room in which to move freely and in which to explore and create scenarios expressive of understandings. Given a reading or a discussion topic, the stage was then an open one on which players could improvise, each bringing his or her perceptions to bear on the collective theme.

There would also be an audience. The audience was interested, critically aware, and, unlike the traditional theatrical audience, directly involved in the drama. In fact, this audience was a combination stage manager/audience/player — one who performed a variety of roles — sometimes suggesting props and stage-settings, at other times responding empathetically and intellectually to a player's improvisation, but at all times inevitably present on the stage as well, engaged as much as any individual actor in the shape of the play.

I stepped into this environment as a graduate student embarking on her first course in curriculum studies. I had enrolled in a graduate studies programme not because I was planning to 'advance' my career, but because I thought I would probably remain a classroom teacher for the rest of my professional life.

Teachers in British Columbia spent the spring of 1987 involved in political action, protesting against government legislation affecting teachers' professional lives. Faced with yet another September and another 26 desks, battered from the round of strikes and instruction-only campaigns, I questioned whether my practice served any purpose other than providing me with an income and my students with an illusion. To feel any integrity I had to search for an answer to this question. After an initial interview with Dr Oberg to investigate the curriculum studies programme at the University of Victoria, I thought graduate school was the setting in which I might begin my search. This first course in the programme convinced me that my instincts were correct.

AO: The invitation for students to devote the majority of a 36-hour course to critical reflection on their professional practice was not issued casually. Although it has been eight years since I first issued this invitation, my journals and papers are still full of my misgivings. How do I explain to students what the course is about? How do I best guide the search for ground? How do I know when someone has turned down a dead-end road? How do I respond to, let alone judge, the individual discoveries made? After all, I am the course 'instructor', and an instructor is normally expected to be expert at initiating students into a subject matter and in judging their mastery of its tools.

The fear that nothing valuable will happen for students unless I provide the wherewithal has usually caused me to supply an abundance of theoretical frameworks and key questions to help students interpret assigned readings. I rest more easily when I know that students are being exposed to both the substance and syntax of the field. These are, of course, the most valuable tools for knowledge growth, and knowledge is taken to be the basis for expertise. By not prescribing the particular knowledge to be gained, I always believed I was avoiding the imposition of predigested conclusions on students, and instead allowing them to develop their own understanding of the material at hand in relation to their own professional practice, thus fostering the development of what is frequently called 'personal practical knowledge'.

Eventually, I came to realize that the frameworks and questions which I had thought were enabling were actually restricting. They limited rather than expanded the possibilities for students to gain significant insights into the ground of their practice. Somehow, students had to be given more freedom to construct their own understandings. The errors of the 1960s also had to be avoided: suitable structures to facilitate critical reflection had to be devised. These were not the theories of hegemony and reproduction of the critical theorists, for these would function in the same debilitating way as the other frames already discarded, separating students from the daily events of their practice and directing their attention to someone else's construction of reality. Nor was the aim for students to develop their own versions of theories implicit in their practice, theories with an already established shape waiting to be filled in with the specifics of a particular person's practice.

SU: We were to keep a journal. We began by telling stories about our teaching and from these stories we were asked to interpret values and formulate questions. In 15 years of teaching, no one had asked how I viewed my practice. For several years I had been involved in professional development, establishing conferences, workshops, policies and projects for my school and district. The focus, however, was always on improvement, on 'updating', on implementation; in other words, I was always less current, less experienced, less knowledgeable than the 'expert'. I had been 'supervised'. I had been judged 'satisfactory' as opposed to 'unsatisfactory'. But no one had offered to listen to the story of my practice. For someone to suggest that I speak, write about and reflect on my experience after 15 years of silence, opened doors that somehow I had not noticed were part of the wall.

AO: Beginning with actual stories from teachers' daily practice was more than a capitulation to teachers' natural tendencies to tell stories of their professional life experiences. Rather, it was the mandatory starting-point for insights that would be firmly anchored in teachers' everyday realities. Insights that originate in someone else's theory are often difficult to connect to one's own everyday actions, but new perceptions of one's own situation and one's own place in it can often transform not only the way one grasps one's world but also the way one acts.[1] The aim is to set up a spiralling dialectic between the general and the particular, at first using theories that originate outside self-selectively and idiosyncratically to build a richer understanding of self and situation,[2] later theorizing the deep structure of one's own experience.

The pedagogical question is how to initiate the dialectic, how to enter the hermeneutic circle. More specifically, it is how to elicit the kind of writing about professional experience that can profitably be mined for the deeper meaning that constitutes new understanding of self-in-the-world. Of course it is impossible to say much more than has already been said about how to start. It is not that something in practice must be made problematic. Rather, a thoughtful attitude must be adopted, a tendency to direct attention towards that which appears not to be problematic, a willingness to have second thoughts even before they are called for (in the second reflective move). How does a teacher invite students to adopt such an attitude?

Perhaps the only answer is to show that which cannot be explained. While my own practice must continuously be a demonstration of that for which we aim, a concrete example from a student is likely to be more effective. Susan's first piece of writing for the course was an ideal example. Her frank and honest portrayal of her own heartrending experience of the death of two of her students surprised and deeply impressed me as well as the rest of her fellow students. The poignancy with which she told the story showed clearly where she stood and who she was, and in doing so it also showed the power of personal life-stories to reveal the ground of professional practice. With that vivid and heartfelt description of some events from her practice, Susan set her stage for more and more penetrating writing about her professional practice and about her place in the educational system. How had she found such a profitable register of discourse so quickly and easily?

SU: From the moment Antoinette asked us during the first class to write a vignette of an incident from our professional lives, my mind was alive with stories. But two memories, disconnected in time though similar in theme kept pulling me toward pen and paper. I wrote; I rewrote. And as I did so, I wondered what was drawing me to revisit this pain. I wrote in my journal, 'Why had I written what I had? Why not about the one million other ideas that streamed through my head? What did that say about me? In other words, I have learned something. My own story was my teacher.'

In fact, I learned as much from what I had not written as from what I had. In writing about the deaths of two of my students, I had abandoned stories that might have been deemed more appropriate for a course in curriculum studies. I had chosen not to write about the way I teach writing, or about the development of a successful curriculum project. What I had written about, what I had to write about, had nothing to do with goals or objectives or lesson plans or units or philosophy of education.

Translating these experiences into words was neither quick nor easy. It took time to search for words that did not erase the pain but did not exploit it either. I wanted to express the nature of that experience, not to transform it, though I realized that through writing, the experience would of course be transformed.

AO: Language is crucial to the understanding Susan was building. When commitments and convictions are put into words, they gain an existence of their own, they take on weight and solidity. We can then hold them more firmly. We can share them with others and declare publicly the theory of our practice. We can also distance ourselves from that practice and look critically at it.

Typical classroom discourse is often inadequate to express the kinds of understanding sought in critical reflection. A new but not alien language is needed — a language of being as well as doing, of feeling as well as knowing, of imagining as well as remembering, of creating as well as reproducing, of integrating as well as differentiating. Teachers must be able to appropriate a language which serves their purposes, to make it their own.

SU: Many times, as we discussed a paper or topic in class, I found myself without words, caught like a child on a circling carousel, always moving beyond the blur of the crowd before I could spot a familiar face. But writing, I found, gave me the chance to hold still for a moment, to let the sensations and impressions that created understanding form into words and phrases. Writing was a way to revisit experience, to revivify it and to extend it into new awareness.

In my journal I wrote, 'I had read the chapter once, written my assignment after much mental tossing and turning, and then reread the article. But this time, I felt as though the words were my own . . . I really think that having come to my own conclusions through the experience of struggling to articulate what I believe allowed me at last to experience Novak's writing. Not just read it but feel it'.

The first assignment, to write a description rich in experiential detail of our teaching practice, also engaged me in a reflective process. What do I do when I teach? Why do I do it? The initial difficulty of communicating these experiences of the classroom opened me to an understanding of their purpose and at the same time to the experiences and understandings of others.

AO: Finding someone who responded so eagerly to the open-ended invitation to reflect critically on her own practice was simultaneously elating and frightening. I had marked the start of a path, the boundaries of which I did not know. It would take both the students and myself into terrain we could not know in advance, terrain that would change every time we traversed it. While I was the designated leader, I did not know the way; nor did I know where we would finally arrive. I did have an idea of what reflection entailed and what it promised. Beyond that, I would have to rely as much on students' good sense as on my own. We were all journeying together. How would they (and I) fare?

SU: At the outset of the course, writing without a given framework unnerved me. I was expected, I realized, to 'do' something, but what? Here was no known outcome. No one would tell me what to write about, no one would praise or disapprove by assigning a grade after each paper or journal entry. The uncertainty was comforting while at the same time uncomfortable. On the one hand, I must be trusted and respected to be engaged in this conversation; on the other hand, what if the trust were misplaced? What if I had nothing to say?

AO: My concern not only at the beginning but throughout the course was to arrange the stage and props in such a way that students could find something to say that was both significant to them and meaningful to me in my role of sympathetic critic. I wondered how students could possibly sufficiently trust someone they hardly knew to enter into a play with an unknown script and a potentially disconcerting last act. What was my responsibility in raising the curtain on such a play, and how would I prompt the players?

SU: After the first assignment, we were to write two more. 'I wonder how you will push further ...' had been Antoinette's comment on my first. I floundered. In describing my practice, I felt I had understood it for the first time. I was still basking in the pleasurable recognition of integration within my practice when Antoinette's remark indicated that she expected more extensive reflection on the subject. Where would I go from here? I truly had no idea. I was happy with the picture of my practice. How could I possibly reflect on it further?

Eventually, I faced the deeper conflict that had drawn me to this course and programme in the first place. Reading through my journal entries, my stories, thinking over my responses to the readings and discussions of the class, I recognized their common theme. My question was: Within the institution of public school, where did I, as a human being, belong? In framing this question, I acknowledged my own need for integration, for a drawing together of the strands of my existence, for a sense of wholeness rather than compartmentalization. Writing this assignment involved struggle, more than I can adequately convey. I began the task without a thesis; at times I was afraid of what I might discover. But the writing left me with the dawning of what felt like a new insight: that my teaching was integral to my sense of community. What kept me in teaching was a desire to be more human, to involve myself with the humanity of others.

This revelation, intellectually expressed in the past but more truly created through reflection on personal experience, lifted me beyond the bureaucratic frustrations of a job to an understanding of the nature of my experiences within that context. I recall the intense excitement by which I recognized each new insight. As I began to see connections among the 'theory' which I read, the events that unfolded before me every day in the classroom, and the thoughtfulness with which I reflected upon those events, I began also to experience 'wakefulness' to the possibilities of connections. I began to look for opportunities to deepen those connections. I was no longer a teacher only; I was a teacher/ student.

The final paper was the easiest of the three to write. Turning to my journal and my previous papers, I read what they revealed. Through becoming thoughtful about my practice, through allowing my experience to become my teacher, I was discovering my own tale in the telling, becoming in the process whole, both creator and interpreter of meaning. Through searching for my own questions and listening to my own responses, I had struggled, not for the approval of an external voice of authority, but for that of the inner voice, the one to which I could listen not just for a few months, but for a lifetime.

AO: Susan was finding not only a voice, but also a footing. She could stand gracefully on the groundless ground and express herself with calm confidence. What of the others, especially the ones who might fail to find a footing on their shifting ground? What is the role of a teacher when a student begins to lose his or her balance? What right has the teacher in the first place to throw students off balance, to precipitate the personal and potentially permanent unease and uncertainty that come from questioning the grounds of particular practices?

SU:

> In writing, for the person who follows with trust and forgiveness
> what occurs to him, the world remains always ready and deep, an
> inexhaustible environment, with the combined vividness and
> flexibility of a dream. Working back and forth between experience
> and thought, writers have more than space and time can offer.
> They have the whole unexplored realm of human vision.[3]

The same words could apply to teaching. A teacher who asks students to open
the door to the 'whole unexplored realm of human vision' need not apologize for
the excitement nor the uncertainty that ensues.

At the end of the course, Antoinette read an entry from her journal which
expressed some of her doubts about what she had asked us to do. I felt profoundly disturbed at some of her words, at the thought that perhaps she might
alter the course structure in such a way that another person, like me in search
of a question, might not have the chance to ask it. The quality of one's experience within the teaching profession must surely be reflected by one's willingness to risk discomfort in return for a 'world always ready and deep.' As a
teacher, I need to turn to my own students, my own practice each day with the
sense of a new beginning, replete with perpetual uncertainty. What could be
more interesting?

In my response to Antoinette's doubts, I knew the importance of her way of
teaching to my wakefulness of purpose and I knew I wanted to protect that path
for any future traveller who needed to follow it. Perhaps the strength of this
awareness was due to her willingness to share her own discomfort. So often I
learn so much from these encounters with the teacher as a vulnerable human
being, rather than an Olympian authority.

INTERMISSION

Teacher and student parted company in December, when the foundation course
ended. Our paths parted but, unknown to us at the time, remained parallel. Over
the succeeding months, as we went separately about our academic and professional business, we each worked in different ways at deepening our understanding of the reflection we had undertaken in the course.

A month before the anniversary of the beginning of the course, our common
but separate quests propelled us together again to seek to understand more
explicitly the intertwined strands of our professional development. We knew
that what we had experienced had special significance both within and beyond
our own individual lives. Building on the journals and the academic and course
papers we had written during the preceding 11 months, we began a series of
dialogues. Between August and December 1988 we had eight conversations,

each lasting about one-and-a-half hours, which we recorded either manually or on tape.

Finding each other congenial co-journeyers, we lifted anchor again and set off, seeking to understand the nature of our combined experiences of reflecting and encouraging reflection on our practices as professional educators. We thus embarked on a meta-reflection, or a review of our earlier reflective experiences. In the following pages, we draw on the dialogues to describe this second journey. We step back from the experiences we have just described without severing our connection with them, and attempt to deepen our understanding of professional development and how it may be fostered.

ACT II: DIALOGUES OF REFLECTION

SU: To interpret the nature of self-development as facilitated by a university course, the reflections of teacher and student meet, overlap and at times merge. In writing this paper, we discovered themes which seemed important to both our teaching practices as well as to our experiences within the foundations course. These themes are relationship, response and reflection.

Incorporated within the particular significance of these themes is the context of our lives as teachers. These themes emerge in our reflections about the curriculum foundation course because they are integral to our lives outside the course, and to the experience which we brought with us when we entered, which focused our attention while we were there, and which we extended when we left. That experience is the basis of our understanding.

From that basis, which is ever-shifting, we construct our understanding, that which is situated beneath that upon which we stand. Our experience is our 'ground'; our understanding is that which lies beneath it. Our understanding we must search for, find words for, root out and uncover. It does not lie on the surface and the surface is always changing.

Relationship

SU: A student and teacher, in the best moments of teaching, experience what George Eliot[4] termed 'the double change of self and beholder'. The student is not the only one, in other words, to be affected by the process; the teacher is affected as well. And as each participant becomes increasingly aware of the duality of change, the teacher ceases to be a 'beholder'. The teacher becomes a fellow student, involved in attempting to understand her practice, her experience.

AO: At the beginning of the course, I did not realize how important my own reflective journey was for the students' experience of the class. Over the past decade, I had become accustomed to reflecting privately about my own practice. Students' practices rather than mine were the topic of the course. My role was to foster their professional development. Only in retrospect, from the vantage point afforded by Susan's joining her reflections about the course with mine, did I

171

become more fully aware of the subtleties of the student–teacher relationship.

In describing this relationship from my point of view, it is easier at first to say what a teacher is not: she is not a problem poser, for the problems she identifies arise out of her own experience, which is different from her students'. The teacher is not a guide or leader, for leading takes responsibility for learning away from students. The teacher is not an interpreter of the literature for students, for each person ultimately makes or takes his or her own meanings from another's writing. Lastly, the teacher is not the final judge of students' learning, for only students can know how much and how well they have truly understood.

So what is a teacher to someone reflecting on professional practice? The teacher is someone who makes a space, both physical and psychic, and sets a tone. Neither of these can be completely prepared ahead of time; rather, they come into existence in the act of teaching.

Making space means providing times and places where students can interact with each other, both casually and in focused discussions. It means being patient while students get to know one another well enough to engage openly and authentically in conversations about their practice. It means letting students make decisions about their learning, providing for a direction without setting the direction. Some strategies which are consistent with these aims are setting up an open-ended activity and having students discuss the significance of the results; having students generate questions/issues they want to discuss; or having students discuss and share what they themselves have written.

The way the teacher acts toward students not only structures the space, but also establishes the tone in the class. 'Tone' was first used in an educational context by Schleiermacher to mean 'that special quality in human interaction that allows a person to behave with sensitivity and flexibility towards others'.[5] For me, its essence is respect for individuals, a discriminating respect which balances appreciation for the already developed with positive expectations for the not yet developed. A respectful tone is established when the teacher genuinely appreciates the goodness of students and their work, trusts students to make their own sense out of what they encounter, and acknowledges the legitimacy of students' conclusions. Let me say a few words about each of these in turn.

A respectful tone requires that the teacher should believe in the possibilities and goodness of students and demonstrate that belief to students. For me, this has not been difficult: I have been lucky to have in my classes self-confident, well-respected educators who have chosen graduate work as a means of professional self-improvement. As I wrote in my journal during the last round of the course, 'They write so well, they tell stories so enticingly. I am drawn in to their professional lives quite strongly. As a teacher aiming for strong, clear, insightful writing, I am taken aback when so many demonstrate this so early in a course.' I show my appreciation by sharing such entries with the class.

Students must be respected not only as writers, but also as readers. This is not so much a matter of competence as of attitude. Students must come to believe that the readings assigned have something to say to them, even though the message may be buried under mounds of jargon, that they themselves can decipher this message, and that the message may very well be different for each one of them; that is, that there is no one 'correct' interpretation. The teacher's role in this situation is to make suggestions to students about how to progress in their individual journeys of self-discovery, but to leave the final responsibility for choosing what 'fits' to the students. As I had to confess apologetically to one student in the last round, 'It is evident you addressed the questions I noted after your second assignment. While I appreciate this, perhaps it was not the best thing for you to do. Your writing in this last paper was abstract and more difficult to understand than was your earlier writing'.

It follows that the teacher must respect the results of students' work. Students' conclusions must be given status as the main product of the course. That is, their insights must constitute the course assignments, pieces that are written up formally and handed in to be read carefully by the instructor.

SU: One of the attributes of Antoinette's teaching that I appreciated first was that she allowed us to make our own connections. The readings assigned each week did not provide answers so much as they asked questions, and each week as I travelled to class I eagerly anticipated the responses of my colleagues. At times the readings illuminated an activity which we had experienced during class, rendering the reading much more powerful because of the relationship. Yet no comment was made to lead us to connect the two experiences; we were merely granted the freedom to recognize a relationship or not. Coming to one's own understanding of a text is a far more dynamic adventure than coming to an understanding of someone else's understanding.

Inherent in this freedom to create understanding was the respect with which Antoinette regarded her students. We were expected to be capable of generating knowledge. The structure of the course made this clear, but equally telling were the everyday actions of the teacher. She listened. She did not listen to extracts from the discourse points that were weak, or information that was faulty in order that she might correct or dismiss. She listened, it seemed, in order to understand what the speaker wanted to communicate and to help if necessary in the clarification of his or her thoughts.

When I read her comments in my journal, the same close attention was evident. One question would be posed beside my entry but the effect of the question, so simply phrased, would cause me to rethink my previous statement and wonder where its foundation lay.

The answers were not given, nor could they be, even though at times many of us asked for them. In the end I was profoundly grateful that they were not. When I completed the description of my teaching practice, I experienced an awareness of who I was as a teacher, as a human being. I wrote, 'What I am learning . . . is that the choices I have been making, but not articulating, are good ones and have something to do with the real voices with which my students speak'. The consequences for my practice of such a recognition, while indirect, are profound. What does it mean for a teacher to recognize within herself the source of her authority to teach? For me, the awareness deepened my commitment to the quality of each encounter with the children in my care.

AO: It is not easy for a teacher to stand back and make space for students. As teachers, we are socialized to take control, to take the lead, to take responsibility for what goes on in the classroom, even for what students accomplish. Moreover, our superior knowledge of the subject matter we teach is supposed to be the source of our authority and our responsibility to both guide and judge students' work.[6] The teacher who hopes to facilitate students' self-reflection in the manner described above must strike a careful balance between teacher authority and student self-determination. This balance can never be worked out according to a formula. Rather, it must be negotiated (and often renegotiated) with each student group.

The balance sought is one which allows teacher and students to interact with each other as genuinely as possible, given the inevitable status difference that results from the teacher's power to grade students' work. This does not mean that the teacher should try to become as if one of the students. I am not one of the students; my experience and therefore my perspective is different from theirs. By virtue of my having been on the road of self-discovery longer than most of them have been, having met and carefully observed many travellers on the way (other students in other years of teaching), and having drawn many maps of the roads travelled, my perspective is broader than theirs. It is my responsibility to give students the benefit of this broader perspective within which they can view their own practice. They undertake professional development precisely for this reason: to gain a broader perspective, to become more knowledgeable about practical affairs, affairs of their practice. I give the benefit of my perspective by providing critical feedback on their ideas and insights. From the context of a broader understanding of practice in general (both theoretically and practically), I am in a position to comment comparatively on individual students' practice.

For as long as possible, my comments must be non-judgemental, aiming to clarify rather than to correct, to reflect meaning back as an audience rather than as a judge. While, in the end, I am required in my situation to assign a grade to each student's term work, the ultimate aim is not the achievement of a grade but the development of students' abilities to judge the value of their own experiences. The ones who do not achieve this fail to do so because they continue to rely on the teacher's judgement. Both parties are implicated here. For students to take control, teachers must give up their exclusive claim to it. Power shared increases. The students who join the teacher are the ones capable of setting directions, deciding where and how to travel the road of self-discovery, and judging the value of their experiences along the way.

SU: Learning is multi-layered; through dialogue about the experience, new awareness emerges. I form new thoughts about teaching, indeed about all human interaction, through relating to the experience of my teacher, whose insights and intuitions also shift in tune with her reflections. I have been lucky to find teachers who have invited me to reflect upon my experience. But in listening to parts of my story they have also told me parts of their own. What I became aware of during the dialogues was the importance of the 'example' to both my experience as a student and my own teaching practice. As Antoinette pointed out to me, 'Example is the only way that this . . . dimension of teaching can be communicated. And this is what we mean about relationship. . . . You can't . . . insert this dimension into teaching by talking about it . . . that's the ontological dimension . . . It's the example that somebody lives'.

I thought about my own students, who learn from each other as much — or more — than they learn from me; how their writing which they read aloud to each other encourages them to open themselves further to the community of the classroom. I thought of my teachers who continued to consider themselves students; how their reflections and questions encouraged me to look again at my experience, my assurances.

I returned to my journal, searching for examples that had included this dimension of teaching. I found many. The example to which I responded in the journal might be a personal reflection that the teacher read aloud, an anecdote shared, or a situation deftly handled. The example encouraged me to respond in kind to the humanity of the occasion. Doing so enriched me as a student and as a teacher.

Having experienced and articulated the importance of this sense of community within the classroom, I am more conscious of its creation. Creation is nothing more than a beginning, one act which engenders a response which elicits yet another. In this way, we learn through example: one example brings forth another; one story suggests more.

Responsibility

SU: 'Responsibility' for me in my role of teacher/student involves an ability to share 'responses'. It suggests a direct, personal relationship, an empathy between the experiences of students and teacher, a willingness to attune oneself to one's relationships with others. Both student and teacher, in other words, must be willing to move beyond what they have known. For some, this impression of responsibility threatens. The demands are personal, involving all of one's being, preventing a tidy segmentation of 'roles' which never connect.

Within a context of responsibility, both student and teacher let go of the 'power' inherent in their roles. The teacher gives up an attitude and belief that she is, by virtue of her position, the sole director of the classroom experience. She gives up invulnerability, inaccessibility. The student gives up a safe, passive role that allows her to accept or reject, without commitment or personal involvement, the authority of the teacher. She also gives up invulnerability, inaccessibility.

As a teacher and as a student, I have met those who are unwilling or unable to be 'response-able'. They expect a teacher to control behaviour. They are impatient with process, content with product, regardless of its quality or relevance to their interests. 'Power' in this case would seem to be with the teacher, and yet how can it be if the teacher feels uncomfortable with such a situation, if her attempts to engage in a human encounter are rebuffed? Without 'response-ability' between student and teacher, there is no power within the human relationship, only within the institutional.

Institutional power was/is the dilemma of teaching with which I struggle. It was the focus of my reflection in the foundations course. The questions Antoinette asked of herself were similar to questions I asked in my role of teacher within the public education system. However, as a student within a university programme, I could respond to those questions from a different perspective. The value of our sharing responses, of our 'response-ability', lay in both the similarity of our questions and the variability of our experiences.

Reflection

SU: Reflections in the still waters of a bay, pond or lake shift continuously, every second mirroring and simultaneously distorting myriad images. In becoming reflective about one's experience, one recognizes a similar mutability. Experience is not tangible and cannot be caught. Its images are multiple and fluid, involving the interplay of several individuals. The tension involved in coming to terms with this ineffability is a sensitive one — not unlike the tension of water, involving a delicate balance of elements.

AO: In this chapter we have sought to capture the reflections of our experiences and hold them still long enough to understand the professional lives of which those experiences speak. It is like describing what happens when a pebble is thrown into a still pond. We throw the pebble not to trace its course, but to reveal something about the water which is not evident when it is still. Some of the essential physical and aesthetic qualities of the water are revealed by the way it undulates without breaking the surface, by the way the undulations are perpetuated in ever-increasing circles, by the way the edges of the ripples catch the sunlight and send it back in blinding flashes. If we look carefully at what happens when the act of throwing the pebble is performed, we come to understand why we were drawn to the water in the first place.

NOTES

1. Novak, M., *Ascent of the Mountain, Flight of the Dove: An Invitation to Religious Studies.* New York: Harper & Row, 1971.

2. Pinar, W., 'Whole, bright, deep with understanding: issues in qualitative research and autobiographical method'. *Journal of Curriculum Studies*, 13 (1: 3), pp. 173–188, 1979.

3. Stafford, W., *Writing the Australian Crawl*. Ann Arbor: University of Michigan Press, 1977.

4. Eliot, G., *Middlemarch*. Cambridge, MA: Riverside Press, 1956. (First published 1871–2.)

5. Van Manen, M., 'On the tact of teaching'. *CACS Newsletter*, October 1988.

6. Frye, N., 'The teacher's source of authority'. *Curriculum Inquiry*, 9 (1), pp. 3–11, 1979.

Chapter 11

Understanding Reflection through Collaborative Research

William Louden

Donald Schon's descriptions of professional knowledge and reflection[1] have been received with enthusiasm by educational researchers and policy-makers. His orientation towards knowing *how* rather than knowing *that* and the respect he shows for the skill required to manage the uncertain and changing problems of practice have been appreciated by an educational community disillusioned with the means–ends rationalism which has dominated educational discourse. The examples he uses in developing his memorable distinction between reflection-on-action and reflection-in-action are not drawn from work with teachers, but his orientation towards knowledge-in-use has complemented developments in research on teachers' knowledge in the past decade.[2] Like most research on teachers' knowledge, however, Schon's work on reflection is based on *observation*: reports of action generated by observers rather than by participants. In the case of the wide range of professions described by Schon — design, management, engineering, planning, counselling, music — this is an inescapable consequence of the researchers' own professional knowledge. He is a scholar, not a musician, manager or designer.

In educational research we have opportunities to move beyond observation and towards participation in the action we wish to understand: most of us have, after all, been schoolteachers ourselves. As teachers *and* researchers we can bring our own craft knowledge to bear, to attempt to understand from the inside how reflection contributes to the action teachers take in their classroom work. Such participative research, however, can only take place in the context of well-developed collaborative relationships between teachers and researchers, relationships built on mutual respect, trust and complementary interests. The commentary on teachers' reflection which appears in this chapter was developed in the context of such a collaborative relationship. Much of the literature on reflective practice in teaching concentrates on the prescriptive questions of how teachers' *skills* reflect on their work and of how we might develop that sort of reflection. This chapter is concerned less with prescribing than with understanding; with understanding the often neglected or misunderstood way that teachers already *do* reflect on their practice. Collaborative relationships of the kind described in this chapter, it is argued, are essential to developing the depth of understanding necessary for appreciating these forms of reflection. From

February 1988 to February 1989, I worked closely with Johanna, a teacher at an alternative middle school. Gradually, I moved from being a visitor to the school, an observer of the action, to becoming a full participant in the life of the school and in Johanna's classes. Throughout the most intensive phase of the study, from September to December 1988, I shared with Johanna the responsibility for planning, teaching and assessing lessons in writing and science for all three of her grade seven and eight classes at Community School.[3]

Drawing on this collaborative experience and connecting it with the literature on reflection, this chapter develops a conceptual account of teachers' reflection. Briefly, this conceptual framework includes two complementary dimensions of reflection which I call the *interests* and *forms* of reflection.[4] These two dimensions are developed from the work of Habermas[5] and Schon[6] respectively. The term *interests* refers to the goal or end in view of an act of reflection: is the goal of reflection fidelity to some theory or practice; or deeper and clearer personal understanding; or professional problem solving; or a review of the conditions of professional action? *Forms* refers to the characteristics of the act; is it a matter of introspections, of thinking and feeling; of replaying or rehearsing professional action; of systematic enquiry into action; or of spontaneous minded action? These dimensions, it will be argued, are both different and complementary. A particular act of reflection thus has both an interest and a form, and in principle all reflective acts may be described in terms of both dimensions. The way in which these dimensions are related may be suggested by the four-by-four matrix in Figure 11.1.

As the 16 boxes in this figure suggest, it is — at least in principle — possible to describe the intersection of each of the four forms and interests. For example, one might use a form of reflection such as enquiry into action with the end in view of critique, or problem-solving, or personal growth, or technical fidelity to theory. Equally, one might serve a critical interest by introspection, or by rehearsing a range of options, or by a process of enquiry, or through some spontaneous discovery made in the midst of professional action. In the discussion which follows, I first describe the four interests and then connect them with the four forms of reflection.

REFLECTION AND INTERESTS

It has become customary in the educational literature to make distinctions about interests according to three traditions of enquiry, often using a form of words drawn from Jurgen Habermas's theory of 'knowledge-constitutive interests'.[7] Habermas distinguishes among the interests of the empirical-analytic sciences the hermeneutic-historical sciences and the critical sciences. Thus, a series of studies which have attempted to review and reconceptualize fields within education have made similar three-way distinctions.[8] Habermas associates each form of enquiry with a cognitive interest: empirical-analytic enquiry

FORMS

	INTROSPECTION	REPLAY and REHEARSAL	ENQUIRY	SPONTANEITY
TECHNICAL				
PERSONAL				
PROBLEMATIC				
CRITICAL				

INTERESTS

Figure 11.1. Forms and interests of reflection.

with technical control by discovering rule-like regularities in an objective world; historical-hermeneutic sciences with practical control through understanding and communication; and critical sciences with emancipation through critical reflection on the conditions of social life. This paper builds on Habermas's framework, following the *technical* and *critical* interests he distinguishes and separating the practical interest into two categories, a *personal* interest and a *problematic* interest. Both of these latter interests share Habermas's sense that the historical-hermeneutic sciences serve the interest of practical control, but what I have called the personal interest emphasizes the personal meaning of situations and the problematic interest emphasizes problem-solving in professional work. Although Habermas first offered his theory of knowledge-constitutive interests as 'quasi-transcendental', that is, as fundamental to the human condition in general, this claim has been the subject of a series of critiques concerning the possibility that such interests could transcend culture and language.[9] The issue at stake here, however, is not the transcendental status of such interests but their usefulness in explaining the range of interests in reflection. For this reason, I have chosen to use Habermas's categories as a point of departure.

Technical Interest

The technical interest, an interest in controlling the world by attending to rule-like regularities, is a powerful force in education. It stands behind quantitative research into effective schools and teachers, competency-based teacher evaluation, and much of the research into curriculum implementation. Key issues in technical reflection include fidelity of teachers' practice to some set of empirically or theoretically derived standards and the development of technical skills of teaching. For example, the kind of reflection required in a programme of supervision based on Madeline Hunter's model of teaching[10] emphasizes fidelity to the propositional knowledge of the model and attention to the conditions under which each principle ought to be applied.[11] Similarly, there is a technical interest in Cruickshank *et al.*'s[12] 'reflective teaching', a programme of initial teacher education using a kind of peer or micro teaching. The lesson content, objectives, time allocation and materials are all predetermined, and what is 'reflective' is the discussion among peers and with instructors which follows each peer-teaching episode.[13]

In all of the discussions I had with Johanna during a year of collaborative work, there were no clear examples of reflection with such technical interests. In general, Johanna was suspicious of the plans and programmes promoted by her school board and unimpressed by the possibility that she would improve her teaching by following prescriptions of people who were no longer involved in classroom teaching. The closest Johanna came to using propositional knowledge during the study was to refer several times to her reading of a pair of books by Thomas Gordon, *Teacher Effectiveness Training*[14] and *Parent Effectiveness Training*.[15] On the day we first talked about the possibility of participation in a collaborative study, she mentioned that she had recently read one of these books and that it had made a substantial impact on her.[16] Much later, when she was planning a curriculum night, she considered looking in these books for activities which might help parents understand her approach to problem-solving with their children.[17] She had discovered these books at a time when she was trying to improve her communication with her daughter, and thought of them as symbolic of the changes she had been making as a teacher in the time just before we met. As she said to me one day towards the end of the intensive phase of our work together:

> 'My memory of the very beginning of your being here had to do
> with my involvement with *Teacher Effectiveness Training*. I
> found the books the summer before you came and they had really
> changed the way I was working with kids. I found that I was

> having tremendous difficulty here — tremendous success in many
> areas but also tremendous difficulty . . . .I really wanted to be
> here and I was trying to figure out how I was going to do that.'[18]

Johanna had not attended a training programme using this approach, and she did not make detailed references to skills or principles she had drawn from these books, but they had come to symbolize something special and important about her philosophy of education and the approach to children she had been trying to bring to community school. She rarely talked about teaching in terms of skills, preferring to talk in terms of 'tricks' which she might trade with other teachers at, for example, drama conferences.

> 'For instance, working in groups of three I have got in my bag of
> tricks different things I can have them do with the same
> information. I can have the kids sitting back to back so that they
> can't see each other while they are talking, and both doing a
> running monologue about how they are feeling at the same time.
> It's another way of approaching the same problem. I can switch
> and have them do whole group work, and if kids are finding it too
> hard, too embarrassing, I can take the focus of that and put it
> somewhere else . . . .You have to have those skills and that's why
> I go to drama workshops, because people will teach me different
> things to do with kids, things that I wouldn't have tried that
> work brilliantly. And once that becomes part of your repertoire,
> then you can trot that out at any time.'[19]

Of course, the kind of reflection involved in trading these tricks barely fits the notion of technical reflection. Johanna's interest was not in fidelity to prior theory or practice, but in expanding her repertoire, not unlike the way that Habermas, in his chapter, describes how experienced teachers constantly expand their classroom repertoires. And as Johanna pointed out in this same discussion, 'You only take it in as it relates to your own life, anyway.' This brings us to personal reflection.

Personal Interest

Much more common in Johanna's work was reflection with a personal interest, an interest in connecting experience with her understanding of her own life. Such a personal interest in reflection informs Connelly and Clandinin's narrative method in teacher education.[20] Narrative, they explain, is 'the study of how humans make meaning of experience by endlessly telling and retelling stories about themselves that both refigure the past and create purposes in the future.'[21] Johanna told many stories about herself which explained the biographical connections between her experiences and her actions, and which shaped her sense of how she ought to act in the future. She talked, for example, about the biographical roots of her very earnest and serious approach to teaching. As a child at primary school she felt that her job was to be intelligent, helpful and well-behaved, and she took life very seriously:

> 'That all came from the fact that I was the child after a Down
> syndrome kid, and I think that when I went into that school I
> was a kid with a purpose. I knew exactly what I had to do in life.
> These were things that were expected of me and I knew really
> clearly what I had to do. I was really serious. I can remember my
> Dad . . . saying to me, "Who's the funny one in the group?" And
> I said, "Well, I guess it's me." And he just laughed. He said,
> "You!" as if it was totally impossible that I would be funny. And
> I thought, "Oh, I guess I'm not funny." But there must have
> been some of the big me — that loves a joke — in the little me. I
> still do take life very seriously, and I don't think that there's
> anything I can do to change that. That's who I am.'[22]

In the past, one of the consequences of her serious approach to teaching has been that Johanna had sometimes taken on more commitments — shows, parental interviews, problem-solving with students — than she could manage, and she had often felt guilty and dissatisfied that she has not lived up to her hopes and dreams. In her private life she had been trying to give up the debilitating expectation that life always ought to be perfect, and to take more pleasure in the present. Her strategy had been to surround herself with friends who supported her to appreciate the moment — the journey — rather than the destination.[23] As she looked back at the experience of reading the field notes and early drafts of this study, she realized that she had been making some progress on this personal and professional issue.[24] She was now more ready to accept that she was a good teacher and less inclined to be critical of herself. Our collaboration, she said, came at 'exactly the right time' for her, and it had captured the 'artistry' of her work:

> 'I was embarking on something totally new, I was having to
> rethink everything, I was feeling very open to understanding and
> being willing to accept my being a good teacher and not being so
> hard on myself as a teacher. It fit perfectly. Although I have
> always been interested in looking at what I do, this was probably
> the best time to catch me . . . .It is as if someone had been able to
> capture the artistry of what I was doing and that felt good to
> know that it was recorded somewhere. This thing that I had
> worked on and honed had actually made it down on paper.'[25]

Similarly, she talked about the connection between her commitment to helping students to become more independent and her own experience of uncertainty at college during the 'druggy times' of the 1960s:

> 'It really affects what I do with kids. My feeling about why that
> time was so absolutely terrifying for so many kids is that the
> world didn't make any sense to them in terms of their own

independence. They were not strong, they were not solid and I
certainly wasn't. I'd never been given practice in decision
making. I was looking for some sort of meaning for life, for some
sort of truth that I was told was very important, and then
handed Catholicism. So, for me that was a terrifying time because,
although it was very exciting, you were being blown about by
winds that were bigger than you and you could be so badly hurt.
People were dying, people were going crazy. It was heady,
because you finally had your freedom and you were beginning to
do things together as a group, but we were such children.'[26]

Her education and upbringing had not helped Johanna learn to make decisions about her own life, she thought, and this had consequences for her actions
as a teacher:

'You don't have to be a baby at 18 and 19 and 20. But our society
made us children and kept us children. It is something I feel is
terribly dangerous to children. You have to give them the
strength to go out and be able to protect themselves and be
independent and make it in the world and not be led by peer
pressures into stuff that is going to be destructive. So, that
experience of being so totally unprepared led to how I feel I ought
to deal with kids now.'[27]

For Johanna, one of the effects of personal reflection is that it supports her
sense of agency, her sense that she controls her own destiny. From her father —
'who always wanted a boy', she said — she received permission to be the one
who decides what she should do, to be the wage-earner, to take control rather
than be controlled by others.[28] Subsequently, and through a series of changes in
country of residence and subject specialty as a teacher, she has struggled to
construct a safe and comfortable working environment. Now, at Community
School, she feels that she has achieved the freedom to do what she wants to do as
a teacher:

'As a career, right now I have the freedom to really do what I
want to do with the kids, which is an unbelievable freedom. Very,
very few teachers have that freedom to work in an environment
of people that I know and love, and do what I want to do without
having too much interference from people who are trying to tell
me what I ought to be doing. I am in a wonderful situation at the
moment. If I can make it less work for myself and less
exhausting, then it is a great position to be in.'[29]

Problematic Interest

Unlike reflection with a personal interest, which connects biography and experience, the problematic interest is concerned with resolution of the problems of

professional action. This is the interest most fully represented in Schon's work on reflection.[30] The problems that most concern Schon are problems which fall outside the established technical knowledge of a profession: cases, for example, which are not 'in the book'[31] and situations which are 'uncertain, unique or conflicted'.[32] Such problem-solving may occur in informal frame experiments which take place while it is still possible to alter the outcomes of action — Schon's reflection-in-action — or after the event, as in Schon's reflection-on-action. In either case, his interest is primarily with the situations that learners or practitioners already see as problematic: occasions where people are surprised by what happens and are moved to rethink their professional practice.

There were many examples of reflection with a problematic interest as Johanna and I taught writing and science together. Some of this reflection was what Schon calls reflection-on-action. We talked, for example, about problems with content, alternative patterns of teaching, ways of pursuing independent learning goals, and the problems we had with particular groups and students. More interesting, and less well-documented in the educational literature, are those examples of the reflection with a problematic interest Schon calls reflection-in-action.[33] The excerpt below, from a writing lesson on 28 October, 1988, provides several such examples. This lesson was part of a long sequence of lessons during which Johanna's classes prepared the text for their own illustrated books.

About two weeks into the illustrated book project, Johanna had asked students to complete the text of their books and to be ready to hand them in. When she announced to the students in Group 1 that she was coming round the class to check, some of the students attempted to talk her out of collecting the work, claiming that they didn't know about the deadline or shifting the blame to some third party. Johanna was irritated because she had planned to take the scripts home and correct them before students started to do their illustrations. How could she do this if students were not all finished? She took out her mark book to record those who were ready and those who were not.

> 'How many people are done? I am going to take this down. A
> little language mark. [*Writing in a column of her mark book.*]
> "Story by due date." If you have done what was required for
> today — no excuses count — if you were done by today, raise
> your hand.'[34]

Just as she realized that only five of the 16 students present had done as she asked, a student arrived with a message from the school secretary asking her to check the form which she had prepared for students' first interim reports from the school. Johanna seized the opportunity offered by this interruption, connected the mark she had just allocated for meeting the due date to the interim report, and began reading aloud from the interim report form.

> 'Listen up. Interim reports are coming out soon. Here's what the
> interim report which is going home on Monday is going to say.

> You could be in the "A" category: "This student is making good
> use of Community School", or you could be in the "B" category:
> "This student is progressing satisfactorily. The check marks
> indicate areas which the teachers consider require special
> attention: home work, behavior, punctuality." Punctuality! "C: A
> teacher who places a check mark in one of these boxes does so
> because he or she feels grave concern for this aspect of the
> student's learning and would like to discuss the matter: Math
> skills, reading skills, need for supervision, ability to meet
> deadlines." Ability to meet deadlines! Five of you passed test
> number 1, ability to meet dead lines!'[35]

While students were finding their calendars and marking in their weekend homework, I walked across to Johanna, who had been sitting on a stool on the rug in the centre of the room. She turned to me and said:

Johanna	What shall we do?
Bill	I was just going to suggest that one way of saving you some marking time at home would be for the two of us . . .
Johanna	To travel round?
Bill	. . . to read their stuff while the students who are ready continue with their reading.
Johanna	OK, I'll let the five students who are done do their illustrations. (*To class*) OK, we are going to have two different lessons happen today. The first lesson is for the five people who are ready — and this is what you would all be doing if you were ready — can start to work in their sketchbooks on the illustrations for each page. Those of you who have not finished must catch up and do your proof-reading right now.[36]

While Johanna moved around the room helping students with their proof-reading, I sat at a table and worked through several students' stories in detail. At the end of the lesson, Johanna said, 'That worked well. We can keep helping them while they do their illustrations. This would be better than taking it home to check.' I replied, 'Exactly, the point is that it gives us the chance to teach at the point of error rather than taking it home and practising our own spelling and punctuation.'

There are two instances of the form of problematic reflection Schon calls reflection-in-action and one of reflection-on-action in this story. First, when Johanna was interrupted by the student carrying sample report forms just as she realized that only five of her 16 students had met the absolute deadline she had set, she seized the moment and connected the two events. Like Schon's example of a jazz player's reflection-in-action, she smoothly integrated a new element into her ongoing performance.[37] Second, when she realized the impact this would have on her lesson plan, we had a quick conference about what to do next. Like Schon and his example of reflection-in-action as he built his garden gate,[38] we were surprised by what happened and invented a new procedure in the midst of action. Had Johanna been on her own, she might have taken a moment to have a similar, silent conversation with herself. Third, as the lesson closed we swapped stories about our responses to this unexpected turn of events. As we reflected on what had happened, Johanna commented that the split-second decision we made (our reflection-in-action) had worked well, and I observed that this pattern of teaching might help solve the problem with which she began the book project — finding a way to help students with their sentence construction.

We were both pleased with the effect of this decision to split the class into two groups, but for different reasons. For me, it was an opportunity to introduce an important and well-practised instructional pattern into this writing class. I knew that while some students were doing illustrations I would have time to help others correct their spelling and punctuation and to talk to them about the meaning of what they were making. For this reason it had been my standard practice to structure writing tasks that lasted over a series of lessons. For Johanna, splitting the class represented an appropriate consequence for students who had or had not met her deadlines and the school's independent learning goals. So, in addition to the embarrassment of making public their tardiness and the possibility that this issue would be raised in interim reports and at parent interviews, the tardy students were required to continue writing while the others began the more generally enjoyed task of planning their book illustrations. My presence meant that the other students could get some time and help to catch up without disadvantaging students who had done as Johanna asked.

The difference in meaning for the two of us at the time that we solved this little practical problem is deeply connected to our biographies and to our hopes and dreams as teachers. For me, making class time to correct students' work at the point of error is an article of faith in teaching. Years ago, in my first weeks as an English teacher, I realized that the corrections I made on students' scripts at home made no difference to their writing at school. When, in my fifth year of teaching, I learned how to organize my classes so that there was time to teach at the point of error, I felt that I had solved one of the major pedagogical problems in the teaching of English. Even better, it dealt with the terrible irony that while my students with spelling problems were watching television in the evenings, I was sitting at home using their scripts to practise my spelling.

Similarly, Johanna has always admired schools and teachers which provided students with opportunities to work independently, but believes that students should not be left on their own in the hope that they will discover ways of working independently. Part of the role of a teacher, she believes, is to provide a structure which supports students while they are learning to be more independent. One part of this structure is that teachers make their expectations clear and ensure that there are consequences when students do not meet those expectations. For this reason, she keeps very careful records, so that she knows which kids regularly do and do not meet deadlines. Although Johanna and I had different reasons for coming to the same resolution to this problem, by the end of the grade seven lesson, when she said 'That worked well', she had realized the practical advantage of having students spread across different stages of a longer task.

Critical Interest

Although perhaps the least familiar interest for reflection among teachers, if the reports of Jackson[39] and Lortie[40] are to be believed, what I am calling critical reflection is the most comprehensively theorized of the four interests of reflection.[41] The essence of the critical interest in reflection is that it involves questioning taken-for-granted thoughts, feelings and actions. Through such reflection, teachers may confront and perhaps transcend the constraints they otherwise perceive as normal or natural. Critical reflection begins with the assumption that reality is socially constructed and that people can act to influence the conditions in which they find themselves. To this end, critical reflection involves considering who benefits from current practices, how these practices might be changed, and personal or political action to secure changes in the conditions of classroom work.

One example of critical reflection concerns Geoffrey, a boy who had proved difficult for many of the staff at Community School to manage. As we sat at the lunch table one day, Johanna, Miles (another teacher at the school) and I were talking about problems we had all had with Geoffrey. Johanna was wondering whether or not we were accepting our responsibility to society in the way we dealt with him. He was a very able person, with well-developed academic skills but very little interest in any of the school programmes. More than that, he seemed to be perpetually angry, and this prevented him from being a member of any of the school's social groups. What would happen if we did not try to help Geoffrey?

Johanna Some woman is going to pay for the fact that Geoffrey is so angry, or society will pay. This is our only chance to catch somebody like Geoffrey . . .

Miles Right now his behaviour is reasonably self-destructive but it is directed at himself. It's not masochistic, it's just that he wants to get everybody else as angry with him as he is with himself. It might pass, perhaps with adolescence.

Bill But when will it pass?

Johanna And how much pain is there going to be for us until it does?

Bill And is this a good place for him to be waiting for it to happen? When he goes to high school next year and he is

told to sit down and shut up, he probably will fit in. But any
opportunity he has to learn by someone working with his
anger will have passed. This is the only school where he is
likely to get some help. Everywhere else, he'll just get
school work.[42]

It might well have been easier for the school to accommodate Geoffrey's behaviour, or to ignore it, but Johanna's decision was to accept some of the social responsibility in the hope that she could reduce the price some woman had to pay in the future. She would continue to help him learn to take responsibility for his actions — instead of blaming other people — just as she had when he had quit strings. In just the same way, she defended the school's difficult decision to continue to work with Mark, a much more seriously disturbed boy:

Johanna   The only reason we decided to keep him was that we
couldn't imagine where else in the system he would go
where there was a chance of him learning something.

Bill   The kids say he's selfish but the teachers do look after him.

Johanna   Well we have to, because soon he's going to be out in society.
If he can't control himself. . . You see he has come a long
way in controlling himself. Now, when he feels he is going to
blow, he goes and is by himself. He tries to work it out there.
He has come so far in his social interaction. He is beginning
to see that what he does affects how people see him.[43]

It was not always easy for Johanna and myself to find time for reflection at community school. Often we would have lunch together at the bistro across the road from the school and there, freed from the press of students passing through the staffroom asking questions and looking for company, we were able to discuss a wider range of issues. We talked at length, for example, about the idea of a good school and about the possibilities of educational change.[44] In one of these discussions, Johanna talked about a school board seminar she and Miles had just attended. The topic was 'active learning', a major local priority in the year of the study. She was enthusiastic about the workshop, partly because she agreed with what the speaker had been saying and partly because he had said it in front of her principal:

'Miles's comment was that what he said we all knew 15 years
ago — but he said it to a gathering of every single teacher in this
area. He said it in front of the superintendent and our principal.
He'd been hired to come and say it, so obviously it was approved
of.
What they said was exactly what you and I have been
saying, which is that you cannot pour knowledge into a kid. What

> a kid actually learns will depend on how actively involved in his
> own education and problem-solving he is and that to delineate the
> number of minutes [per week] that you have him doing a certain
> thing doesn't give you any information about what has happened
> educationally for that child.
>
> So it was a vindication and I looked around to see if [the
> principal] was listening to that little bit because it is what we
> have been saying to him.'[45]

I was glad that Johanna felt vindicated by what the speaker had said in
front of her principal, but I wondered aloud what other people might have made
of the session. There was obviously a good fit between Johanna's teaching and
the idea that was being promoted. I wondered, however, whether such a session
would have been any use to a teacher with a more skills-orientated approach to
teaching. Did talking about 'active learning' in fact make any difference? This
attitude seemed a little pessimistic to Johanna, who knew how much she had
changed as a teacher in recent years. She had, she said, spent many years 'trying
to impose the way I felt things ought to be on kids, instead of listening to where
they were'. Perhaps such sessions could help other people to progress towards
active learning. My reaction was that such sessions would have no impact on
Johanna's own teaching. As I put it to her:

> 'What they are ignoring is how deeply connected what you did
> today is to your history. You are an "activity" teacher. When you
> get a subject which lends itself in other people's hands to giving
> lectures and notes, you turn it into an activity subject. Invariably,
> you go for the kid's personal difficulty not the subject content.'[46]

We realized that we had a fundamental difference of opinion about the value and
the possibility of making a particular teaching method compulsory, and were
interested to explore our differences.

> *Bill* It's to do with the difference between being powerfully
> convinced that for you it is the best thing to do, and
> insisting that other people do the same.
>
> *Johanna* You feel that because it happens to be right for me, that I
> should not therefore jump to the conclusion that it would be
> right for everybody?[47]

This was what I had meant, and I went on to suggest that there was more at
stake here than personal preferences. What happened to a person with a skills-
orientated view of teaching, such as a colleague of Johanna's, whose history left
him poorly equipped to take on 'active learning'? I explained:

> 'So, when someone stands up in the staffroom at the beginning of
> the year and announces that the Board has three priorities this

year and one is active learning, what goes on inside [Johanna's
colleague] is that he wipes off the Board or he feels guilty.
Neither of those is healthy for the system or the teacher. My
sense is that alongside the announcement that the Board is
interested in active learning there needs to be space for
something that a black-and-white person can do well.'[48]

The difference between us was not in our vision of good schooling but in our
sense of the practical and ethical problems of communicating our vision to other
people. Johanna, perhaps more committed to the value of active learning than
concerned about what it would be like to have someone trying to impose a
different teaching method on her, responded with an assertion of the need for
change and a practical example of the way she would approach it.

'I still feel that there is a way. When you are at teachers' college
you do courses which are theoretically supposed to help you
understand the human mind. I would like to teach those courses
by having the people actually being involved in the technique of
active listening. If you experience that, the difference that it
makes . . . To give you an example, yesterday I was in this drama
group with a guy from England. I watched what happened in the
group. One of the people in my group was very bossy and I was
put off by her approach. I could sense that there were several
people in the group who had never done any drama before and
were very nervous. Because of what I know about how to listen to
people, I was able to get the group working happily together.
That kind of skill is tremendously useful to teachers because it
makes stuff happen. Now I could teach that to teachers and that
would be a very worthwhile thing, because that's what we
do — work in groups — so I would say that would be a way of
changing people.'[49]

In conversations such as this, one interest in reflection may be dominant
without other interests being abandoned. Here, the interest is primarily critical,
because it concerns the application of power over teachers and the possibility
that well-meaning educational change activities may close down some people's
opportunities to teach in ways that are consistent with their own biography and
experience. But alongside this interest in the ethical conditions of the use of
power is Johanna's personal interest in ways of teaching that are biographically
appropriate for her, and my personal interest in the need for plurality in
educational change. More than this, the critical interest in the discussion is
pursued through the example of a practical problem and the technical skills
Johanna used in overcoming the problem.

The notion of critical reflection developed in this section draws directly on
the emancipatory interest that Habermas has introduced to the debate about

reflection, in that it is concerned with a critique of the social structures within which people act. Because the examples are drawn from the case study data rather than representing ideal types, however, they lack the political edge which proponents of critical reflection may have in mind.[50] Biographically, Johanna's response to uncomfortable social structures has more often been practical action than political action. Uncomfortable with the reaction to her music and drama programme at a previous school, for example, she preferred to move to Community School than to attempt the task of reforming the school. Her personal responses have led her to a safe place on the margin of a large school district; there, rather than attempting to change the structure of regular schools, she holds open the possibilities for her particular vision of teaching by her practical action at Community School.

FORMS OF REFLECTION

These four *interests* of reflection account for the range of reasons teachers might have for reflection, but they do not help elaborate the range of ways in which changes in understanding and action take place. To explore the latter issue more closely, I now turn to the dimension of *forms* of reflection. This set of categories represents a range from reflection as a process of thinking or feeling separated from action to reflection as a process which takes place in the moment of action. Between these extremes stand two categories of reflection which deal with both thought and action.

The reason for arraying forms of reflection across this dimension is that the forms ought to allow for the ranges between tacit and explicit knowledge. Some of Johanna's knowledge as a teacher is tacit and embodied in her practice, in patterns such as the way she conducts class discussions or conferences, the way she begins and ends lessons, and the way she teaches guitar to whole-class groups. Other parts of Johanna's knowledge are more explicit, such as her content knowledge in music and art, and the hopes and dreams for teaching which impel her to work with students' feelings and to prefer content which is relevant to their interests. Some of her knowledge is not knowledge at all — in the sense of knowledge as justified true belief — but a series of unanswered questions on which she is still working, such as how she can best help students to become more independent and how she can find a comfortable way of teaching science.

Consequently, this dimension ranges between forms of reflection appropriate to the two extremes of tacit and explicit knowledge. At one extreme, reflection may be a conscious process conducted at some distance from the stream of action. This form of reflection, which involves both thinking and feeling, may be called reflection as *introspection*. At the other extreme stands a form of reflection so bound up in the moment of action that there is no conscious awareness of thinking about the action, a form of reflection which may be called reflection as *spontaneity*. The two intermediate categories are reflection as *replay and rehearsal*, the sort of reflection which might involve a teacher thinking or talking about events that have happened or might happen in the future, and reflection as *enquiry*, a form of reflection which involves thinking and acting in a deliberate process of inquiry. Whereas Schon's dichotomy of reflection-in-action and reflection-on-action accounts for this range in two forms of reflection, the remainder of this paper explores these four forms of reflection and connects the forms of reflection with the four interests already established.

Introspection

Introspection, which involves looking inwards and reconsidering one's thoughts and feelings about some issue, is the closest form of reflection to the ordinary language sense of reflection as contemplation or meditation. Boyd and Fales,[51] for example, talk about 'reflective learning', a process of 'internally examining and exploring an issue of concern, triggered by an experience, which creates and clarifies meaning in terms of self, and which results in a changed conceptual perspective'.[52] For Boyd and Fales introspection clearly has a personal interest, but this need not be the case. Mezirow,[53] for example, has outlined a process of introspection with a critical interest which he calls 'perspective transformation'. By confronting the psychological and cultural assumptions which constrain the way people see things, he argues, they may transform their perceptions of the world. He describes a series of levels of reflectivity which include affective reflectivity, which refers to the process of becoming aware of how we feel about our preconceptions and habits of action, and psychic reflectivity, which leads a person, for example, to consider unresolved childhood dilemmas.

In Johanna's case, most of the introspection she shared with me had a personal interest: the relationship between her family of origin and her attitudes to life and work; the relationship between her experience of the 'druggy times' of the 1960s and her determination to help students learn to accept more responsibility for their own decision-making; the effect of learning clarinet as an adult on her attitudes to praise in music teaching. Less often, this introspection led to reflection with a critical intent, such as in the following story about the experience of growing up during the second wave of feminism:

> 'There was an interesting episode in high school with my two
> crazy friends, who certainly were not the twin-set-and-pearls
> style. One of them was on the committee where they could elect
> the Prom Queen, and my name came up. My friend told me about
> it later. She said, "I couldn't do it to you Johanna, I just
> couldn't. I got you out of it." At the time I had the feeling that it
> was bizarre that I would want recognition from that world, of
> being the female symbol of sexuality. I was saved by my friend
> but I wasn't sure I was saved. I wanted it, yet it would have
> grated. The same sort of thing continued at college. I didn't know
> where I belonged. At the fraternity, one of the things they did

was hold a huge parade and they would find girls to march along
the parade wearing short skirts and looking sexy. I can remember
doing that and thinking, "Nah. This is not where I want to be.
This is me on a platter, served up."

It was very hard for me to find a way of being feminine and
sexy without going into that world where women are objects. So
for a long time I couldn't pass through a cosmetic department
in a big department store without feeling that the women who
stood behind the counters would recognize that I was not one of
them. I wasn't a type who could do that. Somehow I would like
to have been able to be female in that way, whatever that was. I
had to find that much later, how to be feminine and not be a
possession.'[54]

The interest in this introspection is critical, in the sense that it relates to her
struggle to find a way of being feminine without being a sex object, but the story
would be too private for some people to tell. At an early stage in this study,
fearful that I would exceed the boundaries beyond which a researcher ought not
to pry, I was inclined to close down some of the more delicate and personal
aspects of introspection. During a life-history interview, for example, I stopped
myself in the middle of a line of questioning to ask whether I had exceeded those
reasonable boundaries:

'Part of me — the therapist part — feels like saying, "Can you
tell me some more about that", and asking you to give an
example and go into your inner life. It just occurred to me as you
said that that it is not my role. It's not what I am doing here. I
am just trying to get a good, clean, clear story that gives a sense
of who you are, so that people can understand what you do in the
classroom. . . . It's not my task to help you understand the way
you are. I would need a license to do that.'[55]

Not only did Johanna reject the possibility that I could get a good, clean,
clear story ('Stories don't come good and clean and clear', she said), but she
also rejected my artificial separation of the roles of therapist, teacher and
researcher.

'Well, *there's* an issue, because I don't think so. That's a real
teaching issue. That means that I don't have a license to do what
I do with the kids, to help them understand why they are . . . and
you are my friend, and I'm your friend. I would help you, we all
do that for each other. Which really means that therapists are an
artificial construction of society because we don't do it enough for
each other.'[56]

In our work together, we reached this explicit agreement to include
introspection which might be thought by some to be too private and personal,

but that might not always be the case in other research projects. This agreement was reached in the context of a teacher-researcher relationship which had been developed with particular care, and involved a teacher who was more than usually open and forthcoming. Judging by the reluctance of other teachers on the staff to make any comments on the early field notes I shared with them,[57] other teachers may not have been as forthcoming. Some teachers may regard the depth of introspection required in, for example, journal writing or a research project such as this study, as beyond the reasonable boundaries of research or professional development.[58]

Replay and Rehearsal

Replay and rehearsal is a form of reflection which involves teachers' discourse about events that have occurred or the possibility of future actions. As teachers talk to their colleagues (or write) about their work they make sense of surprising classroom events, draw provisional generalizations which may inform their future practice, make plans for action, and affirm their values. This form of reflection is one step closer to action than *introspection*, but still stands at some distance from the deliberate movement between action and reflection which characterizes *enquiry*. The conditions of teachers' classroom work — immediacy, multidimensionality, simultaneity, unpredictability[59] — mean that it is rarely possible for teachers to think or talk about the meaning of their experience or their immediate plans while they are still in what Schon calls 'the action present'.[60] More often, teachers are fully immersed in what they are doing, too busy juggling burning swords, to reflect consciously on what they are doing while there is still time to change the situation at hand.

Unlike the 'virtual worlds' which Schon describes in the profession of architecture,[61] it is not easy to construct realistic models of teaching where teachers may practise and refine their actions.[62] Real classrooms are usually too busy to allow teachers to step outside the stream of action, and thus usually the 'meaning-making' takes place outside the classroom: in the hallway, in the staffroom, on the journey home, over dinner or at teachers' conferences. On these occasions teachers tell stories about their experiences, replaying events in a form which outsiders may dismiss as unreflective 'war stories'. Replaying the events of a school day and rehearsing alternative courses of action is essential to making meaning of the experience.

In Johanna's case there are many examples of such reflection. Indeed, one of the advantages for Johanna of our collaborative work was that she had someone to tell these stories to. Garth, her husband, was very patient in listening to her stories but he didn't appreciate them in the way that I did:

> *Johanna*   I have never had anyone who was really as interested in what I was doing as I was, and here was somebody who was *totally* interested! How many people does that happen to in life! I mean, can you imagine if someone came up to you and

> said, 'I really want to know all about you. Tell me in
> complete detail.'

Bill   And to actually *be* fascinated as well!

Johanna   Yes, it isn't a lie. No matter how much Garth tries, he could
never be as interested in the actual machinations as you
were. That was wonderful. It worked so well.[63]

Such replays and rehearsals of experience may proceed with a technical, personal, problematic or critical interest. When Shulman[64] talks about reflection, for example, he describes it as when a teacher 'looks back at the teaching and learning that has occurred, and reconstructs, re-enacts, and/or recaptures the events, the emotions, and the accomplishments' of teaching. It is through this process, Shulman points out, that professionals learn from experience. In Shulman's sense of reflection, the interest is essentially technical:[65]

> it is likely that reflection is not merely a disposition (as in 'she's
> such a reflective person!') or a set of strategies, but also the use
> of particular kinds of analytical knowledge brought to bear on
> one's work . . . Central to this process will be a review of the
> teaching in comparison to the ends that were sought.[66]

Other teacher educators and researchers, more concerned with the personal meaning than with fidelity of means to ends, have encouraged teachers to tell stories about their work and lives in order that they may reshape their understanding of their past, present and future.[67] Similarly, researchers with a critical interest, such as Tripp[68] and Berlak and Berlak[69] have argued that teachers should talk or write about their experience in order to understand it in new ways. Berlak and Berlak, for example, suggest that teachers ought to reconsider their present patterns of action, alternatives to these patterns, the consequences of these patterns for children, the origins of these patterns, and the implications for their craft knowledge of making changes in their teaching. The essence of this critique is for teachers to reconstruct what they have previously taken for granted.

In our collaborative work, however, the larger part of the replay and rehearsal of classroom events was reflection with a problematic interest. Johanna and I often talked in very concrete terms about the meaning of events we had just experienced, or about the possibilities for future action. These conversations often involved verbatim rehearsals of what we would say to a class. The examples below include a typical case of replay after the event, and a much rarer example of a time when we were able to step out of the stream of experience to consider our options while a class waited for the decision.

The first of these examples concerns a relatively theoretical discussion we had during a spare lesson period one afternoon.[70] Picture us sitting in the quietest place we could find, the fire-escape steps, interrupted from time to time by a class from the junior division of the school moving up or down from the play-ground. I had lately been reading Gramsci,[71] and was wondering whether his notion of common sense, that unreflective knowledge which is composed of both good sense and bad sense, might be a useful analytic structure for this study. Johanna had read a commentary on Gramsci and a working paper I had prepared on common sense, and thought it was all a little disconnected from reality.[72] I had been talking about some of the common-sense qualities of the teachers' knowledge that I had noticed at the school and mentioned that I had been surprised how context-specific my own knowledge of teaching was:

> *Bill* It's like knowledge of what will work disappears if you
> change classes, or subjects, or — in my case — countries. Or
> if you have a bit of a break.

> *Johanna* Like summer? Which explains why I was terrified on the
> first day of school, although I have been doing this for
> twenty years. The break totally destroys your sense that you
> can do it again. The thing about teaching that every teacher
> knows is that it is like handling animals: the kids, if they
> know that you are scared, will be in control. So it's a
> confidence trick. It will work only if you can convince them
> that you can make it work. This is something that every
> teacher in their heart of hearts knows. Really, this is dicey
> at times. There is no way you could control a group of kids
> who didn't want to be controlled. It has to do with a
> tremendous number of tricks you pull out of your bag, things
> that you know about child psychology, and every teacher
> has their own bag of tricks. There is always a chance that
> those tricks may not work. You have to keep going through
> the bag.[73]

My response to this image of teachers' knowledge as a bag of tricks was to think of several concrete cases where we had needed to dig deep into the bag.

> *Bill* With some kids, like Mark, you just get to the point where
> you think: 'My bag is empty. That's it for tricks'.

> *Johanna* Yes.

> *Bill* Then you get a case like Luke, just then. When you
> approach him, you don't know what's going to happen. You
> think that you can talk him into [rewriting his illustrated
> book], but you don't know whether he is going to pull a face
> and wipe you off for a month.

> *Johanna* Yes, because I had to watch his face really closely and judge
> what to say next. I was looking for the recognition in his

197

eyes that he knew it was rubbish. That didn't come as
quickly as I thought it would come with Luke. He obviously
had more investment in the story than I thought.

Bill I thought it would come as soon as I said, 'You are a smart
guy, you can do better than this.'

Johanna We managed to pull ourselves out of that, having taken the
wrong track to start with, to think of other tricks we knew.[74]

In such ways, Johanna and I spent dozens of hours of spare lesson periods,
lunch hours and breaks exploring our understanding of events we had been too
busy enacting to reflect on at the time. Much less commonly, we had time to
rehearse our options while a class was there in front of us, as we did on 27
October 1988. Our task for the day was to teach a small class of grade seven students how to organize independent field trips (IFTs) to community institutions.
Johanna began by explaining her goals for these field trips:

Johanna First of all, you want to find your way around the city. You
want to get your own education instead of just having the
teachers be in charge of it. You want to be prepared for high
school, where you are going to need some independence.
And, you are actually learning things. It is a wonderful
opportunity for your education. Your destination should
take those things into consideration.[75]

Taking the example of the Ontario Science Centre, Johanna led a discussion about the kinds of information people might get from an IFT visit. She
linked this to the science and nutrition assignments, so students suggested
things such as finding out the life cycle of an animal. Next, Johanna talked
about the ways people might get information, how they might prepare for the
visit by phoning ahead, and how they might plan their travel to the IFT destination. At one point, a student asked how large the IFT groups ought to be.
Johanna stopped the lesson and turned to me, and we thought through this and a
series of other issues:

Johanna Bill, we were talking about starting five people at a time
and you were going to supervise that. Shall we ask for
volunteers now?

Bill We need to decide whether when we say five at a time we
mean a group of five or five people in smaller groups.

Johanna What would be the consequences?

Bill At a place like the Science Centre five is fair, but at lots of
other places five students would crowd the people out. We
could do it on a case by case basis.

Johanna   In a group like this, if we can take a period to work on it with them, can we have everybody simultaneously?

Bill   In this group we could let everyone do it, but not Group 3. There's also a problem with the number of phone lines we have. How could they all plan at once?

Johanna   I was thinking that planning would be done at home.

Bill   The Science Centre would be ideal for the first IFT, because there are lots of different places people could gather information there.

Johanna   The thing about having them all go to the Science Centre at once is that it then becomes free. They wouldn't have to travel together. Otherwise people might not get their first IFT until Christmas.

Bill   As an observer at the Science Centre, it seems to me that the larger the group, the less people seemed to be learning. The worst groups were where one teacher accompanies thirty kids and they roam around the exhibits playing hide and seek.

Johanna   So they should go in pairs.

Bill   Small groups would be better, and also students could be spread among the ROM, the Science Centre, the Museum of the History of Medicine and some libraries.

Johanna   [*Now talking to students*] OK, here's what I would like to do, and you tell me if you have a problem with this. I would like you to pick one or two people with whom to travel, that you find for us a destination, that you will be able to identify the destination, the questions you want to ask, phone the site to ask if and when you can come.[76]

This case is by no means typical of the experience of teaching in general, and it is for this reason I have quoted it at length. Only rarely do teachers have classes of 16, groups of children who will wait patiently while teachers figure their options and the consequences, and have a colleague to discuss these issues with. More often, with one of the school's larger and less biddable classes for example, Johanna would have had to abandon the lesson entirely when she realized that she had not thought it through, or to have responded to the question with an arbitrary number of students and then relied on her spontaneity to deal with the consequences. Because teaching is more typically a stream of unreflected experience, teachers need to tell stories which help them to make meaning of experience. These stories may not be very technical, they may well be boring to the friends and spouses who were not there at the time, but these are stories which need to be told.

Enquiry

Unlike *replay and rehearsal* and *introspection*, where reflection takes place at some distance from action, enquiry is a form of reflection which involves both action and discourse about action. More than this, it involves a process of deliberate movement between action and discourse. In the educational literature on reflection, the kind of deliberate process here called enquiry has been described and theorized by Carr and Kemmis[77] in their work on action research. They describe action research as a 'self-reflective spiral of cycles of planning, acting, observing and reflecting'.[78] In addition to describing the form in which action research takes place, they link it with the critical interest for reflection. They define action research as:

> a form of self-reflective enquiry undertaken by participants in
> social situations in order to improve the rationality and justice of
> their practices, their understanding of these practices, and the
> situations in which the practices are carried out.[79]

Like the introspection involved in Mezirow's perspective transformation, and the replay and rehearsal involved in Berlak and Berlak's critical enquiry, Carr and Kemmis's stipulative definition of action research presumes that the end in view of reflection is emancipatory educational and social change.

The form of reflection here called enquiry, however, may also be undertaken with technical, personal and problematic interests. Grundy,[80] for example, describes a scenario where the action research cycle of planning, observation, action and reflection is followed, but the end in view is fidelity to already established practices of an activity-based mathematics programme. The descriptions of curriculum planning by Connelly and Clandinin[81] also include a deliberate movement between discourse and action, but in the case they describe the enquiry is shaped by a personal interest. Enquiry shaped by a problematic interest is well documented in Schon's work on reflection-in-action and in particular what he calls the 'reflective conversation', a process of conscious on-the-spot experimentation in the action present which occurs when practitioners try to resolve the unfamiliar problems which confront them in their professional practice.[82]

In the collaborative work which Johanna and I did together in teaching writing and science, much of our reflection was shaped by problematic interests. In writing, for example, a chance remark made by Johanna led me to talk about what I would normally do in a writing lesson, and this led to an invitation to teach the lesson I had described to her. Following this lesson, we talked again about what had happened, and Johanna asked me to explain what I had done and what I would normally do next. Then, responding to a chance occurrence in the classroom, we began to develop a pattern of teaching much like the one I had used for teaching writing in the past. During and after these lessons we would talk about what had happened, and Johanna and I both made some changes to our patterns of teaching as we learned more about working together. When we found that the pattern of teaching we had developed worked better for some classes than others, we discussed the alternative courses of action and decided to resolve the problem through a class meeting with Group 3. Following this meeting, we spent some time teaching parts of the class separately and when we recombined them we found that we had resolved the problems of attitude and productivity which had previously concerned us. As the series of lessons on the illustrated book project drew to a close, we talked again about what each of us had learned about teaching writing and about how we ought to resolve the education control dilemma in the context of teaching this subject.

In our science lessons, too, we began by talking about alternative ways of teaching. As I had volunteered to relieve Johanna of the burden of this teaching, I planned lessons that seemed simplest and most accessible to me, but after a few lessons Johanna decided that what I was doing was not compatible with her vision of useful education. We talked again about our goals and the school board's expectations, and decided on an alternative course of action. We left behind the school science I had been trying to master, and embarked on a more independent approach to science. For some time we helped students to find appropriate activities and experiments for the assignments, while leaving them with responsibility for the detailed planning. As the assignment deadline approached, we realized that they might need some more direct help, so we decided to teach a series of lessons geared directly towards each of the questions on the assignment. Johanna and I began the science lessons with a different sense of what would be useful and we never quite resolved our differences: she preferred students to learn to work independently and on material they found relevant, and I preferred the security of teacher-centred lessons and demonstrations. We talked through these differences and acknowledged that our differences reflected our levels of confidence in teaching the subject.

What these two cycles of teaching have in common is that they began with a discussion about educational means and ends, and involved a series of changes in direction as we reflected on the success of the lessons we planned. Throughout both cycles we would talk about our intentions, plan lessons, teach, talk about how well each lesson had gone and what we had learned, and plan new lessons. Unlike Johanna's music and art lessons, where she was working from a long-established repertoire, we had to talk about each step before we could proceed. In science, especially, where neither of us had taught the subject before, we could not rely on what Schutz and Luckman[83] called 'the natural attitude', but had to find a way of connecting the new subject with our established patterns of teaching. Inside this larger cycle of enquiry we used all four of the forms of reflection which are identified in this chapter. The way in which the other three forms may be embedded in a larger cycle of enquiry may be explored through an example drawn from our work together in science. We talked about the content of a lesson Johanna needed to teach and developed a lesson plan; Johanna taught the lesson; we talked about the detail of what she had done and connected this experience to an issue we had been talking about: Johanna's realization that she lacked the content knowledge and commitment required to teach the sort of science recommended in the guideline.

One afternoon[84] during a swimming lesson, while a specialist teacher took the swimming class, Johanna and I sat in the sun and talked about the next step to take in preparing students for the science assignment we had given them. First, we found the section in one of our textbooks that dealt with the assignment tasks we wanted to teach: classification of leaves and the life cycle of animals. As we talked about this material, Johanna wondered why it mattered that students would be able to classify things. We talked for a time about the arbitrariness of the act of classification, that the classification system chosen would then affect the way people saw the world, and the importance of having a system of classification in order to get the world's work done. I suggested that she should carry out an activity like the one suggested in the science guide, asking students to make up a system of classification to explain the objects in the room or a set of objects she chose for them. As we talked about this idea we both became quite enthusiastic. We began rehearsing aloud the kinds of things we might say or do — such as having a student among the 'things' to be classified — and laughing together at the little jokes that might result. By the end she said that this sounded like the sort of science lesson I'd like to do. It sounded like this to me, too, and I was sorry not to be there to do it.

I missed the lesson we had planned, but later[85] asked Johanna to tell me what had happened.

> 'I didn't do any more planning for the class or thinking about it than our conversation at the pool. I had a vague idea of where I was going, what I was trying to do and it seemed to me like the kind of lesson I had done enough of that I could just fly with it. I realized that was wrong when I got into Group 1 and had to teach it. The instant that I began to teach it, I realized that it might be beneficial to pretend to be from another planet and to have collected these things we were trying to identify. So I played that game with them, but it was the kind of thing that I really needed to have thought about ahead of time.'[86]

Although we had talked about what we needed to teach next and planned a way of presenting the ideas, when Johanna began to teach the lesson she realized that she had lost her grip on the lesson we had rehearsed. Instead, she followed an idea she had in class. The first time she used the 'man from Mars' idea it was with one of the relatively easy grade seven classes and the game she played led to a reasonably successful lesson. When Johanna tried to repeat her success in the more challenging context of the grade eight class, she realized that she did not really understand the idea of classification in science which she had set out to teach.

> 'By the time I did it with the second class, the Grade 8's, I realized that I wasn't really clear what I was trying to teach them

about classification. I had a vague idea that what I was trying to do was to let them see that classification is arbitrary, depending on why you are doing the classifying. But that seemed to me to be a really hard concept to imagine the kids getting their heads around. I lacked the conviction that it was going to work . . . I didn't know enough about classification. I couldn't give them examples of why someone would classify. What divides one species from another? I don't know enough science.'[87]

The lesson with the eighth grade did not go well, but the questions which students asked helped Johanna to develop some of her own ideas about classification. By the third lesson she had developed a clearer sense of the value of classification in science, and in the less demanding context of a small seventh-grade class the lesson passed quite successfully.

'Anyway, as I went through the three lessons I realized that there were some little things I could teach, such as that scientists actually *did* this, it didn't come from God, and that it had to do with ways of looking at objects and finding similarities and differences. Those things I could teach and I got better at teaching them.'[88]

We ended this small cycle of our larger enquiry with a moment of introspection. Moving beyond the replay of details of the lessons, Johanna talked about her lack of content knowledge and commitment in teaching science:

Johanna   It's so completely obvious that I don't know enough science and I haven't taught this way and done this kind of stuff to be a good science teacher.

Bill   So what's the difference between you and me in this? I obviously haven't taught science. Do I seem to have more depth of knowledge in science?

Johanna   I think you are more sure of yourself. You are fairly confident that you know as much science as you need to know to be able to help these kids. I don't. Science is a real mystery to me.[89]

This story describes a brief cycle of enquiry, itself part of the larger enquiry into teaching science. In this case, Johanna set out to teach a concept she did not really understand. By the time she had finished teaching three classes she had a stronger sense of what there might be worth teaching about the notion of classification in biology. However, she still lacked the detailed content knowledge of examples from the classification systems biologists use and the purposes these systems serve. With this cycle of enquiry there are examples of replay and rehearsal — in the lesson planning we did and in the stories Johanna told about her lessons — and of introspection. In addition, the process of learning through experience is also a form of reflection — *spontaneity* — to which we turn in the next section.

Spontaneity

The fourth and final form of reflection distinguished is spontaneity, the tacit reflection which takes place within the stream of experience. This is the form of reflection which corresponds with the 'jazz-player' form of Schon's reflection-in-action. In the midst of action, and without turning one's attention back against the stream in order to become aware of this as action in the world of time and space, teachers seize the moment and change the direction of their action. Cole[90] has described a similar process, which she calls 'teachers' spontaneous adaptations' to changing circumstances in the classroom. Building on a sense of teachers' action as informed by their professional knowledge but not necessarily consciously known, she defines teachers' spontaneous adaptation as the 'split-second overt manifestations of a covert dialogue ongoing between the teachers' knowledge and their actions'.[91] Like Schon's jazz player, this is a process of 'reading' and 'flexing'[92] to students, making small and tacit adjustments to changing circumstances in the classroom. Green,[93] too, has described this kind of reflection which takes place when we 'live forward a little' in our teaching:

> [This] kind of thinking or reflectiveness . . . is very different from
> the predictive or the calculative; it leaves possibilities open; it
> opens the way for choice, for the unexpected, for surprise. The
> issue may be as simple as turning aside from the discussion of a
> story in an English class to give students an exercise in paragraph
> construction. It may be as complex as deciding to turn, in the
> same English class, to a discussion of visual art in order to make
> clear the range and distinctiveness of the languages of art. Often,
> we take initiatives that are unexpected even for us; and rehearse
> in imagination as we may, what Dewey called 'the resultant
> action' will seldom be precisely what we had in mind.[94]

The tacit quality of spontaneity poses particular problems for a researcher hoping to document the phenomenon. In some cases, I noticed changes in direction which Johanna was only aware of after the fact. When we tried to talk about such cases more fully, the task of asking about awareness of a process which is by definition tacit led me to uncomfortable and inconclusive cross-examinations of Johanna. On one occasion, for example, I asked her how she came to make a major digression from the plan she had followed in the first of three similar lessons:

Johanna   In the second class I went into the telephone activity just
             because I was bored. I thought I'd basically cover the same

things, but just do a bit of enrichment in the area of telephone interviewing.

Bill   So, did that occur to you in the break between the lessons?

Johanna   It occurred to me two minutes before I did it.

Bill   It actually occurred to you though? You made a decision, there was a cognitive leap, 'I think I'll go on here and do telephone interviews?' The time passed and you saw a moment and then you started?

Johanna   No, the moment came, I saw it and took it. It occurred to me immediately before you took it.

Bill   You actually did think, 'I will do it' before you did it?

Johanna   I probably did actually. I was thinking about Bob, actually, and a lesson I saw him teach last year on telephone interviewing. It occurred to me when I got to that section of the IFT discussion that they were going to be doing a lot of phoning. I don't know when it happened, but I was doing it.[95]

As an observer of the two lessons, it was easy for me to notice that there had been a change in plan. In place of a discussion about the rules for setting up an IFT there was a role-play of the telephone calls students would need to make. But when I asked how the change came about Johanna was not at all certain what had happened. She might have thought about it, she could certainly remember seeing another teacher use the role-play technique successfully, but she was finally unsure whether or not she had thought about it in advance. Because it was hard for Johanna to reconstruct an account of whether she did or did not move out of the stream of experience to consciously reflect on her options, the remaining examples in this section are drawn from my notes about my own teaching. Having wondered from the beginning of the study how to account for the role of thinking in the moment-by-moment inventions teachers make in the classroom, I was more easily able to report on the phenomenon. The first example is of a brief episode of one-to-one teaching in a writing lesson.[96]

After the first two writing lessons intended to help the class prepare the text for their illustrated books, I asked one of the most reluctant writers, Monica, to show me what she had done. She had written almost a page about the camping trip on the first day. Then she had written about three lines after having a discussion with Johanna about 'the time I almost got killed', one of the tried-and-true topics Johanna had heard me use when working with students who were reluctant to begin writing.[97] This had not worked for Monica: she had once fallen out of a car but could hardly remember it, so I asked her if there was a time when she had been lost. This seemed to be a better place to start. She remembered that she and a small group of friends had been lost in the woods just a few miles from their summer cottage, so I asked her to tell me about it. Then I asked her to break it up into steps, numbering each event. When she found this too hard I dictated the first few steps for her, based on what she had told me. Gradually I weaned her from my dictation, so that by the 12th step she was writing on her own. She had filled a complete page in less than ten minutes writing and seemed pleased with the start she had made. I thought she might lose her momentum so I told her that I would talk to her on Thursday and expected that she would have finished it at home by then. She checked with me that I had said Thursday, so I knew that she left the room with the intention of finishing the story, and she did.

In a second example I confronted the familiar problem of a student who was reluctant to commit herself to a written text, too scared that she would have nothing to say or that she would make too many mistakes. This particular problem was one of a group of problems for which I had previously worked out a set of solutions. Although I had no recollection of previously using the trick of numbering the steps and dictating them back to the student, I certainly remember building up a set of sure-fire story starters, such as asking about a time the student was nearly killed or was very scared. Like Schon's jazz player, I did not explicitly search through my experience in the moment of action. Instead, I followed my spontaneity in the expectation that it would provide me with an appropriate way of helping her to produce some text. In the second example of reflection as spontaneity, my action led me to an unpredictable and unfamiliar place and I learned more about how to teach science to my grade seven classes.

A third example comes from my science teaching. During this lesson[98] my students in Group 2 were introduced to the notion that the formulation of problems is the first step in the scientific method. I used a series of activities from the school board handbook, *Science 7*, and began by asking students to formulate a problem based on their observations about the following:

1. Get down on your knees. Place an elbow against your knee and stretch your arm and fingers out on the floor.

2. Stand a chalk board duster on the tip of your fingers.

3. Place both of your hands behind your back. Bend over and knock the duster with your nose without falling over.

4. After doing the activity take a class vote for the results. How many males were successful? How many females?

I asked the class to read the instructions and write down whether they thought more boys or girls would be able to knock over the duster. Overwhelmingly, they seemed to think that it would be the girls. This was a surprise, and two possible explanations struck me. Either they had been talking about it in the hall to the other seventh-grade class, who had just had the same lesson, or they had understood me to ask whether more boys than girls in this class would be successful. Intuitively I felt it better not to check on the first possibility. If they had heard about it in the hall and they knew that I knew, it would seem silly to continue. Instead, I pointed out that there were more girls than boys in the class and asked whether people thought that girls would be more successful in general. This was still the prevailing opinion, but the fact that there were a few waverers made it possible to say, 'Well, let's find out.' So, following the same plan as the last class, I asked one boy and then one girl to try it until we ran out of boys. Once this activity started, the tone of the class completely changed. It was fun, there was lots of cheering, and from the beginning the activity took on a life of its own. Several girls could not do it and several boys could, so I said that I was not sure that science was on my side today. In an aside to Johanna, who had been listening in while she marked essays at her desk, I suggested that the effect of centre of gravity might depend on puberty.

The possibility that they could overturn the official expectations, combined with a boy–girl competition, made the activity lots of fun. After 12 students had tried, the pattern I expected had begun to emerge. I drew their attention to this, but Christine was unconvinced. She asked me to try, and I was able to knock it over. Next, Johanna tried and was not able to. One of the students commented on the puberty aside I had made, so plainly the effect of puberty on my 'centre of gravity' theory was in doubt. I asked people for a statement of the problem, and after several attempted explanations got, 'Why is it easier for women to lean forward than men?' I also asked for guesses about the cause of what we had seen, and got a range from the official centre of gravity explanations to the more frivolous suggestion that girls had longer necks and noses.

We then moved on to an activity involving vinegar, raisins and baking-soda. When the baking-soda was added to a conical flask containing a few raisins, the raisins were supposed to float to the top. I had planned to distribute the materials carefully to avoid confusion, but in the excitement of the duster activity I forgot my plan. Instead of dividing the class into groups and naming the person to collect each piece of equipment, I found myself surrounded by a dozen students clamouring for vinegar, raisins, water, conical flasks, graduated cylinders and measuring spoons. Johanna saw my confusion and put aside her marking to help me. At this point, I called the rest of the students in and began a demonstration around the bench on which I had stored the materials.

The first time, I swished the flask around too enthusiastically and the foam created by the reaction between the baking-soda and the vinegar poured out over my arm and the desk. The students (and Johanna) seemed to like this, and someone said, 'This is what I call science!' Only one of the raisins rose up on the cloud of gas, so I tried again with less agitation, and two of the three rose. With the class gathered around the bench, I asked what the problem was ('Why does the raisin rise when the baking-soda and vinegar were added?'), and explained that the reason was that the reaction between them created bubbles of gas which attached to the raisins and lifted them to the surface. I asked people why they thought that some raisins rose and others didn't, and was offered a series of suggestions relating to size, weight and surface area. It was now time to clear up, so the group broke up, washed the glassware and moved off to the morning meeting.

This last story contains a series of practical teaching problems which were resolved spontaneously. When, for example, I was confronted by the class's surprising response to the duster activity — that they overwhelmingly thought that girls would be more successful — a series of possibilities flashed through my mind in a moment. Had they heard about it in the hallway from the other class? Did it matter if they had? What else could I do, anyway? I had no time to develop or consider alternative strategies, and I felt obliged by the pressure of my audience to move smoothly and confidently on to organizing the activity I had announced, so I put aside the uncomfortable possibility that some of the students already knew what was going to happen.

The second example of spontaneity in this story concerns my decision to abandon the small-group focus of the activity involving raisins and vinegar. Having lost my mental place in the lesson plan, and briefly overwhelmed by the press of students around my bench, I spontaneously called the remainder of the class in for a demonstration of the experiment. Had I been teaching Group 3 this option would not have been open to me, but with 19 enthusiastic and biddable students and the possibility of additional assistance from Johanna, I was able to seize the moment and develop a better lesson than I had planned. And in the process I learned that with a class as small, involved and tractable as this one, demonstrations can be at least as effective as small group experiments.

The third and final example of spontaneous reflection led to one of the best moments in my term of science teaching at Community School. The students liked the theatre of the conical flask overflowing down my arm, and they were curious about why some raisins would not rise. Rather than participating in a lesson where the students guessed at the name of the problem I had prepared, we framed a new problem from our observations and were left guessing at possible explanations. The genuine sense of enquiry raised by this unforeseen outcome was, I think, what the writers of the syllabus had in mind when they contributed their own tried and true lessons on problems, observations and inferences.

CONCLUSIONS

This chapter has outlined the range of reflection in our collaboration, and considered this reflection in terms of two dimensions intended to be as inclusive as possible about the range of forms and intentions which other writers have connected with the notion of reflection. The two dimensions were proposed as complementary, in that each of the interests may be served by each of the forms of reflection, and examples from the literature were provided for each of the possible combinations of interest and form. Some others who have written about reflection have connected a single interest with a single form of reflection, such as Carr and Kemmis's critical interest and enquiry and Mezirow's critical interest and introspection. Other writers have connected a single interest with a range of forms. In Schon's case, various versions of his reflection-in-action and reflection-on-action were represented in all four of the forms of reflection, and are in each case associated with the problematic interest identified in this framework. In the case-study material, however, some interests and forms were more prominent than others. In short, introspection was most often with a personal interest, while replay and rehearsal, enquiry and spontaneity were overwhelmingly pursued with a problematic interest. There were a few examples where Johanna followed the critical interest through introspection, replay and rehearsal, and spontaneity, and there were rather fewer examples which seemed to be informed by the technical interest in any form of reflection.

This framework of analysis emerged from the experience of the collaborative case study, and was not prepared until the empirical phase of the project had been completed. It was shaped by the more intimate and introspective data available from a long-term, collaborative case study in which both the researcher and teacher were involved in reflecting on the experience of teaching. In addition, the framework was influenced by the preconceptions about teachers' knowledge and reflection that I brought to the study, by the particular circumstances of the study, and by the relationship which Johanna and I developed. Because Johanna is such an open and forthcoming person, the introspective reflection tends to be personal. Because she is intuitive rather than rationalist, there was never any prospect that the study would document in detail the technical interest. Because Johanna sees herself as having reached a position of considerable freedom from external constraints in her teaching, she was unlikely to focus in great detail on the emancipatory interest of critical reflection. In a similar way, because I was more interested in how she and I solved the practical problems of the classroom than in reshaping the conditions of Johanna's work, it is not surprising that more attention was devoted to the problematic interest than to critique. In other studies, teachers and researchers working in different conditions and carrying forward different horizons of understanding about their lives and work, might well engage in patterns of reflection which favour other of the interests and forms identified here. These are possibilities which others may choose to explore.

The value of a typology such as the forms and interests of reflection developed in this paper is that it allows for a more subtle and textured account of teachers' understanding than either a Habermasian distinction among three interests or Schon's dichotomy alone can offer. The disadvantage of such typologies is that the effort to make the set of distinctions clear may lead to the impression that a particular typology is offered as the final word on the phenomena it describes. This ought not to be the case with this conceptualization of reflection. The categories in this typology are neither as separate nor as exhaustive as they may appear when represented as sixteen individual boxes on a chart. The categories on each dimension have been separated for the purpose of analysis; one interest of reflection may be dominant without the other interests being abandoned, and teachers may move from one form of reflection to another within a single conversation. By attempting to understand reflection as a participant in the action of teaching, however, it has been possible to provide a more comprehensive account of the kinds of reflection teachers use in understanding their work.

NOTES

1. Schon, D. A., *The Reflective Practitioner*. New York: Basic Books, 1983; and Schon, D. A., *Educating the Reflective Practitioner*. San Francisco: Jossey-Bass, 1987.

2. See Elbaz, F. L., 'Knowledge and discourse: the evolution of research on teacher thinking'. Paper presented at the Conference of the International Study Association of Teacher Thinking, University of Nottingham, September 1988, for a recent review of trends in research on teachers' knowledge.

3. See Louden, W. R., 'Understanding teaching: meaning and method in collaborative research'. Unpublished doctoral dissertation, University of Toronto, 1989, for a discussion of the research method, the development of the collaborative relationship and a conceptual account of the relationship between reflection and changes in the case-study teacher's understanding of teaching.

4. See Weiss, J. and Louden, W. R., 'Clarifying the notion of reflection'. Paper presented at the Conference of the American Educational Research Association, San Francisco, April 1989, for an account of this framework in the context of the literature on reflection.

5. Habermas, J., *Knowledge and Human Interests*, translated by Shapiro, J. Boston: Beacon Press, 1971.

6. Schon, *The Reflective Practitioner* and *Educating the Reflective Practitioner*, op. cit., note 1.

7. Habermas, op. cit., note 5.

8. See Habermas, op. cit., note 5, especially pp. 301–17. See also Van Manen, M., 'Linking ways of knowing with ways of being practical'. *Curriculum Inquiry*, 6 (2), pp. 205–28, 1977, for theory of the practical in curriculum; McCutcheon, G., 'On the interpretation of classroom observations'. *Educational Researcher*, 10 (5), pp. 5–10, 1981, for a description of approaches to enquiry; Soltis, J. F., 'On the nature of educational research'. *Educational Researcher*, 13 (10), pp. 5–10, 1985, for a description of educational research; May, W. T. and Zimpher, N. L., 'An examination of three theoretical perspectives on supervision: perceptions of preservice field supervision'. *Journal of Curriculum and Supervision*, 1 (2), pp. 83–99,

1986, for theoretical perspectives on supervision; Carr, W. and Kemmis, S., *Becoming Critical: Education, Knowledge and Action Research*. London: Falmer Press, 1986, for work on educational theory and practice; and Grundy, S., *Curriculum: Product or Praxis*. London: Falmer Press, 1987, for a description of forms of curriculum practice.

9. See, for example, Bernstein, R. J., *Habermas and Modernity*. Cambridge, MA: MIT Press, 1985, pp. 13–21; and Held, D., *Introduction to Critical Theory*. Berkeley and Los Angeles: University of California Press, pp. 389–98, 1980.

10. Hunter, M., *Mastery Teaching*. El Segundo, CA: Tip Publications, 1983.

11. On Hunter and reflection, see the debate between Sergiovanni, T. J., 'Landscapes, mindscapes and reflective practice in supervision'. *Journal of Curriculum and Supervision*, 1 (1), pp. 5–17, 1985; Sergiovanni, T. J., 'Understanding reflective practice'. *Journal of Curriculum and Supervision*, 1 (4), pp. 353–9, 1986; and Goldsberry, L. E., 'The reflective mindscape'. *Journal of Curriculum and Supervision*, 1 (4), pp. 347–52, 1986.

12. Cruickshank, D. R., Kennedy, J. J., Williams, J., Holton, J. and Fay, D. E., 'Evaluation of reflective teaching outcomes'. *Journal of Educational Research*, 75 (1), pp. 26–32, 1981.

13. See Cruickshank, op. cit., note 12, for an account of this programme, and Gore, J., 'Reflecting on reflective teaching'. *Journal of Teacher Education*, 38 (2), pp. 33–9, 1987, for a critical commentary.

14. Gordon, T., *TET: Teacher Effectiveness Training*. New York: P. H. Wyden, 1974.

15. Gordon, T., *Parent Effectiveness Training: The 'No-Lose' Program for Raising Responsible Children*. New York: P. H. Wyden, 1970.

16. 8 March 1988, p. 38. Dates and page numbers refer to the field records of the study. These records include narrative field notes and audio-tape transcriptions of lessons, entered into personal computer files at the end of each day of fieldwork.

17. 1 November 1988, p. 368.

18. 21 November 1988, p. 464.

19. 9 August 1988, pp. 112–13.

20. Connelly, F. M. and Clandinin, D. J., 'On narrative method, personal philosophy, and narrative unities in the story of teaching'. *Journal of Research in Science Teaching*, 23 (4), pp. 293–310, 1986; Connelly, F. M. and Clandinin, D. J., 'On narrative method, biography and narrative

unies in the study of teaching'. *Journal of Educational Thought*, 21 (3), pp. 130–39, 1987; and Connelly, F. M. and Clandinin, D. J., *Teachers as Curriculum Planners: Narratives of Experience*. Toronto: OISE Press, and New York: Teachers College Press, 1988.

21. Connelly and Clandinin, *Teachers as Curriculum Planners*, op. cit., note 20, p. 24.

22. 2 November 1988, pp. 139–40.

23. 29 June 1988, pp. 59–60.

24. 5 November 1988, p. 401; 17 February 1989, pp. 483–8.

25. 17 February 1989, pp. 485–6.

26. 6 September 1988, p. 144.

27. 6 September 1988, p. 145.

28. 2 September 1988, p. 143.

29. 9 August 1988, p. 116.

30. Schon, *The Reflective Practitioner* and *Educating the Reflective Practitioner*, op. cit., note 1.

31. Schon, *Educating the Reflective Practitioner*, op. cit., note 1, p. 34.

32. Ibid., p. 35.

33. Turner-Muecke, L. A., Russell, T. and Bowyer, J., 'Reflection-in-action: case study of a clinical supervision'. *Journal of Curriculum and Supervision*, 2 (1), pp. 40–9, 1986, for instance, has provided a personal account of reflection-in-action in their own clinical supervision.

34. 28 October 1988, p. 358.

35. 28 October 1988, p. 359.

36. 29 October 1988, p. 359.

37. Schon, *Educating the Reflective Practitioner*, op. cit., note 1, p. 30.

38. Ibid., p. 27.

39. Jackson, P. W., *Life in Classrooms*. New York: Holt, Rinehart & Winston, 1968.

40. Lortie, D. C., *Schoolteacher: A Sociological Study*. Chicago: University of Chicago Press, 1975.

41. See, for example, Van Manen, M., 'Linking ways of knowing with ways of being practical'. op. cit., note 8; Mezirow, J., 'A critical theory of adult

learning and education'. *Adult Education*, 32 (1), pp. 3–24, 1981; Berlak, A. and Berlak, H., *Dilemmas of Teaching*. New York: Methuen, 1981; Carr and Kemmis, *Becoming Critical*, op. cit., note 8; and Zeichner, K.M. and Liston, D.P., 'Teaching student teachers to reflect'. *Harvard Educational Review*, 57 (1), pp. 23–48, 1987.

42. 17 November 1988, pp. 458–9.

43. 5 October 1988, p. 261.

44. 21 September 1988; 25 October 1988; 8 November 1988.

45. 25 October 1988, pp. 342–3.

46. 25 October 1988, p. 343.

47. 25 October 1988, p. 344.

48. 25 October 1988, p. 345.

49. 25 October 1988, p. 347.

50. The account by Bertola in Grundy, *Curriculum: Product or Praxis*, op. cit., note 8, is more quintessentially 'critical' than any of the examples available in the case study.

51. Boyd, E. and Fales, A., 'Reflective learning: key to learning from experience'. *Journal of Humanistic Psychology*, 23 (2), pp. 99–117, 1983.

52. Ibid., p. 100.

53. Mezirow, 'A critical theory of adult learning and education'. op. cit., note 41.

54. 2 September 1988, p. 143.

55. 2 September 1988, p. 140.

56. 2 September 1988, p. 141.

57. 8 March 1988, p. 38; 11 March 1988, p. 46; 29 June 1988, p. 60.

58. Here I am thinking of the difficulties which may be experienced in inservice education which touches people too closely (see Lewis, M. and Simon, R.I., 'A discourse not intended for her: learning and teaching with patriarchy'. *Harvard Educational Review*, 56 (4), pp. 457–72, 1986); and school board-sponsored programmes of peer or mentor supervision where pairs of teachers are chosen for reasons of administrative convenience rather than established trust between teachers (see Hargreaves, A. and Dawe, R., 'Coaching as unreflective practice: contrived collegiality or collaborative culture?'. Paper presented to the American Educational Research Association, March 1989).

59. This conceptualization of classroom environment is drawn from a literature review of the conditions of teachers' knowledge use in Huberman, M., 'Recipes for busy kitchens: a situational analysis of routine knowledge use in schools'. *Knowledge: Creation, Diffusion, Utilization*, 4, pp. 478–510, 1983.

60. Schon, *The Reflective Practitioner*, op. cit., note 1.

61. Schon, *Educating the Reflective Practitioner*, op. cit., note 1, pp. 75–8.

62. Peer or micro teaching such as 'reflective teaching' in Cruickshank, op. cit., note 12, is one example in initial teacher education, but it may be argued that such artificial situations have a difference that makes all the difference: they lack the press of 30 youngsters' conflicting preferences and intentions. A more convincing example from inservice education is role training based on Moreno's role theory, described in Williams, P. A., Colliver, R. and Simpson, A., *Lessons from Teaching: The Classroom Relationships Project*. Perth, Australia: Education Department of Western Australia, 1986.

63. 17 February 1989, p. 486.

64. Shulman, L. S., 'Knowledge and teaching: foundations of the new reform'. *Harvard Educational Review*, 57 (1), p. 19, 1987.

65. See Munby, H. and Russell, T., 'Educating the reflective teacher: an essay review of two books by Donald Schon'. *Journal of Curriculum Studies*, 21 (1), 1989, pp. 71–80 for a review of Schon, op. cit., note 1, in which they make a similar comment on Shulman's notion of reflection.

66. Shulman, op. cit., note 64, p. 19.

67. See Butt, Raymond and Townsend's and Oberg and Underwood's contributions to this volume.

68. Tripp, D. H., 'Teachers, journals and collaborative research'. In Smyth, W. J., *Educating Teachers*. London: Falmer Press, 1987.

69. Berlak and Berlak, *Dilemmas of Teaching*, op. cit., note 41.

70. 8 November 1988, pp. 414–19.

71. Gramsci, A., *Prison Notebooks, Selections*, translated by Hoare, Q. and Newell-Smith, G. London: Lawrence & Wishart, 1973.

72. 7 November 1988, p. 412.

73. 8 November 1988, p. 418.

74. 8 November 1988, pp. 418–19.

75. 27 October 1988, p. 350.

76. 27 October 1988, pp. 350–1.

77. Carr and Kemmis, *Becoming Critical*, op. cit., note 8.

78. Ibid., p. 162.

79. Ibid., p. 162.

80. Grundy, *Curriculum: Product or Praxis*, op. cit., note 8, pp. 149–50.

81. Connelly and Clandinin, *Teachers as Curriculum Planners*, op. cit., note 20.

82. Schon, *Educating the Reflective Practitioner*, op. cit., note 1, pp. 26–31.

83. Schutz, A. and Luckman, T., *The Structures of Life-World*, translated by Zaner, R. and Englehardt, H. T., Jr. Evanston, IL: Northwestern University Press, 1973.

84. 7 November 1988.

85. 8 November 1988.

86. 8 November 1988, p. 414.

87. 8 November 1988, p. 414.

88. 8 November 1988, pp. 414–15.

89. 8 November 1988, p. 416.

90. Cole, A., 'Teachers' spontaneous adaptations: a mutual interpretation'. Unpublished doctoral dissertation, University of Toronto, 1987.

91. Ibid., p. 2.

92. Hunt, D. E., 'Teachers' adaptations: "Reading" and "Flexing" to Students'. *Journal of Teacher Education*, 27, pp. 268–75, 1976.

93. Greene, M., 'Teaching as project: choice, perspective and the public space'. In Bolin, F. and Falk, J., *Teacher Renewal: Professional Issues, Personal Choices*. New York: Teachers College Press, 1987.

94. Ibid., p. 198.

95. 27 October 1988, pp. 254–5.

96. 25 October 1988.

97. 13 October 1988.

98. 6 October 1988.

Chapter 12

Cultures of Teaching: A Focus for Change

Andy Hargreaves

INTRODUCTION

The various contributors to this book indicate very clearly that there are many ways in which teachers can and do develop professionally. They can do this alone by reading up on new ideas or simply by reflecting on and reformulating what they do in their own classrooms. In Huberman's not at all disparaging terms (see Chapter 7), teachers frequently 'tinker around' with their practice in this way.

Teachers do not develop entirely by themselves, however. They also learn a great deal from contact with many other people who are knowledgeable about and have experience of teaching and learning. They learn from 'experts' by taking courses, studying for higher degrees, or undergoing programmes of staff training in new techniques and approaches. As Thiessen points out in Chapter 6, teachers also learn a lot (but perhaps not nearly as much as they should) from their students through getting feedback on their own teaching, evaluating the effectiveness of new methods or materials, and so on. Teachers learn from many groups, both inside and outside their own schools. But they learn most, perhaps, from other teachers, particularly from colleagues in their own work place, their own school.

There is no simple way for teachers to learn from their colleagues. They may learn from relatively formal discussions and meetings accompanying the planning and introduction of new programmes, for example. They may learn from structured processes of feedback on and review of their own practice as in systems of performance appraisal, clinical supervision or peer coaching. They may be asked to exercise leadership over their colleagues, perhaps as 'subject experts' developing a new programme with their colleagues in science or computers, or perhaps as mentors responsible for the induction and professional growth of new teachers. As leaders in some areas, such teachers may equally be led by their colleagues in others.

These somewhat structured forms of occupational learning have their merits and their place, as we shall see. They also have their critics. The inclination to evaluate and judge often both undermines and overtakes the intention to help, especially in many systems of performance appraisal, clinical supervision and mentoring.[1] Structured systems of feedback and review within the classroom, as in some peer-coaching programmes, for example, may, as Louden points out in Chapter 11 and as Huberman notes elsewhere, require quite exceptional conditions of trust and understanding among participating teachers of a kind seldom found in ordinary schools.[2] Furthermore, sometimes, as I shall argue later and as I have documented elsewhere, collegial energies may be harnessed less for the purpose of giving teachers a say in the development of their own initiatives and the management of their own professional growth than to squeeze out dissentient voices and secure commitment and compliance to changes imposed by others.[3] But perhaps one of the main criticisms of these more deliberate and planned forms of collegiality, is that they are not representative of the way that teachers usually learn from one another. Much of this occupational learning is much more informal and day-to-day in nature. It is part of, and in many respects it constitutes, the very way that teachers do or do not relate to their colleagues. What this chapter sets out to show is that the way teachers relate to their colleagues has profound implications for their teaching in the classroom, how they evolve and develop as teachers, and the sorts of teachers they become.

Teachers do not develop their strategies and styles of teaching entirely alone. New teachers do not need to reinvent the pedagogical wheel when they begin their professional lives (even if that is what it often feels like!). Teaching strategies are not an exclusively individual matter. Most of the problems that the teacher encounters, the issues he or she confronts, have faced many similarly placed colleagues in the past. Over the years these colleagues develop ways of doing things, along with whole networks of associated educational beliefs and values in response to the characteristic and recurrent problems and circumstances they face in their work. Teaching strategies, that is, arise not just from the demandss and constraints of the immediate context, but also from *cultures of teaching*; from beliefs, values, habits and assumed ways of doing things among communities of teachers who have had to deal with similar demands and constraints over many years.[4] Culture carries the community's historically generated and collectively shared solutions to its new and inexperienced membership. It forms a framework for occupational learning. In this respect, the teaching strategies of kindergarten teachers, for instance, evolve differently from those used by teachers of adolescents, because the problems they routinely face are different. In the same way, the teaching strategies of family studies teachers evolve differently from those of mathematics teachers, those of inner city teachers evolve differently from those who teach in the suburbs, and so on. If we want to understand what the teacher does and why, we must therefore also understand the teaching community, the work culture of which that teacher is a part.

Cultures of teaching help give meaning, support and identity to teachers and their work. Physically, teachers are often alone in their own classrooms, with no other adults for company. Psychologically, they never are. What they do there — their classroom styles and strategies — is powerfully affected by the outlooks and orientations of the colleagues with whom they work now and have worked in the past. In this respect, teacher cultures, the relationships between teachers and their colleagues, are among the most educationally significant aspects of teachers' lives and work.[5] They provide a vital context for teacher development. What goes on inside the teacher's classroom cannot be divorced from the relations that are forged outside it.

UNDERSTANDING TEACHER CULTURES

Since the early writings of Waller and, much later, of Sarason on the subject, our knowledge of cultures of teaching on both sides of the Atlantic has expanded significantly in recent years.[6] Yet some important questions in the analysis of teacher cultures remain unresolved. The key one, perhaps, is whether there is a single entity called *the* culture of teaching that characterizes the occupation as a whole; whether there is a multiplicity of separate and perhaps even competing teacher cultures; or whether the two somehow coexist side by side. Writers like David Hargreaves have pointed to the existence of a pervasive culture of individualism among teachers — so pervasive, in fact, that it might be deemed characteristic of the entire occupation.[7] Hargreaves's concern, like Waller's before him, is whether there is something fundamentally 'teacherish' about all teachers. Others, however, have described examples of numerous and diverse teacher cultures, such as academic and 'pastoral' (or guidance-orientated),[8] incorporative and developmental,[9] and academic-elementary and developmental cultures.[10] In their extensive and widely cited review of (mainly North American) literature on cultures of teaching, Feiman-Nemser and Floden come down on the side of diversity, arguing that 'the assumption of cultural uniformity is ... untenable'.[11] Pointing to differences in age, experience, social background, gender, subject matter and so on among teachers, they take the case for diversity to be self-evident. Yet in doing this, they overlook the possibility that teaching might easily sustain various cultures or subcultures while at the same time still retaining certain generic features — like individualism, perhaps — that pervade the occupation more generally.

A second and related issue that still needs to be resolved in the study of teacher cultures is the clarification and explanation of those cultures. At present the tendency is to assert the diversity, rather than to identify the criteria, the dimensions along which teacher cultures are arranged, that give that diversity some form. In Feiman-Nemser and Floden's review, and in many articles like it, teacher cultures are described and listed more than they are classified and explained, so that their interrelationships throughout the teaching community as a whole, and the factors that create and sustain them, remain unclear. We now know quite a lot about particular teacher cultures — like the culture of English teaching or the culture of developmental teachers, for example — but we know little about the overall classification and configuration of teacher cultures throughout the occupation more generally.

The interrelationships among teacher cultures and the connection of these particular cultures to wider features of teaching, to a generic culture of teaching as it were, are therefore areas about which there appears to be a good deal of confusion and lack of understanding. Some (although not all) of these difficulties, I believe, can be resolved by making a fundamental distinction in the interpretation of teacher cultures between *content* and *form*.

CONTENT AND FORM

The *content* of teacher cultures consists of the substantive attitudes, values, beliefs, habits, assumptions and ways of doing things that are shared within a particular teacher group, or among the wider teacher community. The content of teacher cultures can be seen in what teachers think and say and do. The essentially normative concept of sharing, of explicit or implicit consensus, is central to the content-driven view of teacher cultures — a view which underpins and pervades the wider literature on organizational cultures.[12] It is the *content* of teacher cultures we are describing when we discuss academic cultures, pastoral (guidance) cultures, subject cultures and so forth. It is here that cultural diversity among the teaching force is most obvious. There is undoubtedly important work to be done in classifying such cultures, in examining their origins, their interrelationships and the ways in which they change over time. This is not the chief concern of the present chapter, however. My main concern here, rather, is with *form*.

By the *form* of teacher cultures, I do not mean substantive attitudes, beliefs, practices and so on. The *form* of teacher cultures, rather, consists of the characteristic *patterns of relationship* and *forms of association* between members of those cultures. The *form* of teacher culture is to be found in the particular articulation of relations between teachers and their colleagues. The normative concept of sharing is not essential to this definition, for the *form* of teacher cultures may be individualistic or antagonistic, for instance. Relations between teachers and their colleagues, or the *form* of their culture, as it were, may change over time. Indeed, it is through the *forms* of teacher culture that the *contents* of those different cultures are realized, reproduced and redefined. To put it another way, changes in beliefs, values and attitudes in the teaching force may be contingent upon prior or parallel changes in the ways teachers relate to their colleagues, in their characteristic patterns of association.[13]

The number of *forms* of teacher culture is, I believe, considerably less than the number of cultures described in terms of content. Here resides a good deal of the confusion to which I referred earlier. Much of the debate about whether there are many cultures of teaching or only a very small number can be attributed to blurrings of this crucial distinction between content and form. Clarifying this misunderstanding, this mixing together of content and form, is more than an academic exercise in tidy classification. For it is in the *form* of teacher cultures, in the patterns of relationship through which they are articulated, that change or absence of change in the content of those cultures, in teachers' fundamental beliefs and practices, is secured. To understand the forms of teacher culture, therefore, is to understand many of the limits to and possibilities of teacher development and educational change. Securing change in the *content* of particular cultures and the beliefs and practices associated with them, I shall argue, depends very much on bringing about change in the *form* of those cultures.

There are, it seems to me, four broad forms of teacher culture, each of which has very different implications for processes of teacher development and educational change. My description of these is drawn from three sources: my research in England on the clash between high-school and elementary teacher cultures in the intermediate, middle-school setting,[14] my recent research in Canada into how elementary teachers use their scheduled preparation time,[15] and innumerable conversations with teachers on both sides of the Atlantic over many years.

Individualism

Across the world most teachers still teach alone, behind closed doors in the insulated and isolated environment of their own classroom. Most elementary schools still have what Lortie described as an egg-crate-like structure to them: segregated classrooms dividing teachers from one another so they see and understand little of what their colleagues do.[16]

Classroom isolation offers many teachers a welcome measure of privacy, a protection from outside interference which they often value. I have known numerous teachers who have been reluctant to exchange their outside huts — with their seasonal extremes of heat and cold — for space and comfort in the main building where they would be exposed to the prying eyes of their colleagues and the corridor patrols of their principal.

Yet classroom isolation carries its own problems. If isolation purges the classroom of blame and criticism, it also shuts out possible sources of praise and support. Isolated teachers receive little adult feedback on their value, worth and competence. In the culture of individualism, teachers rely on the thinnest threads, the tiniest shreds of evidence, to assess one another — noise from next door's classroom (so teachers learn that it is often best to limit the amount of student discussion),[17] or the quality of class performances given to the whole school (it is teachers as much as their classes who are on show here: hence all the effort).[18]

In the culture of individualism, teachers develop characteristic orientations to their work which Lortie calls *presentism, conservatism* and *individualism*.[19] Elementary teachers, he argued, concentrate on short-term planning in their own classrooms where their energies are more likely to make a difference (presentism); they avoid discussing, thinking about or committing themselves to more fundamental changes which might affect the context of what they do or raise substantial questions about how and what they teach (conservatism); and they shy away from collaboration with colleagues and from the feared judgements and criticisms that may come with that (individualism). Like caged birds, teachers within the culture of individualism, it seems, stick with what they know. They are reluctant to fly free, even when given the opportunity.

Paradoxically, perhaps, the staffrooms of schools characterized by individualism are often rewarding places to be, as an important kind of sharing does go on. Classroom anecdotes and 'war stories' are related. News is traded about particular students and their parents ('Oh, was he like that with you too?'). Bearings are checked with colleagues ('Is your class really "funny" today? Mine's awful!'). There are jokes — lots of jokes — often at the expense of the kids, or their parents, or the administration. Teachers also spend their free time in the staffroom, playing cards perhaps, doing crosswords, or just chatting. Particularly in the 'toughest' schools, these staffrooms are a retreat from the 'front line' of classroom teaching.[20] They are places of relaxation and relief where social, humorous, morale-boosting behaviour relieves some of the stresses and eases some of the pains of the school day. For the classroom-isolated teacher, there is a compensating kind of solidarity to be found here.

Staffroom solidarity and sharing in individualistic schools has its limitations, however. As Nias records, student teachers and new teachers are often appalled by the low intellectual level of staffroom conversation.[21] In effect, such conversation sticks to a lowest common denominator of themes and issues on which staff are unlikely to disagree professionally.[22] Subjects are avoided and opinions withheld which might expose differences in professional approach, or which might make teachers vulnerable to invidiously comparative appraisal by others. So, in these staffrooms, educational theory, long-term plans, discussions about basic purposes and underlying assumptions are virtually absent features of teacher talk. Sharing is confined instead to stories, tips and news — to things that will not intrude upon or challenge the autonomous judgement of the classroom-isolated teacher.

These points about the kinds of co-operation to be found within the individualistic culture of teaching are important, for some recent writers on teacher cultures have taken evidence of sharing, among elementary teachers in particular, as a sign of impending decline in the culture of individualism. Schneider and Hochschild, for instance, in interviews with almost a hundred elementary teachers about their relations with other teachers, claimed widespread instances of co-operation among teachers on the grounds that teachers in their study more often turned to their colleagues for help and advice than to their principal. This evidence, they claimed, constituted a serious challenge to Lortie's individualism thesis.[23]

Yet close inspection of Schneider and Hochschild's findings reveals that much of what they call collaboration amounts to teachers sharing information about pupils and good lessons with each other. While they interpret this as a challenge to Lortie's thesis, it is instructive to note that Lortie himself acknowledged the existence of such talk and help among teachers, finding it revolved more around 'tricks of the trade' than around underlying principles of instruction or classroom practice. In this way, the collaboration identified by Schneider and

Hochschild does not appear to be searching or wide-ranging in the way that Lortie would require it to be to counter the existing culture of individualism.[24]

More than this, what evidence there is of more collaborative teacher cultures has mainly been drawn from atypical case studies where collaboration might most be expected to be found. Indeed, many of these case studies were selected precisely for that reason: as sites for investigating collaboration in action.[25] Many years after the publication of Lortie's influential work, though, studies drawing on much larger and more randomly spread samples indicate the persistence of individualism as the overwhelmingly dominant form of the teacher culture.

Zielinski and Hoy, for instance, drawing on data collected from 417 teachers in 15 New Jersey elementary schools, draw attention to 'an intriguing albeit incidental finding' concerning 'the extreme degree to which elementary teachers were isolated in their work setting.'[26] When asked to list five other members with whom they co-operated in school, most of their teacher respondents were unable to name even that many. Similarly, Zahorik's study of collegial interaction in six elementary schools reveals that while rates of collegial interaction appear higher than in Lortie's seminal study, most of that interaction focuses on materials, discipline, activities and individual student problems rather than on curriculum goals or teacher behaviour.[27]

Notwithstanding some notable exceptions, to which I shall return, the culture of individualism would therefore appear to be alive and well in most schools. Its grip on most of the school system remains as tight as ever. This does not mean that what is often labelled as individualism is unremittingly a bad thing. Indeed, elsewhere I have argued that dispositions towards individuality and preferences for solitude among teachers may be of considerable value in many instances. Individualistic behaviour understood in these terms may be less a source of weakness and diffidence than an expression of creative originality and principled disagreement.[28] In this respect there are real dangers that efforts to eliminate the culture of individualism in its less restrictive forms may also unwittingly entail suppressing individuality of choice and disagreement among the teaching force.

These qualifications notwithstanding, when individualism is less a matter of choice and preference than of habit, of lack of opportunity to work in other ways, or simply of accepted and unquestioned ways of working within a community of teachers, then the consequences for teacher development and educational change are not so beneficial. For if, as Lortie claimed, individualism carries with it a concentration on what is immediately applicable in the teacher's own classroom, then serious contemplation of alternative practices and purposes is unlikely. It is for this reason that writers on educational change, such as Fullan, have suggested that we search for ways in which the 'walls of privatism' can be cracked.[29] The caveat about protecting rights to individuality and solitude within such a project remains important. But generally speaking, developing an understanding of other forms of teacher culture, of the conditions of their existence and of the alternative possibilities they offer for development and change, is a helpful step to take.

Balkanization

In some schools, while teachers associate more closely with their colleagues, they do so in particular groups more than in the school as a whole. Such schools have a *balkanized* teacher culture — a culture made up of separate and sometimes competing groups, jockeying for position and supremacy like loosely connected, independent city states.

Teachers in balkanized cultures attach their loyalties and identities to particular groups of their colleagues. These are usually colleagues with whom they work most closely, spend most time, socialize most often in the staffroom. The existence of such groups in a school reflects and reinforces very different group outlooks on learning, teaching styles, discipline and curriculum.

Balkanization may lead to poor communication, indifference, groups going their separate ways in a school. This in turn can produce poor continuity in monitoring student progress and inconsistent expectations of their performance and behaviour. At worst it may generate squabbles and conflicts, even institutionalized feuds over space (room allocations, storage space), time (priority in scheduling) and resources (budgets, student numbers, etc.).[30] The urgency and necessity of defending territorial status against claims from other groups explains the great seriousness and importance teachers attach to apparently petty disputes over things like rights to shelf and cupboard space in a school corridor.[31]

Balkanized cultures are a familiar feature of high-school life, mainly because of the strong subject-departmental structures on which high schools are based. They can be observed in almost any high-school staffroom. The physical education teachers or 'jocks' in their tracksuits; the large English department with its slight aura of bohemian intellectual smugness; the absent science teachers gathered around their kettles and coffee in the labs; the actual and aspirant 'power' group seeking influence with the principal and vice-principal; perhaps a group of middle-aged (usually male) 'complainers' out of favour with and cynical about the administration and its preferred policies — all these are commonly seen in the high-school setting. Because of its large and differentiated nature, the high school is, in fact, particularly vulnerable to the informal balkanization of its teachers. This is why agreed whole-school policies are so difficult to secure in that setting.

The size and complexity of high schools is by no means the only determinant of balkanization, however. The balkanization of high-school education also has its roots in deep-seated distinctions of status and priority that spread far beyond the individual school and extend into the educational system as a whole.

The curriculum is at the centre of this. The division of learning and the curriculum into specialized domains that we call 'subjects' creates not only different categories of knowledge but different communities of teachers who teach them, identify with them and invest their careers in them too.[32] These distinctions and divisions often have strong status associations that can give rise to enmity, jealousy and rivalry between more-favoured and less-favoured teacher groups. The groups most likely to be marginalized, to receive less staffing and resources and to have lower levels of worth and recognition bestowed on them, are the teachers of lower-status, non-academic subjects. This is because it is academic knowledge in the intellectual-cognitive domain that secondary schools and school systems most value. Once this point is grasped, it is then easier to appreciate that marginalized, disaffected staff cultures in any school arise not simply because of management's failure to recognize and value members of those cultures and the subjects they teach, but because of the narrow range of subjects and achievements that are valued and recognized in the educational system as a whole. The priority attached to higher-status academic subjects creates lower-status subjects and lower-status cultures of non-academic subject teachers *by definition*.[33] The balkanization of secondary-school teacher cultures is, in this sense, very closely tied up with differentiation and divisiveness in the school curriculum more generally. What appears as an administrative problem of teacher development is, in fact, fundamentally a problem of curricular purpose and curriculum development. This echoes Ingvarsson and Greenway's point that 'professional development is . . . influenced more pervasively by administrative and contextual features of the particular educational system within which teachers work than by the particular forms of in-service education available'.[34]

Balkanization is not an exclusively secondary-school phenomenon, however; it can also be found in elementary or primary schools. Canadian French immersion schools, for instance, where both French and English are used as the language of instruction, sometimes have 'French' and 'English' teachers sitting in completely different parts of the staffroom. I have come across 'English' and 'French' teachers who share responsibility for the same class — one teaching them in the morning, another in the afternoon — who consult minimally about the class; teachers who, for administrative reasons, cannot easily be scheduled to plan and consult together in preparation time; who would not dream of using such time to sit in on each other's classes; whose rooms and wall displays have a completely different ambience about them; and whose students even have to take out different sets of pencils, crayons and other property as they move from one classroom to the other.[35]

In regular elementary and primary schools I have seen special education teachers effectively marginalized with their segregated classes in some distant part of the school, rarely troubling to come and socialize in the staffroom as a result.[36] This poses serious problems for the effective integration of 'special needs' students into the mainstream life of the school. In particular, it impedes the development of those informal staff relations and understanding which support the more formal business of consultancy between special-needs teachers and their colleagues as schools try to make integration work.[37]

An even more common form of balkanization is the formal and informal separation of elementary teachers into different divisions: primary, junior and intermediate. In a study of teacher preparation time, I have witnessed many instances of co-operation and joint planning among teachers *within* particular grades and divisions. Preparation time is sometimes cleverly scheduled to encourage this by same-grade teachers being released at the same time. Co-operation and liaison on a regular basis *across* grades and divisions is a comparative rarity, however.[38] Other published research shows similar findings — that elementary teachers consult much more often with same-grade teachers than with other colleagues.[39] This grade-based insulation means that while commendable attention is often given to *lateral* curriculum coherence *within* grades and divisions, *vertical* continuity in the curriculum from one division — or sometimes even one grade — to the next, is disconcertingly weak. So too is associated monitoring of and consultation about students' progress as they move through the school: too many teachers treat their new classes like a 'clean sheet', as if all their skills and understandings began at the same level.

It is sometimes assumed or recommended that vertical continuity can be sufficiently secured through written guidelines or through clear procedures for consultancy between relevant teachers.[40] These things are, of course, important. But ultimately, effective continuity is secured more through human understanding, communication and agreement at an informal level and the necessary openness, trust and support that come with that. It is this that helps avoid unnecessary gaps or duplications in students' learning as they move from one grade to the next. This interpersonal network is what holds the formal business of continuity together. Without it, formal consultancy procedures are but a brittle administrative shell. The tight insulation between division- or grade-based teacher cultures in elementary schools therefore has profound implications for curriculum continuity — not continuity as it is tidily listed in published guidelines, but continuity as it is experienced in the life of the learner. Securing such continuity, I have argued, is more than a matter of implementing appropriate administrative procedures, writing clear job descriptions and the like. Effective continuity ultimately depends on building a community of teachers whose experiences and commitments are not confined to a single grade, division or subject but to the school as a whole. More important still, it depends on having a broad curriculum in the school and the school system, where many different kinds of educational experience and achievement have equal value — a curriculum which does not drive invidious and insidious wedges of status distinction between teachers and their colleagues.

Balkanized teacher cultures and divided teacher communities result not merely from principals or headteachers failing to develop their teachers by valuing them. They result from failing to value many of the things that they do, the things for which they stand. They result from valuing academic studies (and their teachers) over practical ones; from valuing teachers who wholeheartedly support new methods (some might say 'fads') like active learning or whole language, over those who don't; and from valuing new crops of enthusiastic, energetic young teachers over their older, steadier colleagues. For educational leaders, balkanization may appear to be an issue of who you value and how well you value them. Ultimately, though, as we have seen, it is also a matter of *what* you value and the breadth of what you value. Here, teacher development rests on more than generosity of spirit. It rests on breadth of educational vision too.

Collaborative Culture

In a small number of primary and elementary schools a different form of teacher culture prevails. This is a culture of collaboration. Here, teachers are more united than divided. Researchers studying a group of English primary schools exemplifying positive collegial relationships have described the collaborative teacher cultures they found there in terms of routine help, support, trust and openness which operated almost imperceptibly on a moment-by-moment, day-by-day basis.[41] Cultures of collaboration are not formally organized or bureaucratic in nature; nor are they mounted just for specific projects or events. They are not strings of one-shot deals. Cultures of collaboration are constitutive of, absolutely central to, teachers' daily work. They are found in the minutiae of school life: in the small gestures, jokes and glances that signal sympathy and understanding; in kind words and personal interest shown on corridors or outside classroom doors; in birthdays, treat days and other little ceremonies; in the acceptance and intermixture of personal lives with professional ones; in overt praise, recognition and gratitude; and in sharing and discussion of ideas and resources.

In collaborative cultures, as Nias and her colleagues point out, failure and uncertainty are not protected and defended, but shared and discussed with a view to gaining help and support.[42] Teachers do not waste time and energy covering their backs here. Collaborative cultures require broad agreement on educational values, but they also tolerate disagreement, and to some extent actively encourage it within those limits.

When they are in full flow, collaborative cultures exude an apparently 'natural' warmth in human relationships. But they do not just arise by a kind of emotional spontaneous combustion; they have to be created and sustained. Like good marriages, they have to be worked at. Leadership is especially important here — particularly leadership through example; through frequent praise; through helpful, personal notes placed in staff mailboxes; through principals or headteachers indulging their staffs with little treats like cakes or flowers which show caring and thoughtfulness; and through principals' having high visibility around the school, revealing an interest in what is going on there and pleasure in making contact with teachers and students alike.[43] Dispersion of leadership and responsibility also helps, playing down formal differences of status and investing visible administrative trust in the skills, expertise and professional judgement of ordinary teachers. In the main, it is through such small, interpersonal details of elementary school life more than through its official business and procedures that a collaborative culture is sustained. These details take time to weave their pattern; they are slow to evolve. Patience is the vital but often neglected administrative virtue that helps make them possible.

The creation of cultures of collaboration has for a long time been called for to counter the widespread individualism and isolation that impair and inhibit many teachers' classroom performance and their willingness to change and improve. But the need for such cultures has never been greater than in the modern primary and elementary school. In Ontario, for instance, expectations for programme support for elementary students have risen remarkably in recent years, creating a complicated configuration of specialized staff responsibilities and a wide network of adults with whom ordinary teachers have to consult. The integration of special education students, the direct involvement of library resource teachers in programming and the growth of curriculum co-ordination and specialization have, along with the continuing role of the divisional programme leader, created increased needs for staff collaboration and co-ordination to secure overall programme coherence and support for individual students. Elementary teachers' work is considerably more skilled and complex than it was in the times when most parents and trustees were themselves students. Ontario elementary teachers are consulting more with their colleagues than ever before.

In British primary schools, consultancy has become particularly important in the area of curriculum leadership. Once regarded almost exclusively as a generalist teacher of his or her own class, the British primary school teacher is now usually expected to take responsibility for leading and supporting colleagues in at least one designated area of the curriculum, not least since the introduction of the subject-based National Curriculum. As Campbell has noted, these newly developed demands of consultancy require a wide array of interpersonal skills and qualities such as tact, sensitivity, diplomacy and (interestingly) 'charm' — just the kind of personal prerequisites for effective consultancy and collegial leadership that we might expect an established collaborative culture to provide.[44]

The growing demands of collegial consultancy and leadership could potentially present important challenges to the culture of individualism among teachers. The important point to be determined is how meaningful and effective those consultations turn out to be in practice. A highly developed, informal culture of collaboration may be just the context needed for consultative business to be dealt with effectively.

Unfortunately, existing research suggests that the culture of collaboration is a rarity. That culture has been difficult to create and even more difficult to sustain. As Judith Warren Little has observed in the USA, the reason is that it goes right against the grain of all the pressures and constraints that normally come with teachers' work.[45] The preferred *culture* of teaching is just not compatible with the prevailing *context* of teachers' work. Two aspects of that context are particularly significant in restricting the possibilities and scope of collaboration. These are time and curriculum demands.

On the first matter, elementary teachers have traditionally had almost no scheduled time away from their classes to work and plan with colleagues. Elementary teachers' work has been overwhelmingly classroom work. Consultation has had to be done after school, at the end of an exhausting day, or in the few available moments that can be snatched between classes, at recess, or over lunch. Such conditions are not at all conducive to sustained collaboration. Where collaboration has been achieved against these sorts of odds, it has been achieved only with the most remarkable investments of energy and commitment. In this sense, the provision of scheduled preparation time for elementary teachers in Ontario of around 120 minutes minimum per week constitutes an important advance in creating the working conditions necessary for extended collaboration. Teachers interviewed in the preparation time project have been consistently positive, often glowingly so, about the benefits of preparation time for relieving the stresses of their work and creating opportunities to consult with colleagues. However, as we shall see later and as I have documented elsewhere, preparation time provides only opportunities for developing collaborative cultures, not guarantees. Issues of administrative behaviour and political control are also important.[46]

A second constraint on the development of collaborative teacher cultures is to be found in the programme, in the mandated curriculum. Where national, provincial and/or school board administrators produce highly detailed, heavily content-laden curriculum guidelines, teachers are left with little to collaborate about. When new programmes are introduced or teachers are moved from one grade to another, many teachers' energies outside the classroom get diverted into mastering the details of the new programme, so that there is little time, energy or scope left to develop programmes with others. For these reasons, where collaboration does exist, it is often not particularly searching or wide-ranging. Most teachers interviewed in the preparation time project focus their collaborative energies on relatively immediate, small-scale targets such as the next unit of work.[47] There is little scope for anything more fundamental — for collaboration in relation to the curriculum of a school concerning the purpose, value and direction of what it teaches. External implementation is given priority over internal development.

In circumstances such as these, it seems to me that a particular realization of the culture of collaboration is occurring, which I call *bounded collaboration*. Bounded collaboration is collaboration which is restricted in its depth, its scope, its frequency or persistence, or in a combination of these factors. It is collaboration which does not reach deep down to the grounds, the principles or the ethics of practice, but which stays with routine advice-giving, trick-trading and material-sharing of a more immediate, specific and technical nature. It is collaboration which does not extend beyond particular units of work or subjects of study to the whole purpose and value of curricular and pedagogical judgement.

It is collaboration which focuses on the immediate and the practical to the exclusion of longer-term planning concerns. Or it is collaboration that is focused on special events and initiatives, on one-shot deals, instead of collaboration which is embedded more firmly and more continuously in the routine interpersonal relationships that make up the life of the school. The emergent findings of the preparation time study, and close inspection of the existing literature on teachers' relations with their colleagues, reveal that what passes for collaboration is, in fact, almost always bounded collaboration in one or more of these senses.[48]

In this respect, we should be wary of prematurely celebrating the triumph of collaboration over individualism in teachers' relations with their colleagues. Collaboration is less pervasive than commonly imagined. And its form is weaker, more bounded, than is often implied. In particular, we have seen that while a greater focus on collaboration might well be leading to a weakening of individualism among elementary teachers, this is not necessarily bringing with it an end to other characteristics of the teacher culture of which writers like Lortie were critical. Collaboration, that is, does not appear to be correcting teachers' conservative avoidance of large-scale, fundamental planning and change. Nor does it seem to be modifying teachers' present-time orientation to immediate issues rather than longer-term questions of overall programming.[49] Weakened individualism, in other words, is carrying with it no guarantees of weakened presentism and conservatism too. While scheduled time away from class may help eliminate individualism, the weakening of presentism and conservatism appears to require something else in addition. Time is not enough. Modifications in programming, in the whole process of curriculum development and in who holds responsibility for that are also needed.

If collaboration is to triumph not just over individualism but over presentism and conservatism too, teacher development must be reconnected to curriculum development, so that there is something sufficiently broad and significant about which to collaborate.

Contrived Collegiality

Whatever the form of teacher collaboration, be it bounded or extended, a key issue for schools is how to get there, how to move from an individualized or balkanized teacher culture to a collaborative one. The most common route that schools and their systems have adopted has been one which I call *contrived collegiality*. This pattern is not well described in the research literature but is certainly on the increase, not only in Ontario but throughout North America. Contrived collegiality is characterized by a set of formal, specific bureaucratic procedures to increase the attention being given to joint teacher planning and consultation. It can be seen in initiatives such as peer coaching, mentor teaching, joint planning in specially provided rooms, formally scheduled meetings and clear job descriptions and training programmes for those in consultative roles.[50] These sorts of initiatives are administrative contrivances designed to get collegiality going in schools where little has existed before. They are meant to encourage greater association among teachers; to foster more sharing, learning and improvement of skills and expertise. Contrived collegiality is also meant to assist the successful implementation of new approaches and techniques from the outside into a more responsive and supportive school culture.

At its best, contrived collegiality can be a useful preliminary phase in the move towards more enduring collaborative relationships between teachers; a way of putting teachers in touch on which principals can then build those informal elements of recognition, trust and support which are essential to creating an effective teaching community. Contrived collegiality can also help teachers already in collaborative cultures to focus on specific tasks and changes that may need to be dealt with. It can act as an insurance against collective complacency.

At its worst, however, contrived collegiality can be little more than a quick, slick administrative surrogate for more genuinely collaborative teacher cultures, cultures which take much more time, care and sensitivity to build than speedily implemented changes of an administratively superficial nature. In this sense, contrived collegiality can no more guarantee a teaching community which works effectively, openly and supportively together than the introduction of Esperanto can bring about world language unity.

Of course, collaborative cultures do not arise spontaneously, completely by themselves. They too require managerial guidance and intervention. But broadly speaking, this is intervention which is supportive and facilitating, which creates opportunities for teachers to work together in school time through shrewd and sensitive scheduling; which encourages team-work through discussion, persuasion and thoughtful room assignments; and so forth. Collaborative cultures do not mandate collegial support and partnership: they foster and facilitate it. This is what distinguishes them from schools characterized by more superficial versions of contrived collegiality.

In some of the most questionable forms of contrived collegiality, colleagueship and partnership are administratively imposed. Examples include schemes, in some school boards, where teachers are required to select a colleague with whom they will have a peer-coaching relationship by a fixed date. They include teachers I have interviewed who are required to use particular preparation periods to meet with the special education resource teacher, only to find (especially when the teacher concerned has a special education qualification) that there is no business to discuss that week. The consequence is that the teacher guiltily 'sneaks away' and does something else, against the principal's wishes.[51] Examples of contrived collegiality also include teachers who report that when their board superintendent required divisional team leaders to send minutes to all their meetings back to the board, this led to a decrease, not an increase, in the number of meetings they were having.

To sum up: despite some of the benefits of contrived collegiality when it is used in a facilitative, not a controlling way, I have three reservations about its overhasty adoption in many school systems. First, like attempts to introduce language unity by legal statute or other administrative contrivance, contrived collegiality cannot legislate a collaborative culture into existence, nor can it provide an adequate 'instant' substitute for such a culture with all the time and care that is needed to help that culture evolve and develop. A sign outside an Ontario small business reads: 'QUALITY; SPEED; PRICE – PICK ANY TWO!!'. This, in a sense, describes the problem of contrived collegiality. A quick solution, and an administratively visible one that can easily be committed to paper, may be able to demonstrate publicly that something is being done about staff development, but it is unlikely that the quality of what goes on among staff will be significantly improved by this kind of change.

Second, contrived collegiality may sometimes affront the dignity of teachers by failing to recognize what is already going on collegially in a school. It may even discourage existing collegial relations by making them more administratively cumbersome (as in the required minuting of divisional meetings for board purposes). Contrived collegiality may, in other words, not only fail to develop collaborative cultures but actually impede the development of those which are already evolving.

Third, contrived collegiality can lead to a proliferation of unwanted meetings so that not only might teachers eventually suffer from administrative overload, but the small spaces of informal life in a school — the laughing, the jokes, the coffee-time conversation and all the other small talk that holds a staff together — may get eaten away. In the rush to ensure that all non-classroom time is being used in a 'productive' collegial manner, the immense importance of the informal and apparently 'purposeless' aspects of staffroom life in building a collaborative culture may all too easily get overlooked. Administrative colonization of the informal 'back regions' of teachers' working lives might in this sense not just interfere with teachers' private and stress-relieving relaxation.[52] By intruding upon, reorganizing and undermining the spontaneity of informal, open, personal talk between teachers and their colleagues, it may also undermine the vital interpersonal foundations on which collaborative cultures rest.

CULTURE, CONTROL AND CHANGE

Teacher cultures, we have seen, have both content and form. The contents of teacher cultures are many; the forms are few. I have reviewed four of the most dominant of such forms in this chapter; individualism, balkanization, collaborative culture and contrived collegiality. These forms constitute the dominant patterns of relationship that are currently to be found among teachers and their colleagues. They are one of the main regulators of their development as teachers.

The forms of teacher culture are important, for it is through them that the contents of teacher cultures — the norms, values, beliefs and practices of teachers — are reproduced or redefined. It is through working with their colleagues in particular ways, or working apart from them altogether, that teachers either persist in doing what they do or seek and develop ways to change their practice. Understanding the major forms of teacher culture can therefore help us understand much about the dynamics of educational change or its absence, about why teachers do or do not persist in using 'traditional' teaching styles, about why teachers support or resist innovation, and so on. It is in the patterns of relationship between teachers and their colleagues — in the forms of teacher culture — that much of the success or failure of teacher development and educational change is ultimately to be found.

The *individualistic* culture of teachers, I argued, is still the most pervasive of all the forms of teacher culture. This culture of individualism isolates teachers from their colleagues and ties them to the pressing immediacy of classroom life. In most respects, it is a seedbed of pedagogical conservatism.

In *balkanized* cultures, teachers work in separate and sometimes competing territorial groups which bestow identity and provide bases for the pursuit of power, status and resources. Balkanized cultures can exist in circumstances of open warfare or in climates of uneasy peace, but the competing territorial claims and the identities to which they give rise make the definition and pursuit of common goals across the whole school community very difficult, if not impossible.

Most teachers work in schools where these two forms of teacher culture coexist. While teachers may plan and consult, and perhaps even connive and conspire, within their different territorial groups — in their subject departments or their divisions — they rarely co-operate on issues which threaten their classroom autonomy and which open up their practice to intrusive inspection. Materials may be shared and discussed, tricks may be traded, but even within the most closely knit departmental group the autonomy of the teacher's classroom judgement usually remains sacrosanct.

In not engaging with the details and fundamentals of classroom practice, this combination of individualism and balkanization offers few prospects for educational change and professional development of any substance. The possibilities for curriculum development among a community of colleagues which would challenge, cut across, or move beyond existing subject identities and preferred pedagogies are not strong. Equally, individualism and balkanization inhibit the responsiveness of teachers to externally imposed innovation, making many teachers protective of their own classroom and departmental domains which new programmes, newly advocated methods of instruction or new cross-curricular initiatives often appear to threaten.

Individualism and balkanization, then, suit neither the advocates of locally generated, school-based curriculum development nor the supporters of top-down, bureaucratically imposed models of curriculum implementation. Both models of educational change — top-down and bottom-up — are equally ill-served by these two prevailing cultures of teaching. This explains the widespread nature of the support for developing greater collaboration and collegiality among teachers. Reconstituting the relationships that teachers have with their colleagues enhances the potential for both school-centred innovation *and* externally imposed implementation. However, beneath this superficial consensus and behind this unholy alliance lie very different collaborative intents and effects. One set of intents and effects is compatible with the interests of local development and the exercise of discretionary judgement which forms the heart of teacher professionalism. It supports the professional empowerment of teachers in the collective formation of their own lives and work. The other set of intents and effects is more suited to the interests of administrative control which regulates and reconstitutes teachers' collegial relations in line with bureaucratic purposes: deprofessionalizing and disempowering teachers so that they will uncritically implement the ends of others.

Collaborative cultures are most compatible with the interests of local curriculum development and the exercise of discretionary professional judgement. They foster and build upon qualities of openness, trust and support between teachers and their colleagues. They capitalize on the collective expertise and endeavours of the teaching community. They acknowledge the wider dimensions of teachers' lives outside the classroom and the school, blurring the boundaries between in-school and out-of-school, public and private, professional and personal — grounding projects for development and change in a realistic and respectful appreciation of teachers' broader worlds. Teachers' work is deeply embedded in teachers' lives, in their pasts, in their biographies, in the cultures or traditions of teaching to which they have become committed. Developing the teacher, therefore, also involves developing the person, developing the life. In this respect, the interweaving of the personal and the professional in collaborative cultures, and the qualities of trust and sharing within those cultures, provide the most collegially supportive environment for change.

But even this change is slow. Collaborative cultures do not evolve quickly. They are therefore unattractive to administrators looking for swift implementation expedients. They are difficult to locate, to fix in time and space, living as they do mainly in the interstices of school life; in the corridor conversations and exchanged glances that weld teachers and their school together in a working community. Collaborative cultures are also unpredictable in their consequences. The curriculum that will be developed, the learning that will be fostered, the goals that will be formulated — these things cannot be confidently predicted beforehand.

For control-conscious administrators this unpredictability can be a threatening prospect. What is fostered, formulated and developed by these collaborative cultures may not correspond with administrators' intentions and purposes. This might explain why most collaborative cultures take the form of *bounded collaboration*, where the grounds of practice, of curriculum and pedagogy, are not investigated in a searching way, on a continuous basis, across the whole school community. More extended forms of collaboration would require formal devolution of responsibility for curriculum development, for something significant for teachers to collaborate about, to schools and teachers themselves. This is a responsibility that most administrators and politicians are unwilling to yield. It is this administrative retention of curriculum control which confines most kinds of collaborative culture to the bounded form and makes more searching, extended forms of collaboration a rarity.

The administrative retention of curriculum control also explains the growing bureaucratic preference for forms of collegial relations among teachers which are less unpredictable and threatening than those which can evolve in more collaborative teacher cultures. The particular collaborative form therefore preferred among many administrators is one of contrived collegiality.

Contrived collegiality binds teachers in time and space to purposes and procedures devised by their superiors. It mandates teachers to meet at particular times in particular places to deal with administrative agendas determined elsewhere — as in some collaborative planning procedures, for instance. For the openness and unpredictability of naturally occurring and slowly evolving patterns of human interaction, it substitutes administratively contrived and bureaucratically controlled procedures of clinical assessment, feedback and review — as in some peer coaching, mentoring and teacher appraisal schemes, for example.

Contrived collegiality reconstitutes teacher relations in the administrators' own image — regulating and reconstructing teachers' lives so that they support the predictable implementation of administrative plans and purposes, rather than creating the unpredictable development of teachers' own. Contrived collegiality also regulates the pace of change, so as to 'force' human growth among teachers, like so much rhubarb; speeding it up and synchronizing it with administratively convenient timeliness and expectations. The contrast between collaborative cultures and contrived collegiality as ways of constituting teachers' interpersonal relations and the relationship of each of these things to administrative intent, is not unlike the contrast between 'natural' and 'medicalized' childbirth described by Fox:

> From the masculine point of view of obstetrical caregivers, those
> elements of childbirth which are most troublesome, and which
> they strive to overcome, are its unpredictability, its hiddenness,
> its irrationality. . . . Thus the mechanism of defence against
> these fearful elements is to overcome expectancy: the modern
> obstetrician does not stand by the woman, waiting for the birth
> to resolve itself, but hastens to intervene. Not only is labour
> accelerated, or indeed induced, and the birth of the baby speeded
> . . . but indeed the whole of the pregnancy . . . is subject to
> scrutiny and intervention.[53]

Medical intervention in the birth process, Fox argues, is impelled by male, administrative interests in control and in technological efficiency and productivity. The world of teaching, especially at the elementary level, is also largely a world of male administrators supervising the lives and work of women. Collaborative cultures have deeply 'feminine' characteristics. They are spontaneous, evolutionary and unpredictable. They intermix the private and public, openly placing teachers' work in the context of their wider lives, biographies and purposes. Such cultures do not mesh well with the control-centred, accountability-inclined and efficiency-orientated interests of (mainly) male administrators. For such administrators, the preferred mode of the teacher culture — one which will be collectively responsive to the interests of externally imposed implementation — is commonly that of contrived collegiality (see Table 12.1).

Table 12.1. Collaborative Cultures and Contrived Collegiality

Collaborative Culture	Contrived Collegiality
Pervasive across time and space	Bounded in time and space
Evolutionary	Imposed
'Natural'	'Forced'
Spontaneous	Regulated
Unpredictable	Predictable
Public intermixed with Private	Public superimposed on Private
Development-orientated	Implementation-orientated
'Feminine' in style	'Masculine' in style

Contrived collegiality is more strikingly 'masculine' in its characteristics. It is administratively contrived, formally bounded in time and space, and bureaucratically predictable. It superimposes the public on the private, keeping apart these two important domains of teachers' lives. Contrived collegiality preserves the hierarchical separation between development and implementation, creating a system whereby teachers can deliver others' purposes instead of developing their own. And, in doing so, it retains a system whereby (mainly) female teachers remain the technical servants of predominantly male administrators and their purposes.

The challenge in developing extended cultures of collaboration, in overcoming presentism and conservatism as well as individualism within the teacher culture, is therefore more than a challenge of administrative contrivance, of reconstituting interpersonal relations within the teaching community. It is also a challenge of purpose and power; of redistributing the responsibility for curriculum *development* (and not just curriculum *implementation*) from the centre to the periphery, from administrators to teachers and from men to women. It is a challenge of linking teacher development to curriculum development. Ultimately, the challenge is one of administrative humility: in sharing out the responsibility for educational purpose and in deferring to the inevitably modest pace of human growth that underpins the development of teachers (as, indeed, of anyone else). Attempts at teacher development and educational change will meet with little success unless they engage with the purposes of the teacher, unless they acknowledge the person that the teacher is and unless they adjust to the slow pace of human growth that takes place in the individual and collective lives of teachers.[54] Short of relocating inservice training somewhere on the road to Damascus, there are few better starting-points for proponents of teacher development than this.

NOTES AND REFERENCES

1. Such criticisms are developed in relation to performance appraisal in, for example, McLaughlin, M. and Pfeiffer, R. S., *Teacher Evaluation, Improvement, Accountability and Effective Learning.* New York: Teachers College Press, 1989; in relation to clinical supervision in Smyth, J., 'A critical perspective for clinical supervision'. *Journal of Curriculum and Supervision,* 3 (2), pp. 136–56, Winter 1988; and in relation to mentoring in Little, J. W., 'The mentor phenomenon and the social organization of teaching'. *Review of Research in Education,* 16, forthcoming.

2. Huberman, M., 'The social context of instruction in schools'. Paper presented to the annual meeting of the American Educational Research Association, Boston, MA, April 1990.

3. Hargreaves, A., 'Individualism and individuality: reinterpreting the culture of teaching'. *International Journal of Educational Research,* forthcoming.

4. In this sense, occupational cultures in teaching are not unlike the group perspectives described by Becker, H. and his colleagues in *Boys in White.* Chicago: University of Chicago Press, 1961.

5. A point first made by Waller, W., in *The Sociology of Teaching.* New York: Russell & Russell, 1932.

6. Waller, op. cit., note 5; Sarason, S., *The Culture of the School* and *The Problem of Change* (2nd edn). Boston: Allyn & Bacon, 1982.

7. Hargreaves, D., 'The occupational culture of teachers'. In Woods, P., *Teacher Strategies.* London: Croom Helm, 1983.

8. Ball, S., *Beachside Comprehensive.* Cambridge: Cambridge University Press, 1981; Burgess, R., *Experiencing Comprehensive Education.* London: Methuen Books, 1983.

9. Metz, M. H., *Classrooms and Corridors: The Crisis of Authority in Desegregated Secondary Schools.* Berkeley, CA: University of California Press, 1978.

10. Hargreaves, A., *Two Cultures of Schooling.* New York: Falmer Press, 1986.

11. Feiman-Nemser, S. and Floden, R. E., 'The cultures of teaching'. In Wittrock, M. C. (ed.), *Handbook of Research on Teacher Thinking* (3rd edn.). New York: Macmillan, 1986.

12. There is wide literature on organizational cultures and on their relationship to education. Key examples can be found in Deal, T. E. and Kennedy, A., *Corporate Cultures.* Reading, MA: Addison Wesley, 1982; Ouchi, W. G., 'Markets, bureaucracies and clans'. *Administrative Science Quarterly,* 25, pp. 125–41, 1980; Schein, E. H., 'Coming to a new awareness of organizational culture'. *Sloan Management Review,* pp. 3–16, Winter 1984; Schein, E., *Organizational Culture and Leadership.* New York: Jossey-Bass, 1985; Wilkins, A. E. and Ouchi, W. G., 'Effective cultures: exploring the relationship between culture and organizational performance'. *Administrative Science Quarterly,* 28 (3), pp. 468–81, 1983.

13. This is not unlike the concepts of classification and framing used by Basil Bernstein in his classic essay on the 'The classification and framing of educational knowledge' in his *Class, Codes and Control,* vol. 3. London: Routledge & Kegan Paul, 1977. For Bernstein, classification refers to the relationships between contents, whereas frame regulates 'the modality of the socialization into the classification'. Frame is not quite the same as form in curriculum — a point made by Goodson, I. in his essay on 'Curriculum Form', London, Ontario: University of Western Ontario, 1989, but it does point interestingly to the ways in which relationships between contents are constituted and regulated. Form has a similar relationship to content within teacher cultures.

14. Hargreaves, A., *Two Cultures of Schooling,* op. cit., note 10.

15. This project has been funded with the support of the Ontario Ministry of Education Transfer Grant and the Social Sciences and Humanities Research Council of Canada.

16. Lortie, D., *Schoolteacher.* Chicago: University of Chicago Press, 1975.

17. On noise and its importance for teachers' work, see Denscombe, M., 'Keeping 'em quiet: the significance of noise for the practical activity of teaching'. In Woods, P. (ed.), *Teacher Strategies.* London: Croom Helm, 1980.

18. A point made by David Hargreaves in *The Challenge for the Comprehensive School.* London: Routledge & Kegan Paul, 1982.

19. Lortie, op. cit., note 16.

20. See Woods, P., *The Divided School.* London, Routledge & Kegan Paul, 1979; and Hammersley, M., 'Ideology in the Staffroom?'. In Barton, L. and

Walker, S. (eds), *Schools, Teachers and Teaching*. Lewes: Falmer Press, 1981.

21. Nias, J., *Primary Teachers Talking*. London: Routledge & Kegan Paul, 1989.

22. Pollard, A., 'Primary school teachers and their colleagues'. In Delamont, S. (ed.), *The Primary School Teacher*. New York: Falmer Press, 1987.

23. Schneider, B. and Hochschild, J., 'Career teachers' perceptions of the teaching culture'. Unpublished monograph, University of Chicago, 1988.

24. The same levels of misinterpretations can be found in Rosenholtz, S., *Teachers' Workplace*. New York: Longman, 1989.

25. See, for example, Nias, J., Southworth, G. and Yeomans, R., *Staff Relationships in the Primary School: A Study of Organizational Cultures*. London: Cassell, 1989.

26. Zielinski, A. E. and Hoy, W. K., 'Isolation and alienation in elementary schools'. *Educational Administration Quarterly*, 19 (2), p. 37, 1983.

27. Zahorik, J. A., 'Teachers' collegial interaction: an exploratory study'. *The Elementary School Journal*, 87 (4), pp. 385–96, 1987.

28. See Hargreaves, A., op. cit., note 3.

29. Fullan, M., *The Meaning of Educational Change*. Toronto: OISE Press, 1982.

30. Work on the relationships among interests, resources and power in subject cultures is to be found in Ball, S., *The Micropolitics of the School*. London: Routledge & Kegan Paul, 1987; and in Goodson, I., 'Subjects for study: aspects of a social history of curriculum'. *Journal of Curriculum Studies*, 15 (4), 1983.

31. This is a specific case involving a social education department which is referred to in Hargreaves, A., Baglin, E., Henderson, P., Leeson, P. and Tossell, T., *Personal and Social Education: Choices and Challenges*. Oxford: Basil Blackwell, 1988.

32. See Goodson, I., op. cit., note 30.

33. For an extended discussion of such issues, see Goodson, I., *The Making of Curriculum*. New York: Falmer Press, 1988.

34. Ingvarsson, L. and Greenway, P., 'Portrayals of teacher development'. *Australian Journal of Education*, 28 (1), p. 46, 1984.

35. Presentation and discussion of these and other data in the preparation time study can be found in Hargreaves, A. and Wignall, R., *Time for the Teacher*, final report of project 1070 funded under the Transfer Grant, Toronto, Ontario Institute for Studies in Education.

36. Ibid.

37. Ibid.

38. Ibid.

39. Zahorik, op. cit., note 27. Also Hargreaves, A., *Two Cultures of Schooling,* op. cit., note 10.

40. For example, in Campbell, R. J., *Developing the Primary Curriculum.* London: Cassell, 1985.

41. The following account of collaborative cultures draws extensively but not exclusively on the work of Jennifer Nias and her colleagues — see notes 21 and 25.

42. Nias *et al.*, op. cit., note 25.

43. More details are recorded in Hargreaves and Wignall, op. cit., note 35.

44. Campbell, op. cit., note 40.

45. Little, J. W., 'Seductive images and organizational realities in professional development'. *Teachers College Record,* 86 (1), pp. 84–102, Autumn 1984.

46. For an extended discussion of uses and interpretations of time in teachers' work, see Hargreaves, A., 'Teachers' work and the politics of time and space'. *Qualitative Studies in Education*, forthcoming.

47. Hargreaves and Wignall, op. cit., note 35.

48. This can be seen by reviewing studies like those of Zahorik (op. cit., note 27), Schneider and Hochschild (op. cit., note 23), Nias *et al.* (op. cit., note 25) and Rosenholtz, S., *Teachers' Workplace: The Social Organization of Schools.* New York: Longman, 1989. For a penetrating critique and review of the different and often limited forms that collaboration appears to be taking within such studies, see Little, J. W., 'The persistence of privacy: autonomy and initiative in teachers' professional relations'. Paper presented at the American Educational Research Association, San Francisco, 27–31 March 1989.

49. See Lortie, D., op. cit., note 16.

50. For a critique of peer coaching as a form or contrived collegiality see Hargreaves, A. and Dawe, R., 'Paths of professional development: contrived collegiality, collaborative culture and the case of peer coaching'. *Teaching and Teacher Education,* 4 (3), 1990.

51. Hargreaves and Wignall, op. cit., note 35.

52. On the administrative colonization of the 'back regions' of teachers' lives,

see Hargreaves, A., 'Teachers' work and the politics of time and space', op. cit., note 46.

53. Fox, M., 'Unreliable allies: subjective and objective time in childbirth'. In Forman, F.J. and Sowton, C., *Taking Our Time: Feminist Perspectives on Temporality*. New York: Pergamon Press, 1989.

54. See Louden, W., Chapter 11 in this volume.

Index